ENDORSEMENTS

Fortunately, you don't have to be either crazy or a cat lady to enjoy this book! (Of course, if you are either you will absolutely adore it.)

I wasn't sure what to expect - a collection of funny cat stories, or an autobiographical "memoir". In fact, it is both, and more, as Kathy shares the precious life lessons she has learned, especially from her cat family.

I first met Kathy online while I was teaching the Silva Method as an elective during her training in Animal Communication with Joan Ranquet. Even on a tiny screen her sense of fun and love of life already shone through. So I was delighted to be offered the chance to be one of the first to read and review her book before it was even published. To my surprise I discovered my classes got a mention towards the end of the book. I am honoured to have contributed towards Kathy's life story, and hence to her book.

Another nice surprise was her discovery of animal reincarnation. Thank you, Kathy - I am now hopefully looking forward to my own late beloved Ginger finding me again in another body! (Ginger, I am so proud to say, actually did learn to use the toilet, (see chapter 15) - no need for even one litter box!)

There are a lot of events and emotions packed into this life story, so don't expect to devour it in one sitting. I recommend that you read it as a series of tasty little snacks - you can savour and digest all the yummy bits even better!

Kathy writes in a lovely, easy, chatty style, and the readers will soon feel as if they know her personally, and are spending time with an old, dear friend.

— Lee Pascoe,
Silva Method Director and Instructor,
author of The Magic of Make-Believe

Kathy Boyer is truly a crazy cat lady...she is brilliant, funny, smart, and knows how to make a book readable and delicious. Her truth is spoken honestly with humor and emotion that will make you want more and more. This book is great for any animal lover as it will make you laugh, cry, and eager to turn to the next page. I love the way it is organized and methodical, as it flows like a symphony as Kathy expresses herself so wonderfully. I couldn't wait to see what happens next. 4 PAWS UP!!!

— Jill Todd, DVM, CVA, CVCP, CAC

With warmth, wit, and a dash of the mystical, Kathy Boyer takes readers on a journey that celebrates the joy and purpose animals bring to our lives. This memoir blends heartwarming cat tales with reflections on healing, intuition, and the unseen threads that connect us all. It's a delightful and meaningful read for animal lovers, spiritual seekers, and anyone open to seeing life through a different lens.

— Nancy Duval,
Award-Winning and International Bestselling
Author of Whispers from Beyond

At first, I thought this was going to be a charming cat memoir— and it is. But it's also a full-hearted, life-spanning adventure filled with unexpected wisdom, spiritual surprises, and plenty of fur-flying antics. Kathy Boyer writes with a twinkle in her eye and truth in her soul. If you've ever wondered whether your pet knew you better than you knew yourself, this book is your answer.

— Judy O'Beirn,
President and CEO of Hasmark Publishing

Memoir of a Crazy Cat Lady is more than just a tale about a woman and her cats. It is an open-hearted journey of self-discovery, healing, and the unshakable bond between humans and animals. Kathy invites readers into her world with honesty and tenderness, sharing how her "fur family" has not only filled her life with unconditional love but also offered wisdom, comfort, and playful perspective. The cats' voices and comments add a layer of richness and humor, creating a multidimensional story that feels both intimate and expansive.

Kathy has a true gift for planting subtle seeds throughout her writing, hints of what is to come, while weaving together the present moment with the promise of future insights. This creates a rhythm that pulls the reader in, allowing the unfolding to feel both natural and magical.

Her exploration of spirituality, soul connections and reincarnation are entertaining and credible.

At its heart, this memoir is a story of expansion, beginning with the simple act of loving cats and growing into the deeper realization of how these soulful beings can become mirrors, guides, and companions on the path to self-acceptance and spiritual awakening. Through her connection with her cats, Kathy shows us how opening to love, even in its most unexpected forms, can reveal profound truths about who we are and the gifts we are here to embrace.

— Carolyn McGee,
discernment mentor, animal communicator

"Would you throw off tradition, stability and familiarity to pursue your own heart's calling?" That is what this book asks. It is an adventure of transformation.

As a diligent student, Kathy assiduously practiced her clarinet. Hard work led her to becoming such a fine clarinet player, that she received first chair designation at the all-state competition. Later she earned her place as an Air Force musician, traveling internationally, enjoying cultural exchanges, and eventually adopting daughters from Russia and Ukraine with her former husband. Throughout the story, her family is rescuing cats, each with its own lesson for her; spiritual guides who wonder, who rescued whom?

Kathy began life as a devout Catholic, later attending daily Mass for 20 years; yet she still yearned for a deeper spiritual connection. She applied her focus and perseverance to her spiritual quest and was somewhat shocked, yet pleasantly surprised with the results. Here is her ascent to finding her purpose in being an animal communicator and healer. I found her book loving, insightful, and meaningful; but most important, her example inspired me to start letting go of the known to find the way to my own higher ground.

— Susan Johnson, attorney

MEMOIR *of a* CRAZY CAT LADY

*My Journey from Air Force Musician
to Animal Communicator*

KATHY BOYER

Animal Communicator
and Energy Healer

Published by
Hasmark Publishing International
www.hasmarkpublishing.com

Copyright © 2025 Kathy Boyer
First Edition

All Rights Reserved.

No part of this book may be reproduced or transmitted in any form or by any means, electronic or mechanical, including photocopying, recording or by any information storage and retrieval system, without written permission from the author, except for the inclusion of brief quotations in a review.

Disclaimer

This book is designed to provide information and motivation to our readers. It is sold with the understanding that the publisher is not engaged to render any type of psychological, legal, or any other kind of professional advice. The content of each article is the sole expression and opinion of its author, and not necessarily that of the publisher. No warranties or guarantees are expressed or implied by the publisher's choice to include any of the content in this volume. Neither the publisher nor the individual author(s) shall be liable for any physical, psychological, emotional, financial, or commercial damages, including, but not limited to, special, incidental, consequential or other damages. Our views and rights are the same: You are responsible for your own choices, actions, and results.

Permission should be addressed in writing to Kathy Boyer at [kathyh@drnetwork.com]

Editor: Jean-Noel Bassior [jbassior@gmail.com]
Cover Design: Anne Karklins anne@hasmarkpublishing.com
Interior Layout: Amit Dey amit@hasmarkpublishing.com

ISBN 13: 978-1-77482-350-7
ISBN 10: 1-77482-350-0

DEDICATION

To my mother, Lorraine Boyer, and my brothers, Steve and Dave Boyer. We have the best Boyerfest family reunions and share many memories of cats, craziness, cooking, and Yankee baseball! Thanks for accepting me as a truly unique member of the family and for encouraging me to write this book – along with contributing to its contents. There would be no Crazy Cat Lady without my Crazy Family Members!

ACKNOWLEDGMENTS

I'm deeply grateful to everyone who accompanied me on this literary adventure. There would be no stories to tell without the actors – human, animal, and Divine. The synchronicities that arose through the interaction of all these forces have given me a unique journey that I wouldn't trade in a million years.

First my mom, Lorraine Boyer, the first Crazy Cat Lady in my life. As I complete this book, she is now 98 years old and still remembers those cat adventures from her childhood. Not only did I inherit her love for cats, but she also gave me her sense of humor, love of music, ability to cook (especially how to make pies and doughnuts from scratch!), love of sports – especially baseball – perseverance, determination, and a structured faith life that led to my acknowledgment of the Divine from a very young age. Perhaps she also taught me how to tell a story! They say that "more is caught than taught," and I believe that to be true. Mom has been my biggest cheerleader for this writing endeavor and will no doubt be my strongest advocate in its sales.

To my other immediate family members: My brothers, Steve and Dave Boyer, and my daughters, Masha, Dasha, and Kristina, who share my love for animals – maybe not to the extreme that I have lived it, but they have shared in many of these adventures. I know that my father, Maurice Boyer, and sister, Karen Wenditz, are with me in spirit, even though they didn't live long enough to see the completed project.

To my ex-husband, Chuck, without whose support during our married years, there would be NO stories to tell or wacky cat adventures with destitute strays who wandered into our lives. Who else would ever have agreed to travel from Japan to the United States with eight cats?

To all my Air Force Commanders and fellow bandmates, with whom I had the pleasure of serving alongside, many of whom I formed lifelong friendships with. I treasure every moment we shared performing and traveling all over the world as musical ambassadors. We formed a unique bond that few would ever understand. Those were some of the best years of my life.

I want to especially acknowledge Joan Ranquet, my Animal Communication teacher extraordinaire, who, through the school she founded (Communication with all Life University), opened a world I never knew existed: communication with all sentient beings. Joan encouraged me every step of the way in this writing project. Thanks for being the leader of this beautiful tribe of Animal Communicators!

To all the other teachers and mentors in my life during this transformational journey – most of whom I've never met in person. I'm grateful for the internet, which makes remote learning possible, and for your willingness to share your knowledge and life experience with those of us who would never be exposed to such tremendous truths otherwise: Lee Pascoe and the Silva Method, Sarah McCrum (author of *Love Money, Money Loves You*) with her vast experience studying energy with Chinese Masters, David Router and his work with Energetics for Highly Sensitive People, the many teachers of

Mindvalley Academy (an online learning platform for transformational living), Suzanne Giesemann, retired Naval Officer and mediumship teacher, Edgar Cayce's A.R.E. (Association for Research and Enlightenment in Virginia Beach), and the 12-Step Recovery groups I've been privileged to be a part of, whose members have stood by me and encouraged me in my growth. These are just a handful of the influencers in my life, as I've gone through this process of healing, growth, and transformation. If I have left anyone out, you know who you are, and I thank you.

To Jean-Noel Bassior, my incredible writing coach and editor, whom I met through a series of synchronicities! It's been a long process working together, but I've treasured every moment of her patience and guidance with me as a novice writer, always encouraging me to move forward and seek perfection. (She even tolerated my "comma addiction"!) We share the same passion for excellence and attention to detail, but the greatest gift she gave was the freedom to express my own voice without trying to alter it or turn me into somebody else! You made this journey incredibly meaningful.

To all my other extended family members and friends who encouraged me to not only write a book, but to FINISH it! A huge thank you!

To all the animals who have crossed my path and been part of my life – however long the duration – you were each sent here for a purpose, and I am eternally grateful! My life has been enriched beyond compare as the result of your being part of it.

And finally, to the Divine Creator of the Universe, who has tugged on my heart my entire life, even when I didn't know it or understand what was happening within me. You have truly guided me, and given me abundantly more than I could ever ask or imagine, just as your Word promises. Speak, Lord, your servant is listening. I'm ready to continue our adventures!

TABLE OF CONTENTS

*Acknowledgments ix
*Preface xvii
*Foreword xxi
*Foreword by the Felines xxv

Early Years
  1. "Can't You See It's Me?" 1
  2. In the Beginning 3
  3. The Making of a Crazy Cat Lady 17
  4. Life on Wellington Street 29
  5. My Humble Music Beginnings 35
  6. Samantha 47

Early Adulthood 00
  7. Big Boy & Little Boy 59
  8. American Village 69
  9. Balloon Cat 77
10. Pretty Girl 83
11. The Tiger Cat 95
12. The Scabies Infestation 99
13. Muffin 107
14. Cyclops 113
15. Potty Talk 119
16. Bashful and Bobtail 125
17. Mr. Peabody 133

18. Eight Cats, Eight Carriers (No Cat Left Behind) . . 137
19. Laurel Oak Lane 147
20. Kristina's Adoption. 155
21. From Georgia Back to Virginia Beach. 163
22. Crazy Cat Lady Paraphernalia 171
23. Parkland Lane 181

Middle Adulthood 00
24. The Move to Staunton 199
25. Fuji 203
26. Another Mama Cat with Kittens. 209
27. Louie 217
28. The Flow 225
29. The Returnees 233
30. Three Horses and a Pumpkin 235
31. Jake's Diary. 245
32. Squeaker (Kathy's Version). 257
33. Squeaker (Squeaker's Version) 261
34. It's Tough Watching Them Decline 265
35. Bobtail's Senior Years 271
36. Lucy AKA Luce 275
37. Cheated Death Again… and Again… and Again . . 279
38. My Spiritual Quest 291
39. Crestwood Drive. 303

Golden Years:. 00
40. I Am a Trailblazer 00
41. Upward Bound. 00

42.	Past Life Regression #1	325
43.	Is Animal Reincarnation Possible?	335
44.	Demolished and Rebuilt	339
45.	Luce's End of Life	347
46.	Past Life Regression #2	355
47.	Jake's Unexpected Death.	363
48.	I Know What I Want to Be When I Grow Up . . .	367
49.	Does This Stuff Really Work?	375
50.	Squeaker the Wise Guy.	385
51.	Chrissy	397
52.	Fuji's Impeccable Timing	403
53.	Lilli	415
54.	Jake's Computer Sabotage	429
55.	We're All in This Together	437
56.	Pumpkin's Decline	447
57.	I Think This Cat's Been with Me Before	457
58.	Simon and Max: I Have No Male Cats	473
59.	A Fairy Tale of Two Kitties	485
60.	Mom, I Brought You a Present	487
61.	The Baby Rabbit	497
62.	Losing Fuji	503
63.	Lessons I Learned from My Cats	511

*Epilogue – A Life Reflection 513
*Epilogue to the Epilogue – *REALLY*? 520
*About the Author 531

PREFACE

One Saturday afternoon in the summer of 2020, I was walking the 1.3-mile loop around our local park to clear my head and spend some time in the fresh air. I was musing to myself about my childhood.

I had heard that if a person reflects back on what their passions were between the ages of 7 to 12, they can usually find guidance for their life's path. There were several things I had loved: playing musical instruments, baseball, cats, helping animals, and being in the outdoors, to name a few.

I was definitely incorporating some of those interests in my life, having been a professional musician for 40 years and helping numerous cats along the way. I've taken in every sick, dying, destitute, and homeless cat that meandered into my life – more than 25. And although I had to give up my dream of becoming the first female major league baseball player, I still love sports and play a pretty mean game of pickleball!

As I continued my walk past a row of magnificent American Sycamore trees, a thought about another passion flashed into my mind. *When I was young, I loved to write!*

Yes, I did love to write when I was a child, using my imagination to write short stories just for the fun of it. And I won first place in a poetry contest one time when I wrote about two of my cats.

Ideas started popping into my head. *I have so many cat stories I could write a book…* I could feel some excitement starting to well up inside me. *Could I really ever write a book?*

At the end of my walk, I sat on my favorite bench by the stream that runs through the park, just past the duck pond, and the idea became larger: *I HAVE SO MANY CAT STORIES I COULD WRITE A BOOK!*

I jotted down a list of more than 10 possible chapters, and the title came to me immediately: *Memoir of a Crazy Cat Lady!* More excitement welled up inside me, but it didn't stop there.

Once I began to write *Memoir of a Crazy Cat Lady,* I realized that it was more than the story of how I became an Animal Communicator. The book chronicled my lifetime spiritual transformation from a faithful, churchgoing attendee serving a distant God who was out to get me (the "Getcha God," as some would say!) to a child of Divine Love, who created me to be an integral part of the Universe.

In the process, I questioned everything I'd ever learned, waking up to the collective consciousness and "oneness" that Jesus spoke of in the Gospel of John. What I discovered was much more than I ever could have envisioned – that we are spiritual beings having a human experience, and that reincarnation is real, a part of the life cycle for people and animals alike.

Imagine my surprise as my cats gradually revealed, through telepathy and similar behavior patterns, that they are souls who have come and gone in different cat bodies throughout my life. Of course, I demanded proof – and I was not disappointed! As I tuned in to my intuition and skills as an Animal Communicator, it all began to make sense. As I queried my clients and others, asking if they've had experiences that made a strong case for animal reincarnation, I began to gather the proof I needed. It turns out that my feline fur family has been my greatest teacher.

I have many stories to share, not only about my cats, but about other parts of my life as well. As I reflect on how my life has unfolded, I've thought many times, *"Am I making this stuff up?"* I couldn't if I tried!

I hope you will enjoy reading about my adventures and not only laugh along with me, but occasionally shed a tear as well. I've learned that it's a package deal, as much as I would like to avoid the pain. And maybe you can relate to some aspects of this unique relationship we share with other sentient beings.

Perhaps, as you read these stories, you'll ask the same questions I did, as the information these animals shared telepathically changed how I perceived them – and life itself – and it may change your views, too.

And just a heads up that my feline fur family likes to occasionally chime in and express their opinions! They wouldn't give me permission to tell their stories unless I agreed to let them tell *their* side, too.

So, join me now on my wacky journey as I learn how to communicate with animals and find out what they *really* think. And in the process, I hope you gain a greater appreciation for the beauty of life that is both within and all around us. May it bring you peace.

FOREWORD

A book can transport you into a mythical world, or you can see yourself in the protagonist's tragic flaw(s) as they, ready or not, proceed through the hero's journey. This book does both. I found myself lost in Kathy's journey and relating to every step of the way.

Even though Kathy has been a student and graduate of my program, Communication with all Life University, a program that teaches people to communicate with animals and facilitate healing through a few proven modalities, while reading her book, Memoir of a Crazy Cat Lady, I put her in celebrity status! I found myself wanting to proclaim my sameness in parallel stories yet feeling like Kathy was some distant author. All the while, she is approachable and human in this epic love story. I had to remind myself I could just call her and profess my sameness!!

But I would have picked up the phone with nearly every chapter.

It turns out that I read most of the book on an international flight with no interwebs. So, I couldn't pick up the phone, nor could I fire off an email. In the end, that scenario was purrfect as I was submerged in each one of Kathy's stories that were just right.

Sometimes the content was painful, yet the message was just right and in a purrfect progression that I know took a while to craft.

Kathy and I both come from an era where mistakes were made with animals that nowadays someone would say "what were you thinking?" Yet, Kathy gracefully shares exactly what she was thinking and how she felt.

Basically, through some mistakes and much love, Kathy reveals the progression of what an animal lover has gone through to become what I call the animal empath.

Kathy very clearly describes meeting me (later in the book) and what that journey has been. And she tells it from her perspective.

From MY perspective, the moment that Kathy arrived after an incident (which I won't blow her story line here), to Edgar Cayce's A.R.E. while I was teaching animal communication and EFT (emotional freedom technique), she endured a big loss. This loss colored her experience over the next few days.

Often, it's those losses that fuel the next step. And she took a big step in becoming an animal communicator and energy healer.

She has known what most people will never know, having a career as an artist and no other day job. Her talent and dedication did that. So it isn't a big stretch for her to move into this work as an animal communicator. It's more like a sidestep.

And with this work came much pondering about how she came to this moment. Lo and behold her reflections were put to the page, and each and every cat that delivered her to his current moment has a full character and place in her writing and her world.

Kathy's spirituality bloom is also highlighted each step of the way. For me it is a refreshing approach. One of the 'samenesses' I share with Kathy is being raised with a strict Catholic upbringing. While I couldn't quote scripture like she can, it lives in every cell of my body. Rather than renouncing it, I appreciate her evolution of that being the framework for her current spiritual embodiment, that physically is manifesting in a continuum of cats!!

One more sameness that I know is becoming more present in the world is sharing the all- important family value of: animals are family.

I know you will enjoy her journey as much as I did.

—Joan Ranquet, animal communicator,
author, founder of Communication with all Life University

FOREWORD
BY THE FELINES

Hello there! This is Kathy's fur family — the cats she writes about in this book — and have we got stories to tell! We're mostly cats, but we agreed to let a "stray" join us. His name is Jake, and he's a horse.

We have to tell you right up front that Kathy is what we would call "a slow learner." Nothing personal, but we all positioned ourselves to enter and leave her life at exactly the right time. We each had something for her to learn. Some of us even had to come back to her over and over again in different cat bodies before she got the message. We admit it was a scheme, and we included her mother in our shenanigans as well.

Kathy had many life lessons to learn, and this is her journey, which we have been privileged to be a part of. She learned about Divine Timing and the immeasurable love of the Creator of the Universe for her. This was not an easy road to travel down, so we figured we'd come along for the ride and occasionally throw in a few moments of comic relief!

Don't freak out, though, because one of our lessons is about — hold on, are you ready? It's animal reincarnation, not exactly something you talk about at the dinner table! Kathy was astounded when she figured it out. It took decades — in fact, her whole life!

Actually, she was reluctant to even use the term or introduce the topic when she started writing our stories, but after enough of us managed to get our point across, she reluctantly gave in to our pressure and included it. There's nothing to be scared about, really! We did all of this in love, with a little humor along the way.

But be forewarned that you might shed a few tears. We can't help it that our lifespans are a lot shorter than hers, and each time we left our animal bodies, we had to watch her grieve. And that's why we couldn't wait to come back in another lifetime and pick up where we'd left off. It took her a while to recognize us in a new body, but slowly, she began to catch on. And once she'd verified that we really were coming and going, she felt she just had to share what she'd learned! We'll let her tell you more about how she unraveled the mystery of animal reincarnation later in the book.

We'll give our human mom some credit, though. Knowing anything about the afterlife of animals was foreign to her, and she needed to learn to communicate with us in a different way than how humans usually talk with their furry companions. Once she understood us better and became a skilled Animal Communicator, she had the confidence to tell others what we revealed to her about animal spirituality that few people know but have probably wondered about, the same way she did. She understands much better now that death is not the end, and that we are still a part of her life, even after we've crossed the rainbow bridge, as you call it.

You see, we're really her teachers. Yes, there were some humans who helped along the way, but she wouldn't have these stories to tell if we hadn't taken center stage and imprinted them in her mind. And frankly, we love being the stars in these dramas!

It was really fun writing this book with our mom. We kept her busy with these stories spinning around in her head for over 60 years! Yes, we wore her out. And now that she's written them down to be shared, we're not sure what she's going to do with all her free time, but we suspect she'll be playing excessive amounts of pickleball and going on more hikes.

We're only part of the story, though. We were here as part of a bigger plan for Kathy's life. We love her so much... (purr, kisses, hugs, kneading, neighs, and body rubs).

We hope you enjoy our adventures together. We'll let Kathy tell most of them, but sometimes we might feel compelled to chime in and speak out of turn... We tend to get excited about all of this!

So, without further ado, let's get to the main event: Kathy's memoir!

PS: We think it's rather funny that Mom had no clue she would become what some people call a Crazy Cat Lady. In fact, we're still laughing! — The Fur Family

Fur Family Members

Oliver, Kimba, Goldy, Reggie, The Gray Kitten, Samantha, Big Boy, Little Boy, Pretty Girl, Spunky, Muffin, TC the Tiger Cat, Cyclops, George, Bashful, Bobtail, Mr. Peabody, Gray Kitty, Georgie, Gumby, Fuji, Callie, Chrissy, Boots, Alice, Louie, Squeaker, Luce, Pumpkin, Lilli, Simon, Max, and Jake!

CHAPTER 1

"CAN'T YOU SEE IT'S ME?"

"Mom, we know you were going to wait and tell this story near the end of the book, but we are interrupting your plan and want you to share it NOW! It's one of our favorites, and since Fuji's picture is on the front cover of the book, we think she deserves top billing! And so what if we 'let the cat out of the bag' when Fuji and Big Boy showed you how we keep coming back in different bodies? We think you should let readers know about that sooner rather than later. You can fill in the details in another chapter, and remember to add those testimonials you got from other humans whose animal friends came back to them, too."

— The Fur Family

Fuji, my 15-year-old calico, jumped up onto a large plastic storage bin on the floor directly in front of me. At the *exact moment* my eyes landed on her — and I mean *exact* moment — I heard a sarcastic voice inside my heart that said confidently, "Can't you see it's me?" *Oh, My God — that's Big Boy's voice! I'd know it anywhere… This is unbelievable…*

I had communicated with over 100 animals by this time as an Animal Communicator and knew immediately when I was hearing them speak. Now, Big Boy's presence filled my heart the same way it had during the 15 years when he was with me!

It was the first time I'd felt his familiar presence since he'd passed 20 years earlier.

A new wave of excitement hit me as I realized what had happened. Big Boy *had* come back to me in another incarnation – and this time, it was in the being of Fuji, my opinionated, quirky feline matriarch! I stared at the relaxed little calico perched on the storage bin, and every intuitive sense within me knew this was real. My heart swelled with the familiarity of Big Boy's presence.

I didn't understand it, and yet I knew with every fiber of my being that it was true. Although I was hearing Big Boy, his "voice" was coming from Fuji, but from a very deep level of her consciousness. I don't know how to explain it any other way.

So how did I ever wind up writing a book about my journey into this fascinating aspect of spirituality? From childhood on, my life has been filled with so many cats that somehow, unknowingly, I became a Crazy Cat Lady who learned to communicate with animals in a different way. Animal reincarnation is just one mystery they've shown me. There's much, much more, and I can't wait to share what I've learned along my transformational path of becoming an Animal Communicator.

My wacky, sometimes upside down, adventure began long ago, in a small town in upstate New York near the Canadian border.

Hop on board, and let's go for a ride...

CHAPTER 2

IN THE BEGINNING

"Dirt here, remember me? It's about time I apologize for being hit by that car when you were four years old. I was chasing a nasty squirrel, and I didn't look both ways before dashing into the street. I know my death was your first animal-related trauma, but I hated that your brother Steve named me, a gorgeous white cat, 'Dirt.' Really? It was hard to live with that label, but it wasn't your fault, and I am deeply sorry for causing you so much pain. But on the bright side, you come from a great family of cat lovers, including your mother, who set the perfect example, and maybe that's why you grew up to become a Crazy Cat Lady."

– Dirt

My family of origin played a huge part in setting the stage for the direction of my life. As I reflect back, my love for music, animals, nature, and wildlife came very naturally, with many humorous stories and ridiculous scenarios modeled to me by members of my family. My mother, Lorraine Boyer, was the first Crazy Cat Lady I knew, and I'm certain that it was her example that led me to follow in those footsteps.

Mom's fascination with cats could be traced to her early elementary school days. Walking to school provided a great opportunity for her to observe all the sights along the way

– including the neighborhood cats. When she saw a cat she liked, she just picked it up and carried it home!

Her mother was less than thrilled to see her with yet another cat and would ask where she got it. She replied, rather casually, "It was lost," to which Grandma's emphatic response was always the same: "Take it back to where you found it." And so, unhappily, she did, carrying the unsuspecting, "lost" cat back through the neighborhood to its rightful home.

Although I never stole any cats from their owners, in my life I have provided room and board – and an outpouring of love – to every vagrant, dying, destitute, lonely, hungry, homeless, begging cat that's ever crossed my path.

Mom was born in 1927, the daughter of Michael and Mabel LaFrancis, and grew up in Malone, New York, a small town of 10,000 people nestled in the foothills of the Adirondack Mountains, an area we commonly referred to as "The North Country."

It is truly upstate New York, approximately five miles from the Canadian border, where you can easily enter the province of Quebec, the French-speaking part of Canada. In the mid-1800s, my ancestors migrated to the United States from an area known as the St. Lawrence Valley. Mom learned to speak French before she spoke English and was sometimes referred to as "the little French girl."

She grew up at a time when there were no buses, and everyone walked back and forth to school daily, including lunchtime, regardless of the weather, which included months of bitter cold and hazardous snow. Yes, those exaggerations the older generation often uses to emphasize a point, like, "We walked 10 miles to school, uphill both ways and barefoot in the snow," were not that far from the truth for my parents.

My father, Maurice Boyer (1925-1996), the son of Ozias and Helene Boyer, also came from a long line of French Canadians who crossed the U.S. border in the mid-19th century. My great-great-grandfather, Bazil B. Boyer, even purchased a large plot of land that he donated to Notre Dame Church to be used as the church's cemetery.

Dad was attending college to become an electrician when he was drafted into the Army at age 18 in 1943 to serve in World War II. After attending various training schools, he was sent to France in September 1944. A month later, during combat, he was wounded in the eye and ear.

While in the hospital, he was ecstatic when he found out that one of his attending nurses was his first cousin, Lt. Madeline LaRocque, who was stationed with an Army nurses' unit in France! Both Dad and Madeline could speak French, which was to their benefit throughout their war experiences.

He returned to the front on December 30th to fight in the Battle of the Bulge and, a week later, was captured in Eastern France. He was taken on foot and by boxcar in freezing weather, along with approximately 7,500 other Americans, to Stalag 4-B prisoner-of-war camp in Germany. This camp, about 30 miles north of Dresden in Eastern Germany, was one of the Nazi regime's largest, with approximately 30,000 prisoners from 33 different nations. Three months later, on April 23, 1945, it was liberated by the Russian Army.

Dad spent his 20th birthday on January 27th at Stalag 4-B POW camp, and in February, was shipped to Plauen, on the border of Czechoslovakia, where he was put on a work detail, helping move German war supplies from buildings bombed by the Allies.

At Plauen, in March 1945, he was wounded again from Allied air strikes and taken to Hohenstein, a German hospital used for prisoners of war shared by 900 Allied soldiers, where he was placed with approximately 100 other Americans under the care of French POW doctors.

The German atrocities were so bad that it was difficult for me to even read through the accounts reported in the local Malone newspaper. Please bear with me as I share these brutal details, because I don't want to minimize or sugarcoat what men like my father endured during this horrendous war.

Men in one ward hobbled about on stumps where feet used to be, having been victims of frostbite caused by bailing out of planes from high altitudes, or winter marches from as far away as upper Silesia (a historical region of Central Europe) with nothing but bread crusts to eat. The Russians fared even worse. They were skin and bones, many with missing limbs and delirious from starvation, clustered around a garbage bin, ravenously licking the insides of empty food ration cans.

According to my dad in an interview, after he returned from the war, "On April 13th, we saw 200 half-starved Polish and Romanian Jewish women slaves being herded down a road by German women guards who lashed stragglers with leather thongs. And then, the next day, the Americans (from the

Fourth Armored Division) walked into the camp. Boy, there was some excitement in that hospital that day. Cheers and tears, it was a wild scene of hilarity. The next day our guards came back and surrendered."

After being liberated, Dad was taken by American ambulances to Gotha, Germany, and then flown to Rheims (then South England). In South England, he was shipped to Wales, where he was hospitalized for 21 days and then sent to London, where he remained 17 days before sailing for the United States. Much of this time was spent putting the weight back on that he had lost. I remember Dad saying that he had lost so much that at his lowest point, he weighed a mere 87 pounds.

My grandparents received news about their son by Western Union telegrams, usually handwritten in pencil, stating that he was Missing in Action, with no other details. Later, another telegram arrived, and without knowing Dad was a POW, they learned he was freed by U.S. troops. I can't even imagine the anguish this caused everyone in the family – and Dad experienced this ordeal when he was only 20 years old!

After his liberation and return to the U.S., his wartime military honors/decorations included the Combat Infantryman's Badge, the Purple Heart with one cluster, the Good Conduct Medal and the European Theater of War ribbon with two battle stars. In 1949, he was awarded the Bronze Star for Meritorious Achievement in Ground Operations Against the Enemy during the Rhineland Campaign.

All the newspaper clippings from the Malone paper, including the interview above, included more details, such as the tremendous weight loss by all the soldiers, the U.S. troops sharing what little food they had with starving and emaciated Russian prisoners who were given nothing, and how Dad and the American POWs traded cigarettes received in ration boxes from the Red Cross for food within the prison camp.

As a veteran myself, in sharing this story, I really want to honor not only my dad, but all the other brave soldiers from both the United States and around the world who fought on our behalf against the atrocities committed in World War II. Dad's story could have had a much different ending, in which case I wouldn't be here. I'm grateful for every breath I take, and the freedom that I experience on a daily basis.

I've been asked if my dad's military background influenced my decision to join the Air Force, and I would have to say no. I felt a sense of kinship that I was also going to be a member of the Armed Forces, but I was very naïve about his war experience.

I was joining the Air Force as a musician – not an infantryman who would be sent to combat in a war situation. I had the opportunity to earn a successful living playing musical instruments and was far removed from the horrors of a battlefield.

In fact, I didn't even read the accounts of my father's POW experiences until after he passed away in 1996, and I was well into adulthood. All of his wartime memorabilia, including newspaper clippings, were stored in a box in our basement, and they seemed like a thing of the distant past. In reality, it had only been 15 years from the time Dad was freed to when I was born. Now, I'm embarrassed that I had such a lack of understanding of his life and what he endured.

I'm the scrapbooker of the family, and while assembling and reading the newspaper clippings he'd saved, I was able to dive deeper into the reality that he had actually been part of the war, part of world history. I compiled all his Army memorabilia into a beautiful scrapbook album for our family to treasure for generations to come.

Through the accounts of Dad's WW II experiences, I learned more about his character, and that is what I appreciate more than anything: his ability to persevere through incredible hardship, maintain his calm, reserved personality, and respond to life with a sense of humor – what an inspiration to me! I hope that I have inherited those qualities from him, and that they are apparent to everyone that I meet.

My Air Force experience took on a new meaning after I read the war accounts, and not only did I feel a special camaraderie with him as a veteran, but I served my country with even greater fervor. Today I use my music skills regularly to help honor other veterans who served.

The men who lived and served during that period in history, including my father, seemed to have more resiliency in dealing with the aftereffects of war than what I've witnessed in more recent conflicts. Times are different, and cultural expectations are different. I'm not even sure that PTSD was recognized at that time within the medical field. My dad and others like him seemed to bury the past and move on with their lives. I can't pinpoint what their coping skills were other than perhaps a deep faith in God.

My parents met about six months after Dad returned to the States. He invited Mom to go to a movie, so they met at the theater in Malone to see *The Bells of St. Mary's,* starring Bing Crosby and Ingrid Bergman, a year after it was released in 1946.

The movie was very popular, and there was a long line to get into the theater, so they stood outside in the cold, waiting their turn. To avoid awkward silence, Mom started a conversation, saying she had heard he was injured while in Europe, and asked about it.

Dad had a coy sense of humor, and casually shrugged off the question, making light of it. Then, totally joking with my unsuspecting mom, he made a fist with his hand and pounded on his knee, making it sound like wood and saying he had a wooden leg, but he's doing OK.

Believing that Dad was serious, Mom was in shock and didn't know what to say. When they finally entered the theater, she couldn't keep her attention on the movie. She kept looking over at his leg, and her heart went out to this man, who she thought was very handsome, with so many years ahead of him. What a tragedy for him to have to cope with that injury for the rest of his life!

After the movie, they walked around downtown for a couple hours, and Mom noticed her date was moving his body pretty well. "I'm just amazed at how well you get along with that leg!" she commented.

Dad looked confused, and replied, "What leg?"

"The wooden one, of course," Mom answered, at which point Dad broke into hysterical laughter, pulled up his pant leg, and revealed a fully intact leg, with a hairy knee! Mom was relieved and felt somewhat embarrassed over her gullibility – a quality that I also inherited.

Overall, it must have been a successful first date, as they were married less than a year later at Notre Dame Church in Malone, where we were all baptized. There were three Catholic churches in town, loosely divided according to ethnic background, and we were part of the one for those of French-Canadian descent.

I was the third of four children: Karen (now deceased), Steve, me, and Dave. There was an eight-year gap between Steve and me, giving us the feeling that we were part of two separate families: First, Steve and Karen growing up together, and then Dave and me.

Karen seemed indifferent toward animals, and never had any pets in her adult life. She apparently had not inherited the animal-loving gene!

Steve, however, kept a steady flow of wildlife coming into our house. We were hardly ever without a living creature, which included a pet squirrel he had tamed, snakes, frogs, and pigeons.

Dad and Steve were avid fishermen, and from their fishing excursions on the nearby Salmon River, we enjoyed an abundance of freshwater trout, which my mother pan-fried slowly in butter with lots of salt and pepper.

Steve loved and played with anything alive that moved on the ground or flew in the air. One memorable incident happened before I was born when my family lived in a modest white house on Fourth Street that Mom described as a bungalow with very small rooms. It was here that the story of Toadville took place.

When Steve was five years old, he and a neighbor girl collected toads and frogs. My father rigged up a bathtub in the backyard with screening on top, and piped water into it from buckets the kids had filled at nearby Colander's Pond. A friend even sold them more frogs to put in the tub, along with a turtle, which brought the occupancy to 39 at its peak. They called it "Toadville."

One fine spring day, my mother went grocery shopping, and when she arrived home, made a beeline for the bathroom, sitting down to do her business just in the nick of time. In her moment of respite, a frog suddenly jumped out of the tub, and landed right in front of her feet, scaring the living daylights out of her!

She bounded off the toilet as if ejected from the pilot's seat of an airplane, and quickly examined the contents of the tub. In front of her were 15-20 other frogs, at which point she screamed, bolted from the bathroom, and went tearing through the house to find Steve.

Taking him back to the bathroom, she demanded, "What on earth are all these frogs doing in here?" to which he proudly responded with a big smile, "They needed a bath!" Needless to say, those frogs did not spend the night in the house with the luxury of indoor plumbing, but were immediately returned to the backyard Toadville tub.

Steve's neighborhood antics continued with cats. When he turned 10, he and another friend collected all the cats they could find and put them up in the loft part of our garage, which could only be reached with a ladder.

The collection had grown to four when the neighbors began to talk amongst themselves about their missing cats. Somehow, "the cat got out of the bag," and Steve and his friend were in big trouble. The confused, displaced cats were promptly returned to their rightful owners.

I was born while we lived on Fourth Street, but was much too young to remember the catnapping incident, or a later adventure when my parents thought they had found the perfect Christmas gift for Steve and purchased a baby alligator all the way from Florida.

Although excited about this exotic gift at first, Steve lost interest within the first six months, not wanting the responsibility or upkeep of an alligator. Desperate for a solution, Mom quietly disposed of the poor little fellow outside in a snowbank, where he froze to death. She didn't confess to this hideous crime until years later when she expounded on her previous story that "he had just died."

After I turned two, we moved to a larger house on Elm Street with two stories, a cellar, and double the square footage. This provided more space for our growing family, which soon included Dave, bringing the total to two boys and two girls.

Dad was actively involved with Boy Scouts, founding Troop 61 at Notre Dame Church, and was its Scoutmaster for over 25 years. Both Steve and Dave earned the rank of Eagle Scout and went on camporees (scouting weekends with scouts from other troops) four times a year at Camp Bedford, the Boy Scout camp 30 minutes from Malone.

One of my earliest memories is when I was five years old and Dave was an infant. It was centered around Steve's love of wildlife, after he and Dad returned from a camporee in the fall.

Steve brought home three garter snakes in large glass jars, which were going to be his *pets!* He housed them in our cellar, but one of the snakes escaped from its jar and went missing, thus becoming a frequent topic of conversation at dinner, with much speculation over what might have happened to it.

After two weeks, we gave up hope of ever finding it, presuming it had somehow escaped and made its way outside to greener pastures. To avoid another missing snake catastrophe, Dad released the other two from their lives of captivity, dropping them in the empty field across the street from our house. Life returned to normal.

After my brother Dave was born, Mom occasionally needed an extra pair of hands to help with the chores. "I'll do it!" became my motto, and I happily walked downstairs one morning to get milk from the refrigerator for Dave's bottle.

As I walked around the corner of the stairwell toward the kitchen, I virtually stopped dead in my tracks, because my heart seemed to have briefly left my body. Right in front of me on the kitchen floor was the missing snake! I didn't move an inch, but shouted upstairs, "Mom, I found the snake!" Thankfully, it didn't move when it saw me. Steve caught it and set it free across the street to join the others.

Steve also loved cats, in addition to wildlife, and his favorite was a white male cat he named Dirt. I was too young to remember Dirt, but there were a few pictures taken of him with Karen, Steve, and myself. Sadly, Dirt's life unfortunately ended when he was hit by a car.

Dad's job was to bury the cats, and I never did figure out whether he actually liked them or not. He had a very low-key personality when it came to animals, and hunted on occasion, mostly for wild rabbits. He did *tolerate* our cats, though, and never complained unless the "gull dang cat" did something it wasn't supposed to do. No cat was exempt from his disgust.

I can also thank my dad for instilling in me a great love and appreciation for nature and wildlife. He particularly loved birds and built numerous birdhouses during my formative years. Swallows, bluebirds, and robins frequented our yards, somehow dodging the fruitless attempts of our cats to catch them.

We had a great park in town where I took swim lessons, played tennis, and spent hours on the teeter-totter, swinging and climbing monkey bars on the playground. Dad enjoyed taking me there during the late fall months when all the Canadian geese would congregate at the lake en route to their southern destinations. With binoculars in hand, he loved to get a closer glimpse of the literally thousands of geese on the lake. After he adjusted the binoculars, he held them up to my face so I could see them as well.

I confess that I didn't know how to correctly look through the binoculars to see anything, and I never got a close-up view of those beautiful geese. I just pretended to see them, and gasped with excitement so I wouldn't disappoint my dad!

Dad's years of experience with the Boy Scouts and the outdoor life spilled over into our family life as well. We owned different types of campers over the years, and spent many vacations at various campgrounds, especially nearby Lake Meacham, which was a state park only 30 minutes from home.

Taking a picnic lunch on every trip we made in upstate New York was one of my favorite things to do. There were lakes in just about every town, with picnic tables galore on the route to every destination. Of all the members of my family, I'm the one who always insisted that we take a picnic lunch. To this day, I *love* picnics and often prefer them to a meal in a fancy restaurant.

I guess it was the combination of my family environment of cats, nature and wildlife that planted the seeds in me to want to return to that type of lifestyle. It has taken over 40 years to cultivate it on my own, but it has been well worth the effort.

Reflecting back on these childhood memories, I now see that my path to becoming a full-fledged Crazy Cat Lady began after we moved across town to Wellington Street when I was six years old.

CHAPTER 3

THE MAKING OF A CRAZY CAT LADY

"Mom, Goldy and I have a few comments to make about animal reincarnation, and I'm going to go first. Even though you didn't know me, Oliver, because I was your mom's cat many years before you were born, my amazing GPS (better than most cats) is going to show up again in a cat you'll meet in college called Samantha, and later on in a cat named Boots. These incredible navigation skills are a special trait that sets me apart from other cats. Each of us has something unique that you will remember, whether it be a behavioral quirk or something in our personality. So, pay attention to these one-of-a-kind traits, and the feelings they evoke in you, as they are subtle clues to animal reincarnation. This will be important later in your life when you become an Animal Communicator and can share our stories of how we come and go in different bodies. Now, Goldy has something to say – and he's more of a jokester than I am."

– Oliver

"Hey, Mom! Yes, many of us were wild things, roaming the streets as unneutered males – which sadly shortened our lifespans – but eventually, you guys will figure out the spaying and neutering thing, and we will become… couch potatoes! Or rather, YOU will become our SERVANTS! Haha!"

– Goldy

We moved to 66 Wellington Street on the west side of town in 1966 into a smaller, two-story white house we later painted yellow, with an enclosed front porch and one-acre lot. My parents purchased the property for $11,000 after the previous owner passed away. We lived there until I enlisted in the Air Force in 1984, and it created a stable home life and comfortable environment for all the cat adventures during my formative years.

I don't believe that anyone actually "trains" to become a Crazy Cat Lady or aspires to be one when they are young. I had never even heard the term as a child! I only knew that I was obsessed with my love for cats and couldn't understand why others weren't.

The first cat I remember was a small, gray kitten who joined us a year later when I was in 1st grade. He only lived for a brief time, and we hadn't even settled on a name yet, when he had a fatal accident. Within a couple weeks after we brought him home, he managed to climb a tree next to our driveway, and sadly, couldn't hold on. He fell onto the concrete surface, *not* landing on his feet, and died instantly.

It didn't seem fair that this little kitten died so tragically, and at such a young age. I will never believe the saying that "a cat will always land on its feet if it falls." Not true. For months, I stared at the only picture we took of that cat, which was an informal family picture with Steve holding him.

I was seven years old, and this was my first experience coping with the death of a cat. Little did I know that over the course of my life, I would live through the deaths of over 25 others.

I've heard it said that cats lived longer back then, possibly due to less toxic influences from their food, vaccines, and the environment. But all our cats were unneutered males who spent most of their time outdoors, and due to this lifestyle, my family's expectation was that a cat would only live to be three or four years old. It never occurred to us that a cat could live indoors, and to this day, I still allow my cats to go in and out of the house as they please. They are all neutered or spayed, however, and stay close to home.

On Wellington Street, they roamed the neighborhood at night, often incurring injuries, such as a torn ear or disfigured face from a cat fight or a brawl with another animal. We waited patiently for them to return, which they did most of the time; but if they didn't come back home after several days, sometimes we never knew what happened to them. And although our street was quiet, with very little traffic, there was always the risk of one getting hit by a car, and it would only take one fast vehicle to end their lives.

In the 1960s, it was not yet a widespread practice to get animals spayed and neutered to manage the stray population and keep them from wandering through the neighborhood. With such a short, anticipated lifespan, losing a kitten like the gray one that fell out of the tree was particularly devastating. And, if any of our cats lived to be five, that would be a miracle, and they would be considered a senior citizen!

Whenever I worried about a cat getting lost, Mom tried to reassure me with much confidence that cats have a stellar sense of direction. When she and Dad were in their 20s, and my sister Karen was a toddler, they had both a dog and a cat at the same time. Rex, the dog, was a beagle mix, and Oliver, the cat, was a stately black-and-white tuxedo shorthair.

With the demands and responsibilities of a young child (Karen), my parents determined it was overwhelming to take care of both animals, so they kept Rex, and found a new home for Oliver. I'm not sure how they came to that decision, given Mom's love for cats, but nonetheless, that's what they did.

After a phone call or two, a woman who managed a farm three miles outside of town agreed to take him in. My parents drove Oliver to his new home and said an agonizing goodbye.

A week later, Mom called the woman to check on him, but was unfortunately told, "The cat? He never stayed here and left immediately!" Mom was distraught and felt as if it was her fault. She was depressed for days, thinking about Oliver, but eventually came to terms with the realization that he was gone.

Well, as unbelievable as it sounds, one month after they left Oliver at that farm, he miraculously navigated his way back to our house, looking a little ragged – but nonetheless, he found it! To say Mom and Dad were in shock is an understatement. They were both thrilled and relieved, and for a solid week, Oliver did nothing but drink milk and purr incessantly!

That story gave me a little bit of confidence that if any of our cats ever got lost or ran away, they would return. *But did that include Kimba, the first cat I ever completely bonded with, that disappeared?* I wondered…

We always adopted cats in pairs, probably to keep Dave and me from fighting over who they belonged to: Kimba and Speedy (sibling black-and-gray striped tiger cats), Mozart and Reggie (also tiger cats, Mozart named after the composer because of his polydactyl paws), Reggie (named after Reggie Jackson, the baseball player), and Goldy and Blacky (gold-and-white, and black-and-white, respectively).

Therefore, we always had two cats, with an occasional overlapping of pairs due to unforeseen circumstances. In those instances, our house became a revolving door for cats, which could have inspired some tricky word problems for math class: If one cat went missing, we got two more, and that made three. Then when the missing one returned, we had four. After we lost two of those, we were back down to two. When one of those disappeared, we were down to one, and we got two more… So how many cats did we have altogether? I don't really know! My answer today would be: "It doesn't matter. You can never have too many cats!"

Kimba was mine, named after the main character in the animated television show *Kimba the White Lion*. I was obsessed with the show and in love with the little white lion. Dave's cat, Speedy, was so named because he was fast.

I bonded with Kimba very quickly, ecstatic to have a cat of my very own. I carried him to bed with me every night, even though he would eventually be let outside to prowl around in the dark. I was so proud of him, and excited to be able to raise this young cat.

Four months later, my bubble burst when Kimba left the house one night and didn't return the following day. Or the next. Or the one after that. *Where could he have gone?*

I waited and waited each day, trying to hold on to the words of my mother's story about Oliver, thinking maybe there was still hope.

After six months of waiting, and anticipating his return, my hope turned into grief and despair, and I had to face the fact that Kimba was gone. My very first cat had disappeared in less than a year. I cried and cried…

My parents' solution was to get me another cat, and when we found out about some kittens available at the end of our street, we brought home Goldy and Blacky.

Since Kimba was gone and I didn't officially have a cat, Goldy became mine, and Blacky was everybody's. Dave still had Speedy. Now, for the very first time, we had three cats in our household! Although today, that seems like such a small number to me, at the time, it seemed like a houseful.

I loved Goldy, even though he was somewhat aloof and independent. I didn't care. He was mine, and I doted on him, even entering him as my exhibit in the 4th Grade Science Fair. We put him in the car with us, and I held him in my arms as we drove to Notre Dame school. I'm not sure how I talked my parents into letting me do that. We had no cat carrier, just my arms. And what on earth did I think he was going to do once we got there? Sit there and pose for everyone? *What was I thinking?*

Goldy was not the least bit interested in being a science fair exhibit and escaped from my clutches as soon as possible. He ran through the exhibits – and all the other people scattered about in the school gym – making a beeline for his freedom.

I was in a panic and desperately scoured every inch of the gym, as well as other parts of the school, searching for him. By the end of the evening, though, when the science fair was over, I had totally lost my beloved cat, and went back home empty-handed.

In my panicked state, my nervous system went into overdrive, well past fight or flight, and into *freeze* mode. I must have dissociated, so devastated that I couldn't focus or think of anything except my missing cat and my stupidity at bringing him there in the first place. *What if he never comes back? What if he's lost forever?* We called the school office multiple times to see if anyone had seen him, either in the building or on the grounds. Nothing.

Finally, after three long, emotionally exhausting days that seemed like an eternity, the school called back, saying that Goldy had been spotted on the school grounds. We rushed there, and I called his name over and over, hoping he would hear my voice and come to me.

It worked! After a few minutes, my scared gold-and-white cat came happily running toward me and easily let me catch him. I scooped him up in my arms, climbed back in the car and went home, holding him with all the strength I could muster! *What a relief…*

I settled down from my hysterical state of mind, and thankfully put the episode behind me. And although the trauma of nearly losing Goldy forever had crushed me, when he came back, I was so thankful! Eventually, I admitted that I'd been quite proud of my creativity in entering my prize possession in the science fair. And to this day, my friends are still talking about my handsome cat!

Goldy was the first cat that showed me true feline ingenuity and resourcefulness, and that cats can totally train humans – after only one attempt.

My parents' bedroom was situated above the front porch. Goldy figured out a way to jump onto the carport, then to the porch roof, and make a grand appearance in their bedroom window. In short, he found another entrance to the house!

With his loud, droning, mournful meow of desperation, he woke up Dad in the middle of the night, clearly demonstrating that he wanted to come inside to find refuge from the cold. *"HELP ME,"* he wailed. Dad succumbed to the pleas of the desperate boy, slowly emerging from his warm covers and restful sleep, and begrudgingly opening the window to let him in. Goldy had succeeded!

The only real issue was having to open the window in the middle of the night and experience Malone's nasty, brutal winter weather: sub-zero temperatures, gusting winds, and snow… Goldy made this ritual a habit, and after that first successful house entrance victory, Dad had no other choice but to continue letting him in every night for the remaining seven months of winter. *"That gull dang cat…"* could be heard throughout the house like clockwork at 3:00 a.m. It didn't bother me, though. My young but logical mind knew that Goldy was cold and needed to come inside to get warm! What a smart cat I had!

Goldy, Blacky, and Speedy filled my childhood world with feline joy. So much so that *I* wanted to be a cat, and decided to literally eat with them. I wanted to know what their wet food tasted like, so one morning, at their designated mealtime,

I dropped to the floor on my hands and knees and assumed the position.

I followed my cats' lead by smelling the food first, then scooping up the first bite with my mouth. Then a second, and a third… My technique wasn't as polished as theirs, and my face was smeared with cat food, but I continued anyway. *This is so tasty!* Mom thought I was nuts and rolled her eyes at me in disgust, but my curiosity had been satisfied. I only did that once.

Having three cats was blissful, and although I missed Kimba, the painful memory of his loss started to fade. But then, over two years later, a miracle happened...

One morning, we noticed a slim tiger cat approaching our house. I took a closer look, and, with utter disbelief, saw my beloved Kimba! He had somehow found his way back to our house, and I was beside myself with joy! *I guess Mom was right about a cat's sense of direction.* Now, once again, with Kimba and Goldy, I had two cats of my very own. And with Blacky and Speedy, that meant we had four cats. Life couldn't have been any better.

My joy was short-lived, however, for within five short months, Kimba was hit by a car overnight, and my father found him lying motionless in front of our house the next morning. He had died instantly. With such a small amount of traffic on our street, it seemed utterly impossible that a cat would get hit there, but it happened. I was in shock.

Now I was grieving Kimba a second time. It didn't seem fair. The first time was slow and agonizing, not knowing what had happened to him – and this time he was taken from me in the blink of an eye.

Dad buried Kimba in the furthest part of our backyard, while I memorialized him with a poem that, as a child, I considered to be my first original literary masterpiece. It was short, but it expressed my sentiments, would help me remember this cat that meant so much to me, and helped me give closure to his life. It read:

> *Here he lies, and here he'll stay, through the hours of each day: My Cat Kimba.*

Maybe it wasn't exactly a literary masterpiece, but the words flowed from my heart, and I've never forgotten it.

Blacky didn't live long after his kittenhood, and he was also hit by a car. I didn't find out until *after* Mom took him to the vet to be put to sleep. I had gone to play at a neighbor's house, and she informed me in the car when she picked me up later that day, saying that he had been hit, had a broken leg, and was in a lot of pain. I was incredibly upset that I wasn't able to say goodbye to him. It was another devastating loss.

So now, we were back down to two cats. At 12 years old, I wrote another poem and entered a poetry contest sponsored by our local newspaper. I couldn't believe it when I was awarded first place, along with the grand prize of $25.00. The topic of my poem? Cats, of course! The title: "My Cats Goldy and Speedy."

Goldy died when he was three years old. He was also hit by a car, but not killed instantly. Instead, he lost his equilibrium when he walked and became disoriented. There was no alternative but to have him also humanely euthanized, like Blacky.

I treasured the years I'd had with Goldy, and at age three, he had lived longer than all my other cats.

When I entered Junior High School, the last of the sibling groups we adopted were Mozart (Dave's cat) and Reggie, the black-and-gray striped tiger cat whom I named after Reggie Jackson, the baseball player. Sadly, Reggie was another one that *had just disappeared* when he was only six months old. It was the heartbreaking storyline of a cat running off during the night and not returning.

It was tough dealing with so much loss, but I'm grateful that we always had a feline presence in the house, and that I was able to recover and muster up enough love in my heart for yet another one. After Reggie, my next opportunity wouldn't come again for many years.

These experiences as a young Crazy Cat Lady created what I have termed *imprint moments* – specific memories or fleeting thoughts that became permanently embedded *in my heart* that I would later recall – and that helped me learn some important spiritual lessons as my consciousness expanded. They were part of a puzzle, so to speak, and many more would follow.

Meanwhile, there were other special memories of growing up on Wellington Street, especially alongside my brother Dave, some of which have given me insights as to why I'm drawn to the things I'm drawn to. I would later recognize these to be steppingstones to the life path I would eventually pursue.

So now, let's take a walk down memory lane… Who would like some fresh homemade pie?

CHAPTER 4

LIFE ON WELLINGTON STREET

"Mom, it's interesting that you were drawn to spiritual matters, even when you were a child. What we, as your felines, are showing you is definitely 'spiritual,' and we understand that it will take you a while to grasp this concept. But don't worry, we're going to persevere in teaching you. This is your life's work, and it will truly take a lifetime, with many steppingstones along the way."

– The Fur Family

Wellington Street was located in a quiet, residential neighborhood with little traffic. The fact that three of our cats were hit by cars seemed nearly impossible, which to this day continues to baffle me.

The road spanned nearly a half mile in length, on mostly level ground, but with a sharp hill at the top just past our house, making it nearly impossible to ride a bicycle without getting winded. Huge poplar and maple trees towered next to our driveway.

We had three bedrooms upstairs, along with the lone bathroom which, before my sister moved out, accommodated all six of us. There was no such thing as a master bedroom and bath in those older houses, and it was normal that we just took our turns using one bathroom. There was a cellar and stairs to an attic, which provided plenty of storage.

Karen had graduated from high school and entered nursing school the year we moved, and Steve went to college just a few short years later, so that left just Dave and me at home to grow up together. We became both the best of friends and the best of adversaries.

The backyard was spacious enough for us to play baseball and Dad to plant a garden, with plenty of room for the cats to romp around in. I loved exploring milkweed pods and other plants that grew freely. We eventually planted some pine trees halfway toward the back of our property, one or two of which eventually became Christmas trees.

Dave and I spent hours playing together, both outside in the sandbox that Dad had made, or just exploring our backyard and the empty field adjacent to us. Sometimes, Dad would make an ice-skating rink in the backyard during the long winter months. I loved to skate! And after multiple blizzards came through town, we made igloos next to the driveway from the massive snow drifts. Sub-zero temperatures were a way of life during the winter months.

Across the street was a wooded lot full of wild blackberry bushes that nobody claimed, where Dave and I furiously picked baskets of fresh berries each summer to give Mom to make her succulent blackberry pies. Along with the hearty rhubarb patch and red raspberry bushes in our backyard, fresh fruit pies with homemade crusts adorned our table for months.

I was not a "girly girl" per se and was never interested in Barbie dolls or other typical "girl" toys. The one exception was

Jane West, a doll that came with a beautiful palomino horse! I dreamed of one day owning a ranch in Arizona with horses. I never did move to Arizona, but I eventually got my own horse and learned how to ride at the ripe young age of 48!

I enjoyed playing with paper dolls, though, and managed to talk my brother into playing with me. We also spent hours on end playing with our Legos – the simple ones where we had to create *everything* with our imaginations.

All our toys required imagination, as there were no electronic options for us. It was a way of life during our childhoods, for which I am eternally grateful. Dave and I created our own stories and scenarios with Tonka trucks in the sandbox, and Hot Wheels, Lincoln Logs, and Tinkertoys in the living room.

We had occasional sibling quarrels, with Dave always pushing my buttons or 'breaking the rules,' but never getting punished when I would tell on him. I later learned that being the youngest child came with an unspoken privilege: the parents are too worn out to care anymore!

Perhaps that's what led me to commit a hideous crime with his favorite soft, baby blue blanket, the satin corner of which he referred to as his "windy." He loved to fan his face with the "windy."

One day, I decided to cut up Dave's blanket, probably to experiment and create something with the fabric, like Batman capes, but it was a failure. All that remained were small pieces, yet I *did* keep his "windy" intact. To this day, he still holds a grudge, and I haven't yet been able to find a suitable replacement for that blanket…

Dave and I still reminisce about our days on Wellington Street, and I also appreciate the fact that in addition to my love for animals, I had other interests at that time that not everyone shared, but were "normal" to me. I loved science fiction and mystical topics, and although I'd never heard the terms "metaphysical" or "quantum" as a child, that's really what I had been unknowingly exposed to. There were signs of my fascination with these topics imprinted all over me.

I loved science fiction books and movies, and watching television shows that explored the unknown, or documentaries speculating about the Bermuda Triangle or Atlantis. I also loved writing my own science fiction short stories, just for the fun of it!

The idea of time travel fascinated me, and I loved shows like *The Time Tunnel,* where two scientists with a secret time travel project wind up in a time stream where they appear in notable periods of history. The work they did while crashing these time periods had an impact on history (or at least it did on the show).

I was particularly enthralled with the popular show *I Dream of Jeannie*, and together with a girlfriend in 2nd grade, we'd dress up in whatever fun clothes we could find and pretend we were Jeannie. Folding our arms and blinking our eyes like Jeannie did to make things happen was magical!

Another favorite of mine was the original *Star Trek* series from the 1960s, which took my imagination well beyond the boundaries of Earth! Today when I watch those reruns, I see signs of Energy Healing throughout the techniques used by Dr. McCoy to treat his patients. I also marvel at the technological advances they used, such as the *phaser*, which to me is now the modern cell phone. I found out later that Gene Rodenberry's writers stole that idea from *Space Patrol*'s "space-o-phone." As a child, the idea that a phone that wasn't connected to the wall could actually work was inconceivable!

I believe my childhood fascination with science fiction and mysticism, along with my love for animals, were the early stages of my soul's attempts from deep within my consciousness to find its purpose and place in life. Embodying the *oneness* that was part of the original creation, along with becoming an Energy Healer, Vibrational Sound Therapist, and Animal Communicator, are some of the results of that search. It has been a long spiritual journey with many struggles, and I consider the work that I do as Sacred.

These professions within the fields of Energy Healing and Telepathic Communication did not exist when I was growing up. While they are still not considered mainstream, everything I have become trained to do is now backed by, and can be supported with, science.

There were several steppingstones along the way which led to my new vocation, without which I would never have found my calling – or grown into a full-fledged Crazy Cat Lady!

The most important one began "officially" in 6th grade when I started private clarinet lessons. Little did I know that I would later become a professional musician of over 40 years.

So how did this come about? Bring on the pots and pans!

CHAPTER 5

MY HUMBLE MUSIC BEGINNINGS

"Mom, one of the 'steppingstones' you've talked about was to survive being humiliated by those disgusting teachers before your parents put you in the right school, where you could develop a love for music and learn a bunch of instruments. You even joined the band! And this might shock you, but we know that one day, you'll live in a foreign country, play music, and collect cats! (That's our favorite part of the book.) But we're getting ahead of ourselves. Get to practicing those instruments, so you can get good enough to make a living at it!"

— The Fur Family

My long, illustrious music career began in the meager surroundings of my bedroom on Wellington Street. Dave and I collected all the pots and pans from our kitchen and eagerly brought them upstairs to create a band! What fun it was!

We perfected the art of creating crashing cymbal sounds with the lids and pulsating rhythms with the pots, using wooden spoons as beaters. Mom's only reprieve from all the racket was to claim that she needed the cookware to make dinner, forcing us to return our orchestral instruments back to where they belonged.

Dave and I both started school at Notre Dame, which is affiliated with our parish by the same name. It was not a good match for me, and I lasted there only five years before my parents transferred both of us to public school. The experience created a huge amount of stress in my life, including my attempts to be perfect in learning how to be a good Catholic.

Attending the parish school meant that we incorporated religious studies into our daily schedule. I was always interested in spiritual matters, and when my class walked the half mile up Main Street to Notre Dame Church during the school day to practice for our upcoming church sacraments like First Holy Communion, Confession, or Confirmation, I tried to sort out the workings of the universe, asking what I considered to be important philosophical questions like, "If God is in the church building, isn't He everywhere else, too?" And "How can He be everywhere? How does He do that?" or "How do I talk to God? Do I have to use formal prayers, or can I just talk to Him in my own words?" I didn't want to do it the wrong way.

This led to even more unanswered philosophical questions, such as, "What is the proper way to fold your hands when you pray?" and "Do I always have to kneel down to say my prayers?" I wanted God to know that I was a good girl, always paying attention and wanting to do things the correct way. Anything less than 100% meant that I wasn't perfect.

I learned to perceive God as the "Getcha God," a tyrant who would *get me* if I didn't "do it right." That has been the biggest obstacle to my spiritual growth over the years and the most insurmountable attitude to overcome. It was the perception ingrained in my heart for as long as I can remember.

But I wasn't just an overachiever in religion – I felt driven to excel in *every* subject, and on all my exams. I attribute that partially to being a middle child – the invisible one – trying to get attention! I didn't do it by acting out and getting into trouble. I took a different approach. One of my best memories and greatest academic achievements was winning a spelling bee in 2nd grade with the word "once," which everyone else spelled with the letter "w."

I had nuns for teachers in 3rd, 4th, and 5th grade, and although my 3rd-grade teacher, Sister James, was a gem, the other two were the complete opposite. Both those nuns humiliated me in front of the class on multiple occasions and showed heavy favoritism toward others. I have no clue why this happened, because, in my mind, I was a model student – I got good grades, was a rule-follower, and an overachiever! What more could they want?

As I reflect back, I believe it was Divine intervention that helped arrange the circumstances so that I couldn't continue to attend this school and have any sanity left! A transfer to public school was looming, which led me down the musical path I would follow for the rest of my life. I could not see this at the time, however. Instead, I internalized the stress, so much so that I dealt with physical symptoms such as hives, allergies, and a "lisp" that required help from a speech teacher to overcome.

I was a full-fledged tomboy, and my obsession with baseball could not be satisfied at school when, in the 5th grade, I was not allowed to play my favorite sport with the boys during recess. I was an avid New York Yankees fan from the womb – another inherited trait from my mom – and nothing would deter my early lifetime dream of becoming the first female major league baseball player. The nuns told me that baseball was for boys, and I had to play with the girls.

Although that might not have seemed like a big deal to anyone else, it was devastating to me, and was ultimately the final straw that broke the camel's back. I was even sent to the principal's office because I was angry and had pleaded my case before the nuns. That scenario created a memory that lingered in my psyche for years.

By the end of 5th grade, after the final "baseball episode," my parents decided to transfer both Dave and me to a public school. The following year, he started 2nd grade and I sixth at G. Burton Davis Elementary School.

There was another reason for the transfer, however, that was to change the course of my life. Mom had a great singing voice, singing with bands in high school in the 1940s when the music of the Big Band Swing Era was popular. She was passionate about music and wanted us to experience that as a part of our lives as well, with the opportunities that public school offered.

Notre Dame did not offer music classes or band as part of the curriculum. The ensuing music opportunities that followed my transfer to the public school were the hidden blessings that I didn't comprehend at the time.

I'm now grateful for the two nuns who made life so miserable for me in the 4th and 5th grades when I struggled so much. That forced my parents to make a huge decision that would set me on the right path to a career that I would embrace for over 40 years!

The change in my perspective from *adversity to gratitude* is one of the greatest spiritual lessons that I've learned, which flows from one of my favorite scriptures in the Bible, Romans 8:28: *And we know that all things work together for good to them that love God, to them who are called according to His purpose.* I've come to rely on that scripture many times over the course of my life.

When Mom enrolled me in public school, she was aware of the music opportunities and approached Tony Maiello, the head of the entire public school band program, asking if I could join the beginning band. I'd never heard of a school band, but it sounded exciting! Mom knew that the school's policy was for students to start band in 5th grade, and I was a 6th-grader, but Mr. Maiello agreed to make an exception, saying that I could start with private lessons and join when my skills caught up to the other students.

The school band policy required that I commit to practicing 30 minutes a day, six days a week, which I readily agreed to. Since I was an overachiever, that was easy. I was a terrific rule-follower, which was an asset 12 years later when I joined the U.S. Air Force as a musician! I was fairly self-disciplined in all areas of my life, and that quality, along with perseverance and dedication to my craft, continues to serve me well to this day.

Mr. Maiello asked me what instrument I wanted to play, but I didn't have a clue. I didn't know what any of the instruments looked like, what they were called, or what they sounded like, because I had never been exposed to band music before. But I *could* tell him the names of all the New York Yankee ballplayers, their batting averages, and all the MLB team standings! I debated whether to offer that important data, but suppressed the urge as he suggested I play the flute, because there were no beginning flute players in my grade.

I wasn't sure what that would entail, so I took out a Montgomery Ward catalog and scrutinized every musical instrument I could find so I could make a decision. I found out that the flute was held up with both arms, pressed up against the mouth, and played to the right side of the face past the body. I figured my arms would get really tired holding it up like that, so I said, "No, that doesn't interest me." It was the alto saxophone, gold and curvy, that got my attention. *That's* the one I wanted to play! But Mr. Maiello said there were already enough saxophone players. Finally, he offered me the clarinet, saying that it was a better instrument to start with, and later on, I could learn the saxophone. That suited me fine, and I was all in!

A year after starting on the clarinet, in 7th grade, I began piano lessons, so now I was practicing two instruments per day. My piano teacher also required that I practice six days/week, and I had to turn in practice sheets. Of course, I did that, in keeping with my overachiever status and rule-following attitude. (My brother Dave also took piano lessons and did *not* practice as much as I did. And once again, he did *no*t get punished!)

It was easy for me to practice, though. I *loved* it, and l wanted to keep getting better and better. I even brought my clarinet on our family vacations when we traveled in an RV (which for us was a Winnebago, back in the 1970s) and practiced at the campgrounds, so I wouldn't miss my practice routine!

I hated to admit it, but my love for music was beginning to overtake my love for baseball. And after my cat Reggie ran away, I didn't have another cat to distract me for the remainder of my adolescence, so I was very focused on music.

After a year and a half of private lessons, I joined the band halfway through 7th grade and quickly moved up within the ranks of the clarinet section to play the more difficult parts.

By the end of 8th grade, I was the first chair clarinetist. What an accomplishment! At the time, I didn't realize that not everyone in the band had the same practice ethic or motivation to play their instruments that I did. I was more scared of making a mistake and not being accepted than worrying about everyone else's practice routine. I never, ever, asked anyone how much they practiced.

At the first concert I performed in, all the other school bands and choirs, both junior high and high school, also performed, and when I heard the high school jazz band – or "Stage Band," as it was called back then – I totally fell in love with it. *I HAVE to learn the saxophone so I can play in that group!* became my obsession.

I started saxophone lessons in 8th grade and joined the Stage Band in 9th grade, playing the large, baritone sax, and practiced three instruments daily. When I entered high school at Franklin Academy, the school my mother had attended, I knew without a doubt that I was going to be a music major in college and have a career in music.

I eventually switched from baritone sax to alto, and it didn't take long to notice that some of the sax parts with the Stage Band called for "doubling" (the ability to play more than one instrument), namely the clarinet and flute. My next step? *Flute* lessons, of course!

Midway through my junior year of high school, I practiced four instruments on a regular basis and took private lessons on each one. I admit that some of my practice time was spent in front of the television in my bedroom, spending hours watching the Yankees play. I became adept at practicing and watching the games simultaneously.

Also in my junior year, I started taking clarinet lessons from the professor of clarinet at Crane School of Music, the music department at Potsdam State University, only 45 minutes from our house. Mom drove me regularly back and forth every Saturday, even taking piano lessons herself from a college student while I was at my clarinet lessons.

In high school, every year, we performed solos with a piano accompanist for adjudication at the New York State School Music Association (NYSSMA) Festival, which also served as an audition for the All-State Band. That's when I saw that the hard work I'd put in, with all the hours of practicing, had paid off. In my senior year, I was selected for the New York All-State High School Band.

The All-State Festival took place at a convention center in Kiamesha Lake, a few hours downstate in the Catskill Mountains. Our Stage Band was also selected to perform at that event, so for the conference, I carried both my sax and clarinet with me. My parents accompanied the band on the trip – which turned out to be a tremendous blessing.

After the final in-person clarinet auditions to determine our seating placement for the concert band, I started walking through the back of the clarinet section, looking for my name, but it was not there. Puzzled, I walked toward the front row, and a huge rush of adrenaline combined with disbelief filled my entire body. *That's my name on the First Chair!* What a *huge*, unexpected honor!

The players next to me were from New York City, and took lessons at the Juilliard School of Music, one of the premier music colleges in the country. Here I was, a simple girl from a small town of 10,000 people, who lived in a remote part of the state near Canada, placed ahead of these very fine high school players! I was very humbled, and so grateful that my parents were in attendance for that concert, proud that they could experience the fruit of what they had supported for so many years.

I loved playing multiple instruments, which fit nicely into the creative outlet I needed to fill on a daily basis. I clearly had inherited my mother's love for music, and although I didn't inherit her beautiful singing voice, that didn't matter. She had given me the opportunity to find my niche in life, all pointing back to that tough decision to enroll me in public school.

In the fall semester of 1978, I entered college at Crane School of Music, where I had taken private lessons during high school, and was fortunate to be part of the music groups that performed at the 1980 Winter Olympic Games in Lake Placid, New York, the year the U.S. hockey team won the gold medal. Potsdam State University, which housed the music school, was only an hour's drive from Lake Placid, and with three performing bands, we were bused back and forth on a rotating schedule, providing music for both the opening and closing ceremonies, along with all the national anthems for the winners in each daily event.

Playing at the Winter Olympics was the highlight of my two years at Crane, and in my junior year of college, I transferred to Michigan State University (MSU) to study clarinet with world-renowned clarinetist Elsa Ludewig-Verdehr. I concentrated on performance and instrumental music education. I didn't know exactly what I was going to do with my music career, or in what direction it would take me, but I wanted to keep all my options open. I had faith that when the right opportunity presented itself, I would know what it was.

That opportunity came after I completed my undergraduate degree in Instrumental Music Education from MSU and continued with graduate school in the Woodwind Specialist program.

One day, while walking by my clarinet professor's office, I noticed a flyer advertising for a clarinetist in the U.S. Air Force Band at Langley Air Force Base (AFB), Virginia. *Hmmm… I wonder what that would be like.*

The thought of playing in a military band intrigued me, and I wrestled with the decision because I had not yet completed graduate school, but a nagging tug inside me said, "Go for it!" – and so I did! I had spent so many years in school as a student that I felt I needed more life experience before I would ever be an effective music teacher. Plus, I loved to perform, and this would be an incredible opportunity to fulfill that dream.

I was also quite eager to leave behind the extreme winters of Michigan and upstate New York for the more moderate climate of Virginia. I loved the four seasons and would still be able to experience them.

I sent my Senior Recital tape as my audition to the commander at Langley AFB, was accepted, and then completed the audition process in person at Wright Patterson AFB, Ohio. In July 1984, I entered Basic Training at Lackland AFB, Texas, and after six long weeks of heat and humidity in the Deep South, I moved to Virginia to play with incredible musicians and begin another phase of my life and music career.

But not before another cat adventure happened by accident, courtesy of a young gold-and-white kitten named Samantha.

CHAPTER 6

SAMANTHA

"Mom, this is Samantha, your college cat. You might find this hard to believe, but my soul has been with your family before in the body of another cat. Pay close attention to the story your mom told you about Oliver! We both had a great internal GPS! Your mom felt a familiarity with both of us, and although I did my best to convince her to let me stay in her home again as Samantha, she ignored it. I don't give up easily, though, and in the future, there will be another cat named Boots that she will fall in love with (who also has a great GPS, hint hint...). Your mom won't understand why she feels so drawn to him, but you'll eventually make the connection between the three of us, and it will make you very happy!"

– Samantha

While practicing my clarinet late one October evening in 1981, in a practice room at Michigan State University's music building, I met my college boyfriend of three years, Jeff, a 6'6" jazz tenor sax player. We both enjoyed practicing late at night, along with the conversations that ensued on our breaks. We got to know each other well, and soon we began dating.

I lived in Spartan Village, one of the university housing complexes, which consisted of several neighborhoods of very small houses. My roommate was another clarinetist, and when she eventually moved out, Jeff moved in with me for seven months prior to starting Law School at the University of Michigan in Ann Arbor and my joining the Air Force.

Spartan Village did not allow pets, but that didn't stop a small, gold-striped female kitten from showing up outside our front door, obviously hungry. We were in a dilemma. I was a good rule-follower, but my love for cats and desire to always help a homeless, hungry animal overruled the housing policy. At least initially.

We snuck the kitten into the house, took care of her, and in no time at all, we bonded. We named her Samantha. She had a very sweet disposition, was undemanding, calm, and yet sociable – the perfect pet! And we thought she would make a great playmate for my mom's older, gold-and-white striped cat Oscar, so we devised a plan.

On my next trip to Malone to see my parents, Jeff and I would drive Samantha all the way from East Lansing, Michigan, across Canada to upstate New York in Jeff's 1970 maroon-colored Pontiac LeMans. We would deliver her to my mother, who would undoubtedly welcome this lovable companion with open arms. What a great solution!

We didn't have a cat carrier, so once again, I transported a cat without one, apparently suffering from amnesia over Goldy's expedition to the 4th-grade Science Fair. I would hold Samantha and let her sit on my lap. *What could go wrong?*

It was a 12-hour drive, and after 11 long hours sitting in the car with only an hour left, we decided to stop at a grocery store. We left Samantha in the car by herself, and when we returned, she was nowhere to be found!

My heart sank as we had safely driven for miles and miles across Canada, only to lose her at the very end. We made several "Lost Cat' signs to put up at that store in hopes that somebody had seen her, and spent about an hour aimlessly wandering around the vicinity looking for her.

We eventually went back to the car, feeling despondent that after all that effort, she was no longer with us. But suddenly, when I opened the car door, we heard a faint sound coming from the dashboard area behind the glove compartment. *Mew...mew...* We looked closer and saw that Samantha had climbed up underneath the dash and was hiding, no doubt traumatized from the endless hours in the car and utterly confused about what was happening to her! *What a relief...*

We were ecstatic that we had not lost her, and that she was safe! Jeff reached up behind the dash with his long arms and slowly pulled her out, with a bit of resistance on her part, but she emerged from her hiding place with no bumps or bruises. We were back to our original plan as if nothing had happened to interrupt our mission! We continued onward to Malone, New York, for the last hour's drive.

The "homecoming" for Samantha was, shall we say, *less than perfect*. Of course, I had presumed that my mother would love to have another cat, but she didn't have the same vision that I did about providing a playmate for Oscar.

I was in my early 20s, still lacking the full development of my frontal cortex and the ability to reason effectively – oh, and did I mention a wee bit hardheaded? If I had even *heard* Mom say, "No, not interested" when I brought the subject up to her, it went in one ear and out the other. I would not take no for an answer! I was confident in my ability to talk her into it, especially when she saw what a sweet cat Samantha was.

After we returned to Michigan, I was sure that Samantha had adjusted to life in Malone with her new friend Oscar, yet at the same time, I was scared to ask if anything was wrong when Mom failed to talk about her. Eventually, I summoned the courage, and she told me that Samantha had run away.

Mom thought Oscar was fine just by himself, and I didn't find out until much later – years, in fact – that Samantha had *not* run away. At the time, I'm sure Mom didn't want to hurt my feelings, especially after all the trouble we had gone through to bring Samantha to Malone.

Years later, Mom told me the truth – that she had found another home almost immediately for Samantha "at the end of Wellington Street, turn left, and go up the hill on Route 11 for about a mile." But about a week later, Samantha found her way back to my mother's house all by herself! *Another cat with an incredible internal GPS… Flashbacks to Oliver, Mom's cat that returned when she and Dad were younger!* This time, though, my mother didn't keep the cat after it returned, but found *another* home for it on a farm farther out of town.

Samantha remained there for what I presumed to be the rest of her life. I can only hope that it was a happy one, and that she was loved. The last time I saw her was when Jeff and I left her at my parents' house and drove back to Michigan.

I was both sad and angry, but I'm not sure if I was angrier at myself or my mother (who I thought dearly loved cats and would love this one, too), or at my powerlessness over the situation. And my heart broke at the thought that Samantha was not wanted in our family. *I had let her down.* I would have kept her, but that was not an option. I had to try to come to grips with the fact that I had made the best choices that I possibly could, given the circumstances.

As I reflect back on this drama that unfolded with Samantha, the entire story could be summed up in four words: *What was I thinking?*

I don't know why I made the choices I did, and I would do *everything* differently today. First of all, animals are not a commodity to be 'dealt with' or used. My cats are an integral part of my family. They have emotions, thoughts, and desires. Samantha deserved better than what I gave her.

Next, instead of foisting her on my mom, who clearly did *not* want another cat, I would have earnestly sought out a family that wanted to give her a loving home. I would have put Samantha's needs first, not my wishful thinking and fear of letting her go to anyone else. I was so intent on keeping Samantha in the family that I had no room in my mind to consider any other possibility.

And driving for 12 hours in a car with a loose cat and no carrier? That was *total insanity.* I was so determined to make it work that I didn't see how selfish I was; then, following through with the plan without my mother's promise that she'd keep the cat was the icing on my cake of stupidity. Which brings me to another life lesson...

Question: What happens when one of your good character traits runs amuck?

Answer: Something that was once an *asset* now becomes a *liability*.

My unwavering determination and commitment to persevering at a task till the bitter end had turned into a terrible urge to control the situation, such that I was imposing *my will* over the circumstances to achieve the result that *I* wanted – much like a human bulldozer!

I would love to say that I learned that lesson quickly about relinquishing control, but unfortunately, I didn't! I'm still wrestling with those tendencies, but I am doing much better at letting go of things that are out of my control and learning to go with the flow.

In other words, *let go of the results*. And sometimes, not making *any* decision is the best course of action!

As with many other choices I made during my younger years, I've come to realize that it's pointless to beat myself up for the bazillion things I should have done differently, not only for Samantha, but in other areas of my life as well. I have to give myself some grace, even though it seemed that the logical side of my brain was missing in action on many occasions. At least my heart was always in the right place, and I tried to make the best decisions I could at the time.

Allowing myself to stop reliving the past and move forward without harboring bitterness in my heart toward myself or anyone else due to poor decision-making has led to a much more peaceful life.

Many years later, a third cat, Boots, would teach me about the tapestry linking him with Oliver and Samantha – and the relationship of all three to my mom. At the time, though, I couldn't see anything except the huge mistakes I made in mishandling my sweet girl Samantha's life.

My not-so-great choices would also make better sense to me later in life, once again confirming the same Bible verse that has guided me before, Romans 8:28: *We know that all things work together for good to them that love God, to them who are called according to His purpose.* For that, I am so grateful.

There would be many more cats coming into my life after Samantha in unexpected ways, each with their own story. But since I was about to start my life as a traveling Air Force musician, how could that be possible?

Early Years

Dad in the Army

Dad and Mom

Me almost 3 years old

Steve holding Dirt, Me (age 4)

Karen (16), Me (4), Steve (12) and Dirt!

Mom and Dad, Me with Goldy, Dave with Speedy

Steve holding the gray kitten, Karen holding Dave, and Me wearing my First Communion dress

Reggie and Mozart

Wellington St in Summer

Wellington St in Winter

Graduation from Michigan State with my clarinet 1983

Goofy Family 1978

Family 1983

Family 1978

CHAPTER 7

BIG BOY & LITTLE BOY

"Hold on tight, Mom… You have no idea how much your life is about to change now that I'm back. It's no surprise that I remind you of your first cat, Kimba – it's more than just our black-and-gray stripes. You and I already have a strong bond from your childhood, although you haven't figured it out yet. We're going to have such a great life together, and years from now, you'll recognize me again in another cat body (dare I say it) – a calico!"

– Big Boy

Jeff and I went our separate ways in July 1984 when I joined the Air Force, braving the intense summer heat of San Antonio, Texas, for six weeks of Basic Training, and then reporting to my first duty station at Langley Air Force Base in Hampton, Virginia.

Within the first week of rehearsal as an Air Force musician, I was totally dumbfounded at the amazing world I had just entered! I performed in a 45-member concert band, was surrounded by superb musicians, rehearsed four to five hours per day, and traveled by bus one week per month, performing community relations concerts in towns throughout Virginia, North Carolina, South Carolina, Tennessee, West Virginia, and

Maryland. We also supported local military ceremonies and patriotic events. I was totally living the dream!

At least in my professional life. My personal life was less than stellar. My relationship with Jeff was the first long-term one that I'd had. There were others that were shorter, but they seemed to end up in a similar fashion, with both of us drifting apart emotionally and/or through geographical separation. I'd known Jeff and I would eventually split up, as our long-term goals were not the same, and we weren't at the "settling down" stage of life while still in college.

I believe my relationship difficulties started as early as age five when a friend of my sister wanted me to touch him in an inappropriate way. Although I *didn't*, being put into that unsafe situation scarred me emotionally for my entire life in ways I never understood. I buried that experience deep within me until the memory of it returned in my early 50s when my marriage was falling apart. It was then that I finally began to understand the deeper cause of my difficulties, as well as my tomboy tendencies as a child.

The relationships I wound up in during my early college years were a combination of my naivete about men and being in the wrong place at the wrong time (#MeToo). I won't elaborate because I don't like to give fuel to negative experiences or memories so as not to perpetuate them.

After a frustrating downhill spiral regarding relationships, I had a "Come to Jesus" meeting, shall we say, with an authentic spiritual conversion experience on October 11, 1985. I remember the date because I was watching the movie *E.T.* by myself at Andrews Air Force Base, where I was spending the night en route to catching a military flight back to Langley the next day.

I earnestly cried out to God for help, and that night, I felt an overwhelming amount of love and acceptance. Multiple Bible passages sprang out at me as I read them, and I felt like I was starting my life over! For the next couple years, I felt "spiritually free," but eventually, the emotional, relationship baggage I carried returned.

I thought that when you began to have a more personal relationship with God through Jesus Christ, it meant that all your troubles and trauma disappeared! Back then, I didn't have the skills or knowledge to understand major concepts like "inner healing." I not only had *stuffed* my feelings surrounding trauma, but I'd totally *dismissed* them, thinking they were gone forever.

Later in life, I would gain a clearer understanding of my deep trust issues surrounding men, resulting in being attracted to relationships that would never last and men who were unavailable to me in some way.

After that powerful spiritual conversion, though, it never entered my mind that I had any underlying emotional issues that would one day surface. I was optimistic about the future, and met my husband of 27 years, Chuck, a Naval Officer, two weeks later.

We met at a Bible study on Halloween night that was also a "Hallelujah" dress-up party. Chuck came dressed like Chuckles the Clown, and I was a New York Yankees fan wearing a Yankee baseball cap and whatever silly clothes I could put together that looked festive. I had just returned from a week-long band tour that afternoon, and it was a last-minute decision to attend. We started dating soon after that, and were married a year later in Hampton, Virginia.

In my church life, I started attending daily mass at the base chapel at Langley on a regular basis, a ritual which I did faithfully for over 20 years. Of course, that kept my childhood pattern of "trying to do as much religion as I could to please God" fully intact.

I was also consciously doing everything I could think of spiritually to ensure that we had a lifelong marriage, since the current divorce rate was nearly 50% of all married couples – and I didn't want that to happen. Daily mass was part of my personal checklist.

Chuck and I became actively involved with a group of other Christians that was an extension of the Charismatic Renewal movement and included prayer meetings, home fellowship groups, and wonderful friendships.

We purchased a four-bedroom townhouse in Virginia Beach, but the thought of having a cat or any other animal was not even on our radar. With my travels as an Air Force musician, and Chuck's remaining time in the Navy – including his deployments – it was not the ideal living situation to bring a cat into.

Just like my own cat-filled childhood, cats were part of Chuck's life, too, while growing up in middle Tennessee. He *liked* them and *wasn't allergic*, fulfilling two of my marital pre-requisites! By this time, it had been 15 years since I'd had a cat of my own, not counting Samantha who only entered my life for a brief time. Actually, I was skeptical about ever having one again, since I was moving around so much, and living in different places had become a way of life.

But our circumstances shifted in the spring of 1988, when Chuck resigned his commission with the Navy, and enrolled in graduate school at Regent University, just a mile from our house. Only one of us would be traveling now. We were still not thinking about a pet, though.

Until...

In September 1998, a portly, divorced woman we knew through our church, "Miss Gail," as we called her, invited me to her home. We had become close friends in a very short time. While there, the cutest little male, black-and-gray striped tiger kitten came strutting down the hallway and decided he wanted to sit on my lap — so he did! *This feels so good! I had forgotten how much I missed holding a cat, feeling its body purring against mine, and oh, the love from their hearts! I'm in heaven...*

This little guy, whom she called Zanny (named after a cartoon character), was about six months old and had belonged to Miss Gail's daughter, Gloria. They were now looking for a new home for him, because Gloria had recently moved into an apartment that didn't allow animals. Living with Miss Gail was only a temporary situation for the kitten, and if she couldn't find another home for him soon, she would take him to a shelter. *I can't let that happen. I want him...*

Zanny's life had a rather rough start. First, he was allergic to his mother's milk and had to be bottle-fed, and then Gloria's boyfriend accidentally stepped on him while walking down the stairs, breaking his leg. They didn't take him to a vet, and it eventually healed on its own, but as a result, Zanny was never able to jump very well or climb a tree.

After I left Miss Gail's house that day, my mind was totally preoccupied with wanting this little guy, and I couldn't think about anything else. Tiger cats were my favorites, going back to Kimba, my first cat that had disappeared, returned, and then been hit by a car. Now I had a chance to have another one. *What is it with Zanny that feels so familiar? I can't put my finger on it.*

Chuck was out of town when all this happened. He and I were involved in pro-life work in the early years of our marriage, and after getting out of the Navy, he participated in some of Operation Rescue's missions of peaceful protesting against abortion laws. He was in Atlanta with some of our friends for a large demonstration at an abortion clinic with hundreds of other people. Nevertheless, I just *had* to call him, because I really wanted this cat that I had become obsessed with. After a wee bit of coaxing, Chuck agreed that I could adopt him, and I was so excited I could hardly contain myself!

When Chuck came home, we picked the cat up from Miss Gail's house – in a carrier, I might add – and changed "Zanny" to "Bartolo*mew*," so named because we wanted a biblical name that we wouldn't name a child. Plus, the "mew" at the end gave it the connection to a feline. That's one of those moments I look back on now, roll my eyes and say, "What was I thinking?"

This playful tiger cat kitten grew quickly into a big boy – and that's what his name came to be: "Big Boy." I bonded with him instantly – actually, from that first moment he jumped on my lap, if the truth be known. And one of the results of his having been bottle-fed as a young kitten was that he bonded to humans more than to other cats.

Miss Gail told me that he liked to sleep on her pillow at night, kneading her hair. He never outgrew that sleeping habit and did the same thing to me! My pillow and hair became his permanent nesting place. I would lie on my right side, and he would plop his growing body against my head and "make bread" in my hair. When I turned to sleep on my left side, he turned his body, too, and always faced the side I was facing. His voluminous, motorboat purr was totally soothing, and this became our bedtime ritual for the next 15 years until his last day on Earth!

To say that I had a connection with this cat would be a total understatement. We were inseparable when I was home, and it tore me apart to leave him alone during the day when Chuck and I were at work. He *always* wanted to play! His favorite game was to paw at something in the slim crack of a partially opened door, specifically the door to our walk-in closet.

When we weren't home, I was imagining him by himself all day, lonely and bored. I felt like a neglectful pet owner. (Years later, when due to a bout with whooping cough, I was forced to stay home for an extended period of time to recover, I observed firsthand that he slept, on average, about 23 hours/day, and I was able to release that guilt.)

It was obvious within just a few months that Big Boy needed a playmate.

In December, we found out about some kittens in the neighborhood available for adoption, so Chuck made arrangements to see them. By the time we arrived, there was only one male left, so we said we'd take him, and with no delay, we walked home carrying a small, black ball of fur with a face and body buried somewhere down in the middle of it! I'm sure this little guy was the runt of the litter.

Our newest family member was the first long-haired cat I ever had – a completely black kitten, except for a white spot on his chest. We brought him home on New Year's Eve and named him Gabriel, after the archangel. It seemed to fit with the season, along with our theme of naming him "something biblical we probably wouldn't name a child." In all fairness to our poor choice of names for cats, we wanted to reserve the other male Bible names for any future children we might have.

Like Big Boy, Gabriel's archaic name didn't last long. Although only six months younger than Big Boy, he was significantly smaller, so this black ball of fur became "Little Boy!" He was a pesky fellow, and his favorite activity was climbing up my pant legs while I was cooking in the kitchen – *ouch!* Those claws were sharp! We quickly learned how to trim both boys' nails. Between my scratched-up legs from Little Boy and my gently clawed face from Big Boy's kneading at night, I had become a pincushion.

Little Boy was a very demanding and needy kitten, and I honestly couldn't wait until he grew out of the kitten stage. He eventually did, and may have actually been bigger than Big Boy, if you counted his long, beautiful, fluffy black fur. The long hair was very difficult for me to get used to, though, and years later, after cutting numerous clumped mats off his body, we happily discovered cat groomers! I don't think Little Boy ever liked the ribbons they put in his hair after he was groomed, but I thought he looked very stylish.

Our four-bedroom townhouse in Virginia Beach was located in a heavily trafficked area with a tiny yard, so it was not safe for the boys to be outside. I wasn't used to having cats that lived exclusively indoors, so I became filled with stress and guilt about leaving them inside all the time. I believed they were missing out on all the cat fun, like catching and killing bugs, mice, birds, chipmunks, etc. Oh, and also the ever-popular grass-eating routine, coming back inside the house after the grass feast and vomiting... *Well, maybe I could get used to having an indoor cat!*

We lived with these two cats in Virginia Beach for two years, and also briefly adopted an older female Maine Coon cat that we brought home from a yard sale... No, not *for* sale, just one that had wandered into the yard, looking for sympathetic humans to help her out and bring her home. That would be *us*, and a sign of things to come – and to come *soon*.

In June of 1990, I found myself sitting stoically in my commander's office at Langley AFB, being told the unbelievable news that the Air Force was transferring me to Yokota Air Base, Japan – a place I had never heard of – much to my dismay at the thought of leaving the band at Langley. *How could this have happened?*

I was number two on the *non-volunteer* list and had even told some friends recently that "it would take an act of God to move me from this place." That was how convinced I was that I would stay at Langley permanently, but, apparently, an act of God was stronger than my wishful thinking.

On the other hand, I thought it would be very exciting to live in a foreign country. I just thought that if that ever happened, it would be somewhere in Europe, not Asia.

But what about the cats?

Thankfully, Japan and the United States had a relationship under the Status of Forces Agreement (SOFA) that allowed us to transport two animals with us, with no quarantine requirements except 14 days in our house, as long as the paperwork, vaccines, and vet health check were completed. If we had not been able to do this, I probably would have refused the assignment and taken my only other option, which was to be discharged at the end of my enlistment instead.

Chuck's mother helped us find a home for the Maine Coon we had named Mitzi. I was disappointed, but at the same time, she hadn't been with us long, was elderly, and would have had a difficult time making the trip. I was happy that she would have a new family that loved her.

For the record, I left for Japan first to secure housing for us, and during the six weeks Chuck was waiting to join me, he drove Mitzi *in a cat carrier* to his parents' house in Tennessee, several hours away.

We were about to embark on a new chapter of our lives with Big Boy and Little Boy. Little did we know about the multitude of other furry additions that would join us over the next five years.

Japan, here we come!

CHAPTER 8

AMERICAN VILLAGE

"Mom, seriously, that was a long plane ride to Japan. Thankfully, we're here now, and we like our new house. We are especially thrilled that we get to go outside and play! But if you feed us any more of that 'healthy food' (barf...), we're going to have to start hunting on our own!"

– Big Boy and Little Boy

I arrived at Yokota Air Base by myself in September 1990, and stayed in temporary living quarters for six weeks until off-base housing was secured, when Chuck, Big Boy, and Little Boy would come and join me.

We would soon be moving into a quiet Japanese neighborhood called American Village, adjacent to a large, beautiful city park, where we frequently rode our bikes on the numerous trails lined with flowering Japanese cherry blossom trees in the spring. The land had previously served as Tachikawa Air Base during WW II for American troops, but after the base closed, it was converted to a park.

American Village was built specifically for the Americans stationed at the base. It consisted of four residential streets with five single-dwelling homes on each side, and since it was only a 10-minute drive to Yokota, it became one of the off-base housing options for both U.S. military and civilians stationed there, along with a handful of Japanese families.

These small, roughly 1,100 square-foot houses were constructed with whatever materials were available after the war. You could actually touch real tree limbs holding up the roof of our house when you climbed into the attic! As the homes began to age, they deteriorated to the point where they were considered "condemned" and no longer met USAF standards until they were renovated.

When I arrived that fall, the house we would live in was still under renovation for six more weeks until Chuck and the two cats – who were in overall good health but looked a little shell-shocked after the nearly 24-hour plane trip – arrived to join me. We were the first occupants of this newly refurbished property, albeit uninsulated, which proved to be a little chilly when we woke up to 40-degree temperatures one morning with frost on the single-pane windows!

We had no telephone – cell phones were not in use yet – and if we needed to call someone, we used the green phone booth in the neighborhood, inserting a prepaid phone card.

I had the best job on the planet! The 35-member Air Force Band of the Pacific had a varied mission, which included Troop Support (from performing for military ceremonies and leadership training graduations on bases throughout the Pacific Rim to background music for official military dinners and occasions like the Marine Corps Birthday Ball in Tokyo, and building community relations with foreign countries throughout Asia).

I loved the community relations aspect of my job, which included performing for students in schools throughout Japan, Korea, and Thailand. It was interesting to me that in many Japanese schools, classical music was piped throughout the loudspeakers between classes while the students walked from room to room.

When the band wasn't needed to perform as a large ensemble like a marching band, we broke into smaller groups: a popular music combo/rock band, a small jazz band/show band, and my group, the Pacific Winds, a woodwind quintet comprised of clarinet, flute, oboe, bassoon, and French horn. I was the clarinetist.

Traveling with the Pacific Winds was a joy. We were an acoustic group that needed very little equipment except our instruments, so we didn't take up much space when we performed or traveled. Occasionally, our transportation was provided on small T-37B jets flown by Air Force pilots looking for opportunities to maintain their flying hours. It was the perfect way to travel, and we were treated like royalty!

One trip to Thailand with the Quintet involved a cultural exchange with one of the Hill Tribes of northern Thailand, sponsored by the U.S. Information Services (USIS). In reality, the efforts of the USIS were to try and stop the use and trade of heavy opium drugs.

We traveled in an all-terrain vehicle onto a secluded dirt road to one of the Hill Tribe villages, where there was no electricity at the job site. By the time everyone had gathered around the open-air pavilion we played on, with no music stands and only tables in front of us to hold our music, it was dark. The only light source was rigged up with an overhead light fixture attached to the vehicle's battery to provide electricity.

After we played our portion of the "cultural exchange," we learned traditional dances from the Hill Tribe members. There were about 70 people total, and all the women were wearing colorful native dresses.

We spent the night in a building that would remind you of a weekend camping trip, complete with bugs and a community bathroom, but at least the sleeping quarters were separated for men and women, and it had electricity and running water!

As a full band, our duties took us to Hawaii, Guam, and Australia. We were sent to Townsville, Australia, twice (via Navy aircraft, where through the back window, we watched our plane being refueled in mid-air) to commemorate the 50th Anniversaries of the Battle of the Coral Sea and the end of WW II.

Among the activities we participated in was a reenactment of the victory parade through the streets of Townsville, where we marched in WW II era uniforms. As we paraded through the streets with multiple other military units and the Royal Australian Air Force Band (RAF), thousands of enthusiastic onlookers were cheering us, and I have never felt prouder to be an American than in those moments.

The Australian people were so grateful to us for our role in their freedom at the end of the war, and it was difficult to play my instrument in that parade with all the tears in my eyes.

Every community relations endeavor included visits to nearby attractions from that locale, such as the Billabong Animal Sanctuary and a Koala refuge in Australia (I even got to hold a koala!), temples and historic sites in Japan and Thailand, and beautiful nature spots everywhere.

To retell all the stories from my five-year musical career in Japan would take volumes, but it remains the highlight of my musical life. I'm grateful that I realized this at the time and cherished every moment as it was happening.

Chuck found employment teaching English to high school students at a nearby Japanese private school and added a part-time job on Saturdays teaching conversational English to adults at a school in Tokyo.

Our house in American Village was the first one visible as you drove into the neighborhood, and only two other houses on the street were occupied. The first by an older Japanese couple, and the second by a constant turnaround of Department of Defense (DOD) teachers who only stayed long enough to complete their tour of duty. Our house and the one belonging to the teachers were the only ones renovated, and the rest of them were all condemned.

Some of the houses directly behind ours were upgraded, with other Americans living in them. We became close friends with one couple, Rhonda and Mike, who also had two cats. Rhonda taught English at the same school as Chuck, and Mike was a C-130 cargo plane navigator in the Air Force.

We settled into a lifestyle of my traveling throughout Japan and other parts of Asia and the Pacific with the Air Force Band, while Chuck taught English. We took one two-week vacation back to the States after a year of living overseas, but the jet lag was too difficult to overcome in such a short time, so we focused our attention on traveling in time zones closer to where we lived. That included Singapore, South Korea, Thailand, Malaysia, Indonesia, Hawaii, Australia, and New Zealand.

Neither Chuck's nor my parents had ever visited Japan, and we were blessed by visits from both of them over the course of our five-year assignment. That also gave us the incentive we needed to travel to historic places such as Nagasaki, Hiroshima, Kyoto, and Nara. Chuck even joined his parents on a hike up Mt. Fuji – I had already done it once, which, in my mind, was enough for one lifetime! With Rhonda and Mike, we took turns finding unique restaurants in Tokyo and planned at least one culinary adventure per month. Those were five of the best years of my life!

Big Boy and Little Boy adjusted to life in Japan fairly well, especially since we gave them the opportunity to periodically venture outside, initially on a collar and leash, and later transitioning to letting them roam freely. They never strayed far from the house, and we kept a close eye on them. Chuck and I were totally overprotective cat parents.

The cats slept on average about 23 hours/day, keeping the bed warm on the cold evenings in our uninsulated house. Other than that, they didn't really do much of anything, so I thought it was time to use some creativity and change their routine.

I've always been super interested in health and wellness, wanting to learn as much as I can about nutrition, supplements, herbal remedies, and natural types of healing and wholeness, even to this day. I'm not sure what possessed me, but this interest – or shall we say, *obsession* – spilled over to the area of natural cat health, and after reading a book on it, which included recipes for homemade cat food, I decided to give it a try. *These two boys are going to love it! Gourmet delights, here we come, and it's sure to be an improvement over the store-bought, processed food they've been eating. I'm so excited!*

I made sandwich-size plastic bag portions of food with ground beef and some sort of vitamin concoction and removed all the store-bought food from the cats' diet, putting the remaining unused dry food bags on top of a tall kitchen cabinet, way out of reach. I'm not sure why I didn't throw it away, except for the fact that I've never liked wasting anything. I froze the extra homemade food packets and took them out as needed.

The first week I introduced the new food, Big Boy and Little Boy seemed to enjoy the fresh ground beef taste, but there was definitely *no variety*, and *no choice*. The novelty wore off quickly, and within two weeks, I'm convinced that their familiar dry food that was situated on top of the cabinet acquired a voice and began calling to them. They responded with a serious case of kangaroo envy, attempting to leap up to the top of the cabinet out of desperation to get to it! They were unsuccessful and, thankfully, not injured…

I thought Big Boy and Little Boy would embrace this culinary change and thank me forever for enriching their lives with tantalizing, vitamin-laced ground beef entrees, but in their minds, I'm sure they believed they were being eternally punished and sent to Kitty Kat Hell's Kitchen for no reason!

The two cats obviously didn't appreciate my brilliant nutritional insights, and I finally paid attention to their mournful pleas to save them from starvation. It was painfully obvious that I was torturing them, so I relented and went back to feeding them store-bought food. My two ravenous boys no longer had to exercise their jumping abilities to try and reclaim their dry "junk food," and I'm grateful they didn't hold a grudge against me.

So much for that brilliant idea! *I wonder what next feline adventure awaits...*

CHAPTER 9

BALLOON CAT

"Mom, I'm so misunderstood! Those vets who labeled me "aggressive"… Didn't they understand that it's my job to protect you, that I've got your back? And if anyone ever tries to muzzle me again, well, they'll learn what I'm made of! And this Balloon Cat episode… Well, I'll let Little Boy talk about that. I'm too embarrassed."

– Big Boy

"Mom, this was freaky. My brother got so big that he looked like the Goodyear blimp! You might even say he got 'too big for his britches,' hee hee… What happened? One day he was fine, and then his body just seemed to blow up! It was scary, and I was afraid it would happen to me, too. At least he wasn't in pain – just oversized. And I know you named him Big Boy, but I have a better one: Frankencat!"

– Little Boy

We were entering into our third year of life in Japan when a stranger-than-fiction episode began brewing with Big Boy. We weren't sure if it was food-related or environmental, but it began the day we noticed that his face seemed slightly larger than normal. Taking a closer look, his throat appeared to be a little swollen. This lasted about three days the first time, and then it returned to its normal size. We didn't think any more about it, until it happened two more times.

After the third flare-up, it became increasingly worrisome and puzzling. *Is he having some type of allergic reaction? If so, what could he be allergic to?* We hadn't changed his food – except that he and Little Boy were no longer subject to my homemade cat food experiment!

We took him to the vet clinic on base, which was becoming an ordeal in itself, as he hated to go there – so much so that they attached a large, bold-lettered note to his records, visible to anyone at least 10 miles away: "Aggressive – Use Muzzle." I didn't like that one bit, and personally thought the vet tech, a large man with a sarcastic personality, was provoking him.

Big Boy was my guardian and protector. Anybody who entered the house had to pass the Big Boy test, and they could only stay if he knew I was safe. He literally approached every visitor, occasionally swatting them if he thought they were a threat. He was not aggressive, just protective, and was a well-behaved boy at the vet clinic in Virginia Beach.

In any case, the vet thought he might have an environmental allergy and suggested we keep him inside for a while. Thanks to the Army Veterinary Program and its mission to treat and care for military working dogs, we were able to access their veterinary services on base.

In my mind, the possibility of an environmental allergy seemed unlikely, because everything in our yard was familiar. Big Boy and Little Boy had been indoor-outdoor cats for nearly two years now, and there was nothing new in our landscape. I didn't realize, however, that an allergy can develop over time, so it was possible that something previously tolerable was now toxic.

The swollen throat cleared up with the help of some medication, and we kept Big Boy inside for longer periods of time. I didn't want him to live this way indefinitely, though, since he was now accustomed to both indoor and outdoor life, so I kept a close eye on what he liked to chew on when he was outside. Through the process of elimination, I noticed that he seemed to be reacting to the bamboo growing in our yard. He liked to chew on the leaves of the bamboo stalks. This would be very difficult to control, but with the medication, the allergy seemed to subside.

Then, something in Big Boy's appearance seemed to change. About two weeks after the last throat episode, when everything had returned to the status quo, we noticed his shoulders, neck, and head seemed to be expanding and were slightly larger than normal. *What is this all about?*

Within a few more days, over the course of a weekend, his *entire body* seemed to be bigger. He looked like the Goodyear blimp with whiskers – not exactly a pretty sight. When we petted him, his fur felt "crinkly" as we rubbed deep into his whole body, but he didn't act like he was in pain, and his personality was normal. We were totally baffled by what was happening to him, causing this grotesque change in appearance.

Big Boy had become Balloon Cat.

We panicked, not knowing if he would keep expanding and eventually burst his skin open, or if he would return to normal, or somewhere in between. *What if he died?* This was Big Boy, my number one cat, and my alarm quickly turned into despair. I was obsessed with this cat and couldn't bear the thought of anything happening to him. He was too young to lose his life this soon.

The base vet clinic was closed on weekends, so rather than wait until they reopened – without a guarantee that they could even see us in the upcoming week – we decided to book the first available appointment with a Japanese vet instead. We were so grateful that he could be seen on Monday morning, and since I had to work, Chuck brought Big Boy in by himself.

We had *never* seen anything like this before – nor have we since – and neither had the vet. As strange as Big Boy looked, the results from the appointment were even stranger. They inserted a needle through his skin to determine what sort of fluid build-up it could be, but there was no fluid – it was AIR! His fur and skin had literally separated from his body, and the gap underneath was filled with air. *What on earth is going on with him?* The vet was just as clueless as we were.

And just when I thought it couldn't get any more bizarre, the instructions from this new vet were even more absurd: He wanted us to confine Big Boy to his cat carrier for six months to minimize his movement.

Frankly, the Japanese vet didn't know what was wrong with him, what caused it, or how to treat it. And to confine my cat to a carrier for six months was *not* going to happen. *Talk about a way to break a cat's spirit…*

We were willing to take the risk of losing Big Boy if it meant letting him live out the remainder of his life where he could be happy, however long that would be. And, I reflected, he was neither in pain nor unhappy.

I admit that over the next two weeks, I never prayed so hard in my life, and all those religious things that Catholics do, like fasting and making sacrifices for a person or cause greater than themselves – well, I did them all, along with a lot of heartfelt begging: *Please don't take Big Boy…*

Every day, we lived on pins and needles as we waited and watched for changes in his appearance. Those were the longest, most nerve-wracking two weeks of my life – living with the uncertainty of my number one cat's outcome was almost unbearable.

Then it happened.

We noticed the swelling in Big Boy's body began to subside. Within 24 hours of the first signs of change, Big Boy returned to his normal body size.

The cause of "Balloon Cat" remained a mystery, and Big Boy never had an allergic reaction on his face or any other part of his body ever again. He even played in the yard, happily chewing bamboo with no medication. Perhaps it was a miracle? I like to think so.

CHAPTER 10

PRETTY GIRL

> *"Mom, thanks for paying attention to that dream that guided you to rescue me, and for calling me 'Pretty Girl' instead of that horrible name from the man who abandoned me, forcing me to fend for myself. And who would ever call a beautiful girl like me 'ugly'? I really like my orange mustache! Now, as I join your family as a mama cat with babies, I have a painful lesson to teach you, but I promise that it will change your beliefs about animal emotions forever."*
>
> – Pretty Girl

Life was fairly calm with Big Boy and Little Boy, and I was certainly not looking to invite any more cats into the family. I started feeding a feral cat across the street, along with a few miscellaneous strays, but nothing more.

In June 1993, I noticed a very thin tortoiseshell cat with an orange mustache marking on her face wandering through our small backyard. I tried not to make eye contact and kept my distance, I'm ashamed to say, because in my mind, if I did, I'd be responsible for doing something about it. But as I looked closer, I could see nipples hanging from her nearly emaciated body. *This cat has kittens somewhere.*

Then I had *the dream*…

Of course, everyone dreams, and it usually plays out like this: You dream, wake up, and if you remember it, you might think about it for a minute. Then it leaves your mind. You forget about it, get out of bed, and start the day. But this dream was different. I can't recall the specific details, but I awoke with a vividly clear message I would describe as a *heavenly mandate* directing me to help this *torti* (a nickname for tortoiseshell cats) and her kittens, wherever they were.

From that day on, I became obsessed with feeding this cat and constantly looked out the kitchen window to see if and when she would show up again. *What was her story? Why was she coming into my yard?*

I didn't know it at the time, but this dream would change my life forever and open the floodgates. More and more cats would "find me" and wiggle their way into my heart and home, serving as catalysts to heal animal-related trauma in both myself and others, and eventually teaching me about animal reincarnation.

More information gradually unfolded after I talked with Rhonda, our neighbor, who referred to this uniquely marked cat as "Mustache." She said that Mustache had been abandoned two years earlier and left to fend for herself by an Air Force man who moved out of an unrenovated house in American Village and into base housing. Mustache kept returning to the house that was now vacant, looking for him.

She was not spayed, and Rhonda remembered seeing her with another litter of kittens about a year earlier. My heart ached.

Heeding the prompting of the dream, Chuck and I left food for Mustache in the backyard, and actively started looking for her hiding place, walking up and down the streets through the neighborhood, hoping to find this feline family.

One evening, as we were walking by an abandoned, unrenovated house a couple of streets behind ours, lo and behold – there she was! We watched her climb up a tree, enter the house through a hole in the roof, and climb down into its interior.

Chuck and I went into the house through the unlocked front door and gasped at the squalor that greeted us. *How long had this house been abandoned? How could anyone live in this filth?* Everything was covered with dirt, the walls had holes, and the structure was collapsing; the whole place reeked of neglect, and a foul odor was everywhere.

We found Mustache caring for four kittens inside a filthy, freestanding, old-fashioned white bathtub whose sides were about 3 feet tall. It was a safe place to keep her babies, who were roughly four weeks old, because there was no way they could climb out. Sadly, the kittens weren't much cleaner than the filthy tub, and the gold-and-white one's eyes were all crusted and tearing.

So, we planned our strategy to help rescue this courageous mama cat and her four babies…

Two days later, we drove our car over to the nasty house in the pouring rain, just in the nick of time to see Mustache trying to relocate her family – no doubt to safety, since her hideout had been discovered. She had lifted each kitten out of the bathtub individually. Although she trusted us enough to feed her, I don't think she had enough confidence that her babies would be safe.

The family of five was slowly trudging away from the house, the babies closely behind their desperate mother. It was a pitiful sight to behold as the rain continued to steadily fall on this homeless family. Mustache was both wet and exhausted, offering no resistance as Chuck and I picked them up one by one. Using the two cat carriers we had brought with us, we gathered the family and brought them to our house, making our second largest bedroom their new home.

We started calling mama cat "*Miss* Mustache" (to give her some dignity!), and temporarily named all four kittens, trying to remain unattached while we looked for permanent homes for them. We planned to keep Miss Mustache, who, along with Big Boy and Little Boy, would only increase our cat household to three. Keeping the kittens seemed impossible with our small house.

Of the four kittens, two were females: a calico and a tortoiseshell who looked like their mother, and two were males: a ginger, who was the largest of the litter, and the gold-and-white one, who was very playful, that we called Spunky – he was my favorite. We isolated them from Big Boy and Little Boy, who were curious but not overly concerned.

Miss Mustache was a wonderful mom to her babies and seemed so happy to finally rest after her life of sacrifice and scrounging for food, so her body would be able to produce enough milk to nurse them. Here, in this quiet bedroom, they now had plenty of food, warmth, safety, a place to play, and lots of love from us!

Although Miss Mustache was her formal name, we soon gave her a nickname like we had done for both Big Boy and Little Boy. We called her "Pretty Girl," because that just seemed to flow out of our mouths when we looked at her. This nickname became very significant when we later found out that the man who previously owned her had called her "Ugly." My heart broke once again for this sweet girl, and I was determined to ensure that she would always feel beautiful and loved.

I would soon learn a very painful lesson from this happy cat family.

Up to this point in my life, with the exception of Samantha from college, all my cats were males, and I had certainly never had a female cat with kittens. I just presumed that, as kittens grew, mother cats were ready to move on with their lives and became unattached to them. Then, when the kittens reached the "adoptable" age of 8-12 weeks, you found a home for them. That's just what everybody did, and I thought it was normal, so we diligently began to look for permanent homes for them as they continued to grow.

We placed a flyer on base, along with an ad in the base newspaper, and tried to spread the information by word of mouth. One of Chuck's students from the Japanese school where he worked adopted the two girls. That was a huge blessing and a relief, because it meant they would be with each other and stay in Japan. One of our permanent neighbors took the ginger-colored male, and that seemed like a safe future for him, too.

Then there was Spunky, my favorite.

A woman who lived on base responded to the ad in the paper, and when she inquired about the calico, we told her that the only remaining one was the gold-and-white male. She agreed to take him, but I should have paid attention to the red flags that were all around this adoption. At the time, I hadn't learned to trust my intuition.

The prospective owner was looking for a playmate for her big, black lab dog, and *really wanted the calico*, but hesitantly said she would settle for Spunky. *Seriously, Kathy? How could you give away your favorite kitten to this woman who didn't really want him, only to become a playmate for her large dog???*

I placed Spunky in the cat carrier that only weeks before had served as his refuge, and now I was uprooting him from everything familiar by sending him to a place unknown with a big, black dog, and to a woman who really wanted his sister. *What am I doing? But I can't turn back… It's too late to change my mind.*

I transported Spunky by myself, and when I arrived at his new home, sadly and with great reluctance, handed the frightened kitten to the woman and said my goodbyes to this little fella that had won my heart. At least I had the presence of mind to tell her to call me if she had any problems.

With all the kittens now relocated to permanent homes, our household consisted of Chuck, me, Big Boy, Little Boy, and Pretty Girl. It was so quiet without the babies. Immediately after Spunky left, though, we noticed that Pretty Girl was wandering around the house, moaning loudly and looking for them. I became distraught as well, sad and guilt-ridden to have gotten rid of her babies without her knowing what was happening. *What had we done?*

If I had been an Animal Communicator back then, the dynamics of the entire scenario would have been different. I don't know if we would have kept any of the kittens, but now that

I communicate with animals, I know we would have resolved the circumstances in a better way. When an animal understands what's happening, it makes a huge difference in how they respond. Watching an animal suffer *without* understanding really breaks my heart.

Although I had never heard the term *empath*, I was highly sensitive, and began feeling Pretty Girl's grief as well as my own – which added to the guilt I felt for betraying this beautiful girl that trusted me so much. Today, I've learned how to manage this intense sensitivity, which has become a gift in the work I do as an Animal Communicator, but at the time, I didn't know how to stop it. It was a traumatic experience for all of us, and the entire household was in mourning.

I've learned that these highly emotional moments as an empath are not always isolated, but can build on themselves from previous similar experiences if the emotions aren't processed in a constructive way when they first occur. Stuffing them and berating oneself out of guilt and regret are not constructive ways to deal with the trauma.

Perhaps my body remembered the emotional impact I'd experienced as a six-year-old watching the Disney movie *Bambi* by myself at the local movie theater. I never recovered after Bambi's mother was shot. And now, here I was almost 20 years later, duplicating those same emotions with Pretty Girl. *Separating a mother from her babies… How could I have done that?*

Today, as an Animal Communicator and Energy Healer, I've learned skills to help alleviate, and even erase, the emotional sting of these animal-related trauma incidents from the past.

It would take almost 30 years, though, and many more experiences along the way before I gained those skills.

Pretty Girl's response to her kittens being given away illustrated to me the powerful bond and range of emotions that the mother of a species can have with her offspring. I *never* wanted to experience this type of grief again.

As fate would have it, the woman who adopted Spunky called me back three days later and told me that the adoption had turned into a disaster, and she didn't know what to do. This frightened little kitten, who had just been removed from his siblings and mother, had been hiding behind a piece of furniture for the entire three days, shaking, and too scared to eat.

I told her immediately that we would take Spunky back. That afternoon, I drove to her house, and we were able to move the furniture to pick him up and load him into the cat carrier. I was beside myself, filled with incredible joy that I had been given another chance with this little boy. What a happy day!

When Spunky and I entered our house, the reunion between Mama Cat and her son was a joyous sight to behold and quickly eased the grief in our household. Pretty Girl doted on him for the rest of their lives, which would be 16 more years when they died within three months of each other!

Spunky, on the other hand, although happy to be back home and reunited with his mom, had been traumatized. He ran and hid whenever the doorbell rang, or if anybody new came to the house, seemingly afraid to be sent away again. He sadly remained that way for the rest of his life.

With his severe separation anxiety, he rarely went outside. In fact, the first time he tried to leave the house after we brought him back, he panicked and hid in a hole underneath one of the houses down the street, shaking. We managed to coax him out, quickly scoop him up, and bring him back home.

In spite of those fears, Spunky had a happy life – even striving daily to become best buddies with Little Boy, but to no avail. This young gold-and-white kitten regularly threw his body on the living room floor alongside Little Boy to *beg* for friendship, but was met with a hiss from a disinterested, large, fluffy black cat that wanted nothing to do with him.

Pretty Girl was a most ingenious, resourceful feline with a very intense, serious, persevering character that was capable of the full gamut of emotions. We had planned to get her spayed but heard that female cats couldn't go into heat while they were still nursing, and we definitely didn't want to put her through surgery while she still had the kittens. But that was definitely wrong information. This emotional, tortoiseshell cat went into heat while still nursing them, and no earplugs on the planet could ease the torture we experienced!

When Samantha, my college cat, went into heat, she was fairly quiet, amiable, affectionate, and made barely audible *mewing* sounds. Pretty Girl was the complete opposite! I was convinced she was at least half Siamese, because she loudly moaned *all the time*, permeating every wall in our small house at all hours of the day and night. We certainly couldn't let her go outside, so there was no relief. Big Boy and Little Boy totally ignored her, since they were both neutered and disinterested!

Pretty Girl's unmanageable moans got even worse, because Chuck and I had scheduled a vacation out of the country, and the cat sitter who agreed to stay in our house was forced to build a "secluded place" for her by the entrance door in an unsuccessful attempt to drown out her wailing so he could sleep!

Finally, after what seemed like months, but in reality was only a few weeks, the moaning tapered down, and her personality returned to normal. We got her spayed, and this was another eye-opening experience for me. I was oblivious to the fact that her stomach needed to be shaved, and when I saw it after the operation, I was shocked. Not only was it difficult to look at that part of her body, but it was full of stitches.

I was 33 years old, had never had surgery, nor had I ever seen anyone who did. To make matters worse, something went wrong during her recovery at home. Her stomach was hanging below her body lower than it should have, almost touching the floor. That sent a wave of panic through us, and we took her back to the vet. The stitches had fallen out, but thank goodness there was no internal damage. He stitched her back up, and she fully recovered. What another ordeal for all of us to experience!

Pretty Girl was as loyal a cat as I've ever had, perhaps even more so than a dog. She did one thing none of my other cats has ever done: go on walks! Not just a casual, feline adventure to hunt for bugs or chipmunks, but she walked *with* us, *next* to us – just like a dog – without a leash.

She followed us everywhere, stopping when we stopped, and walking when we walked. If we diverted from our usual pattern of strolling around the neighborhood, and instead walked to the bus stop five minutes away, we had to be careful that she didn't see us. Otherwise, she kept following. We sometimes had to pick her up and take her back to the house. If she had ventured much farther, it would have been problematic, because I'm fairly certain she didn't speak Japanese!

I treasure my memories of Pretty Girl, forever grateful for *the dream* that directed me to help her. I'm grateful that I followed through, because that decision permanently changed my life. This mama cat modeled so much love to me, so many heartfelt emotions, and so much dedication and perseverance.

Adding her and Spunky to the family truly altered my thinking, because once we had four cats, I didn't care how many we had! We never planned to have more than two, but the Universe had other plans, and several more felines – all with unique characteristics and stories – would join us before we moved back to the States. Years later, their unique attributes would come to the forefront of my mind and seem eerily familiar in other cats that would somehow "find me."

CHAPTER 11

THE TIGER CAT

"Even though I wasn't 'technically' part of your family, I still considered you a mom and want you to know that even the smallest act of love will be remembered."

– TC the Tiger Cat

Occasionally, there is an animal that steps into your life only briefly, yet its impact is forever. One such animal for me was an unneutered male tiger cat that I'll call "TC," fairly tame and good-natured, who stopped by to eat during his wandering life as a Japanese stray. I fed him for about three months, and then he disappeared.

I was disappointed when TC stopped coming by the house, but that is often the behavior pattern of unneutered, male "tomcats," as we called them – they are wanderers. I wondered what happened to him as the ensuing months passed.

About a year and a half later, an animal almost unrecognizable as a cat wandered into our yard in American Village. It had virtually no fur left except a small patch of black-and-gray stripes on part of his face. When I saw the stripes, I knew immediately it was TC. His whiskers looked like they had been snipped, with only about an inch remaining on each one. The sweet boy, who only months before had been a strong, docile, healthy cat, was now an almost lifeless form that had somehow made its way back to our house.

I was sickened at the grotesque figure that was now in front of me and wondered who could have harmed him – before I understood what *mange* was. I later learned it's called *Sarcoptic Scabies*, which are small, parasitic itch mites that burrow directly into the skin and cause the symptoms they refer to as *mange*. You can treat it by bathing the animal with a sulfur shampoo, which we later did with several cats.

I was able to make an appointment for TC at the base vet clinic for the next day and was determined to help him get through this ordeal. I placed him in a cat carrier with a towel to sleep on, and slept on the living room floor next to him that night, ready to take him to his appointment the next day.

That night's sleep was to be his last, however. He didn't make it, and died overnight. I was so distraught, feeling like I had failed and should have done more to save his life.

I attended daily mass in the morning at the chapel on Yokota Air Base. To my surprise, the response to the Psalm for the day was from the book of Deuteronomy, Chapter 39: "I, the Lord, deal death and give life." It felt like those words were completely directed at me and penetrated my heart like a ton of bricks. I understood that I had not failed to save that cat. There were greater forces than me at work, and it was this precious cat's time to transition.

That was, and still is, a huge life lesson for me, more than 20 cats later. I can't save every one, as much as I would like to, but I can give them as much love as possible for the duration of time they are with me. I'm grateful to that beautiful cat that came to see me at the end of his life and taught me this lesson.

In my life now as an Animal Communicator, I'm able to connect with animals that have already passed, and I felt compelled to reach out to this little tiger cat. My communication with him was short and sweet, and he relayed the following message:

"Thank you, you were kind to me. Your love does make a difference to others (both animal and human), even if it's only for a short period of time, like with me."

I believe this cat had been guided back to my house for the end of his life so that he would be loved again and wouldn't die alone. He played an important part in my life's journey, and, in only a brief amount of time, made a huge impact.

CHAPTER 12

THE SCABIES INFESTATION

"Mom, this is George, the black-and-white cat you fed and nursed back to health in Japan. I loved being at your house and wanted to stay there forever. I even did my best to try and talk you into bringing me back to the States when you left. Thanks for taking such good care of me and letting me experience the love of a family. Maybe one day, I'll be able to live with you again. Come to think of it, that's a great idea! Years from now, I'll be back in another cat body, and you'll call me Squeaker! And I will make such a great impression that you'll let me write an entire chapter about how I talked you into it!"

– George

Now that I knew about *Sarcoptic Scabies* and its more common name of *mange*, I would be able to recognize it in the other cats if I saw it, nipping an infestation in the bud. I wasn't prepared, however, for the possibility that those nasty mites could infest a human – namely, *me*!

Chuck and I had planned a full-day whitewater rafting trip in Tokyo, culminating with a bountiful cookout feast for dinner. I couldn't wait to go! The timing of the trip happened to be within a week after the tiger cat died. *I'm sure this will cheer me up. TC's death really devastated me.*

It was late fall, and the weather had a chill in the air – so did the water in the river we would be rafting down. This meant we would have to wear wetsuits as if we were scuba diving. The rafting company supplied us with black, skin-tight, one-piece, rubbery suits with a long zipper down the front.

Rafting down a river in downtown Tokyo didn't provide the outdoor beauty we had experienced on a previous vacation to Bali in the summer of 1994, but we were hooked on whitewater rafting, and were thrilled to have the opportunity to do it again, this time closer to home.

The day started out like any other rafting adventure – procuring the wetsuits, oars, and helmets, receiving a safety briefing, and then being assigned a raft with an experienced guide. It was going to be a great adventure!

We skillfully navigated those rapids with the expertise of our guide, exhilarated by the splashing water and thrill of the moment, when suddenly, I started getting "itchy" under my wetsuit. I have a skin allergy to rubber and elastic, and thought that I might be having an allergic reaction to the wetsuit, since the rubbery material directly touched my skin. I couldn't even imagine it could be caused by something else.

I endured the itching for the remainder of the day, because there was no other choice, but I was not a happy camper by the end of the five-hour whitewater adventure.

As we plunged through the rapids, one after another, I relentlessly tried to get the itching sensation out of my mind and body by distracting myself and thinking about everything under the sun till I was nearly delirious: *What are we going to have for dinner? When is my next band trip? I hope the cats are OK… I wonder if we should try to climb Mount Fuji again… I'm hungry… How much longer do I have to wear this wetsuit? Whose idea was it to do this trip anyway? I'm miserable… Should we stay for the cookout? I HATE RAFTING… The water's freezing… When do we move back to the States? I'll never wear a wetsuit again… I don't care if I ever have a cookout again… And so on.*

We decided to stay through the meal, but when we took off the wetsuits and changed into our regular clothes, I had a rash all over my body and scratched *everywhere* until I was numb. We made the easy decision to stop at the emergency room at the base hospital on the way home, so I could get some relief.

During the two-hour drive back to the base, I had an "aha" moment: *I was infested with TC's mites – they had infiltrated my skin and were holding me prisoner.* I even asked the attending doctor at the ER to call the base vet to get clarification about what type of mites they were and whether they could be contagious to humans. In today's world, I would have asked Google; but back then, cell phones and the internet didn't exist.

"Yes, they can spread to humans," was the answer from the vet over the phone… *of course!* When we got home, I practically flew into the bathtub and bathed with the special shampoo the ER doctor prescribed for me. Then we went on a cleaning frenzy through the entire house, scouring everything in and out of sight, and keeping a close watch on every cat we came in contact with to avoid a further infestation.

Thankfully, none of the cats we called our own were infected, but we eventually bathed several others that we were feeding outside the house. The vet gave us a sulfur shampoo that smelled like… sulfur! I had a flashback to a childhood family vacation when we drove by the paper mill in Savannah, Georgia, in our un-airconditioned Winnebago, and were inundated with the smell of sulfur combined with the Deep South's humidity. I became nauseous for what seemed like days. At least with the scabies, the smell and the mites were gone in no time. The shampoo had worked!

With the cats, though, it took some time for their skin to clear up and heal, and we sometimes had to bathe them more than once. That is, I'm grateful to Chuck for all the ones *he* bathed. I confess I was a bystander, offering unending moral support as, one by one, the cats tried to escape for their lives from the deluge of running bathtub water, destroying many a shower curtain – and Chuck's T-shirts! I held the triple antibiotic cream firmly in hand, ready to do my part when the torturous bath adventures were finished.

One such victim of the scabies pandemic around our house was a short-haired, black-and-white tuxedo cat we'd named George, who periodically walked through our yard, grabbed a snack from our outdoor cat food bowl, and left.

George was a gentle, well-mannered, quiet fellow whose personality was the same as Muffin's when she first arrived: plain. Unlike Muffin, though, he didn't talk much and wasn't starving, because he also dined with a multitude of other cats at a Japanese lady's house a few streets behind ours – another Crazy Cat Lady! *Hallelujah! I'm not the only one.*

I would love to have struck up a conversation with this kindred spirit who also loved cats, but because my Japanese language skills were minimal, I never did. While knowing enough words and phrases to initiate a conversation, I didn't have enough skills to understand what was spoken back to me. This was always an awkward situation for both parties trying to communicate, so I didn't reach out to her.

We noticed that when George came by the house to eat, he didn't look very good – and he was scratching profusely! The pesky mites were starting to invade sections of his body, but since we already had so many cats to take care of, I didn't want to add to that workload. *Oh, no…* George was an outdoor cat, and there was no telling how many others were getting infested.

The heart-wrenching, dying, desperate condition of TC entered my mind, and I couldn't let that happen to George. I had some remote thought tucked in my brain that maybe the Japanese woman would take care of him, but as we monitored him over the course of a couple more weeks, he was definitely getting worse. She might not have even been aware of the source of the problem.

Those aggressive, hungry mites hadn't taken long to infiltrate this unsuspecting victim. Predictably, we brought George into the house and placed him in the "Kitty Cat Hospital" (our third and smallest bedroom), where he could be separated from the other cats to recover. We gave him a sulfur bath that day, and although it provided immediate relief from the scratching and his coat showed some improvement, I knew he'd need weeks or months to fully recover and for his coat to glisten.

I was a bundle of nerves. The cat hospital room had a window that George could look out while he recovered, but if that lady ever walked by our house, she would find her missing boy. Our covert attempt to save George would be discovered, and we would be arrested for catnapping!

Well, those fears materialized one day after George had spent about six weeks recuperating. There was a knock on the door... *and there she was — the Japanese Crazy Cat Lady who had come to demand that we return her cat immediately, OR ELSE! I envisioned paying a huge fine or being thrown in jail. Come on, get it over with quickly. I admit my guilt…*

But the interaction was not at all what I had dreaded. She walked into our house smiling with another Japanese woman who could speak some English and served as our interpreter. This is the essence of what she said: *"I'm so grateful for your helping Fue (pronounced Fu-ay, the name she called him). As a token of my appreciation, please accept these two beautiful Japanese dolls in glass cases, and I would like you to take Fue with you to America when you move back."*

WHAT???

I just about keeled over and dropped dead. *What a relief!* Caught off guard, all I could think of to say was that he was a nice cat and we wanted to help him, but we were already taking several cats back with us and didn't have room for any more. I was glad that George/Fue had a place to live and thanked her for taking care of all the cats in her yard. I knew she loved them all.

What a beautiful moment! And I breathed another huge sigh of relief when she left.

We released George back outdoors after another two weeks of recovery. He had been a very good patient, and didn't seem in a hurry to leave – in fact, he acted like he wanted to live with us! But under the circumstances, we thought that letting him go was the best choice.

The two beautiful dolls in glass cases remained in our home for years and served as a reminder of George/Fue, the gentle black-and-white cat from Japan who wanted to live with us, and that recovered from mange in our Kitty Cat Hospital.

CHAPTER 13

MUFFIN

"This little girl was so desperate to be loved when she wandered into your yard. Yes, her personality was a little boring at first, and you could have called her 'Plain Jane.' But her sweetness — especially when she licked your chin — overshadowed her dullness, so 'Muffin' was perfect. How could you have ever considered parting with her? We're glad you didn't, because she's an important part of our story. Years from now, after she passes, she will come back to you in a dream with a hint that she wants to live with you again."

– The Fur Family

On a crisp, late fall afternoon in 1993, while Chuck and I were standing in our small backyard, a wailing, low-pitched, droning sound came from under the bushes behind the house. It got louder and more desperate... "m-o-a-n... m-o-a-n... M-O-A-N..." *What's that noise?* Taken aback by its mournful tone, we walked over to the bushes to investigate further.

Underneath the bushes stood a black-and-white, paper-thin female kitten about the size of our six-month-old Spunky. Her white fur looked dingy-gray – she was filthy! Her face was even dirtier than the rest of her poor, malnourished body due to the dried, caked-blood under her nose. And her breath – *whew* – it stunk worse than raw sewage!

She was truly paper-thin, and judging by the sound of her wailing, she desperately needed help, including some nourishment. Who knows when her last meal was – if she even had one.

We gave her something to eat, but weren't ready to take any more cats in, as we now had four: Big Boy, Little Boy, Pretty Girl, and Spunky. That was more than enough. I was still recovering from the ordeal of giving Pretty Girl's kittens away, including Spunky's traumatic adoption failure, and needed time for my emotions to calm down.

We fed this little kitten outside for the next three days, and on the third morning, I awoke to the sound of my neighbor Linda's loud voice, yelling at her to go away. She even threatened to get rid of her. Linda was a Department of Defense (DOD) teacher who had recently moved in when she was transferred to Yokota Air Base following the closure of Clark Air Force Base in the Philippines. Her lungs and voice were equally as strong as the desperate feline's.

I'm not sure if it was the constant moaning sounds that angered Linda or the kitten's neediness, but my heart was breaking, and I had heard enough. I wasn't going to let that uncaring woman hurt this cat in any way. I brought the scrawny, desperate little girl into the house that afternoon, and continued my unofficial *Stray Cat Rehab Program*. Of course, that included finding a forever home for her.

Rather than refer to her as "the thin cat," we named her Muffin based on her very sweet temperament. She was definitely an adoptable cat, and we figured it would be easy to find someone who would love her.

We helped clean her fur until she was able to effectively groom herself. Although the discoloration on her face was due to the dried blood, we never found a cut, bite mark, or any other source where it might have come from. It was old, and she didn't appear to be in any pain.

Muffin was ravenous, and like the other malnourished cats we'd found, we tried to pace her eating so it would be easier on her digestive system. Her breath eventually started to smell better. The horrid odor most likely came from her eating whatever garbage she could find, which is probably just about all she ate – if even that. Gradually, she began to groom herself, and her terribly discolored fur became a beautiful, lustrous white.

While indoors, she didn't do anything to disrupt the other cats. In fact, she didn't do *anything!* Muffin had absolutely no personality. She didn't know how to play or interact with the others. She spent all her time sitting on our very plain living room chair, which along with the other plain furniture that was provided by base housing, matched her plain personality. Maybe she was worried about being stuck outside again with no food.

Despite having no personality, she did have the most beautiful face, with a sweet, cordial, gentle meow that now replaced the desperate, mournful, droning wails we had heard coming from under our bushes. *Maybe she does have a personality, and we just haven't seen it yet.*

After two months of rehabilitation, we decided Muffin was ready to be placed in a permanent home and made posters to hang on the various advertising boards on base. A woman called who was very interested in adopting her, and we set up an appointment to come and see this now clean, adoptable, sweet cat. Unfortunately, it would be during the time I would be out of town on a band trip, so I wouldn't be there, and Chuck would handle the adoption by himself.

Her adoption day arrived, and as I carried my belongings to the front door to leave for my trip, I gazed longingly at Muffin as she sat on her chair, and she, in return, did the same to me with her beautiful eyes. I walked out of the house and drove to work. *What a miserable day.* I couldn't stop thinking about her and knew I couldn't let her go to another home. I had become too attached to this little girl with the bad breath and no personality, who trusted me with everything.

I called Chuck before I went out of town and begged him not to give her away while I was gone. I didn't know how we were going to manage with five cats, but I didn't care. I had to keep her, and Chuck reluctantly agreed.

One consolation of having a multi-cat household was that we now, for the first time, had at our disposal the greatest invention since sliced bread: clumping cat litter! We – or I should say, Chuck – no longer had to clean out and replace the litter in the box every week. Unpleasant cat odors in our house were now a thing of the past!

As the months passed, Muffin metamorphized into an even more beautiful girl. She eventually gained weight, developed a loving, yet mischievous, personality with a loud purr, and became a huntress – even sneaking a bird into the house one day when she thought I wasn't looking!

She liked to lick my chin almost raw every time I picked her up! She also became the bathroom kitty who liked to drink water from the sink spigot, even pawing at it herself to coax the water out.

This sweet girl had become the latest victim of my cat adoption failures. Honestly, I really did start out with good intentions…

CHAPTER 14

CYCLOPS

"Hey, Mom! Notice the pattern evolving here: The uglier we look, the more irresistible we are, don't you think? Time for a one-eyed cat to make the scene. And we approve of the name Cyclops. He's super-sweet – maybe even more so than Muffin!"

– The Fur Family

One early evening in the spring of 1994, roughly five months after Muffin joined the family, Chuck and I were riding our bikes through a nearby Japanese neighborhood comprised of single-dwelling homes, much like the size of the one we lived in but older and definitely not renovated like ours. It actually looked more like a ghetto. We had learned that the houses in this neighborhood were to be torn down and replaced with government-managed apartments.

One by one, the residents had vacated their homes, and the neighborhood took on a ghostly feel as we slowly rode our bikes up and down the empty streets, save for a miscellaneous car here and there parked at the few remaining inhabited houses.

We were riding our three-speed Japanese bikes that had upright handlebars with wire baskets attached for groceries or miscellaneous items. They had been abandoned at one of the many train stations outside Tokyo, which was a common practice. There were repair shops that corralled these bikes, refurbished them, and sold them. Most often, they were in good condition or just needed some minor repairs.

As we were riding through the mostly abandoned neighborhood, we heard a cat (of course!) crying from beneath a car. We dismounted our bikes and walked toward the pitiful-sounding cry. Approaching us from the car was a small, short-haired gold-and-white cat – bony, malnourished, and missing his left eye. The socket of that eye looked more like a birth defect or nutritional deficiency rather than from a fight with another animal or abuse from a human.

We said hello, and he started purring as soon as we bent down to pet him. When we continued walking alongside our bikes, the kitten immediately started to tag along. We turned back every few steps in hopes that he had stopped somewhere, but he had his eye on us – literally!

And he kept crying. "He probably belongs to somebody," Chuck commented. The cat was so friendly, it seemed impossible that a nice little kitty like this didn't have a home. But I was thinking to myself, *This fellow's in rough shape, and he's obviously homeless. What do we do next?*

We carried him back to where we had first seen him under the car and tried to walk away once more, but he was not interested in staying there and continued to trot along behind us. Finally, we decided to go knocking on the doors of the few occupied houses we could find and ask if anybody owned him.

Knock knock…

In my best broken Japanese, I blurted out to each blank face, *"Tsugi no nekko, desu ka?"* (Is this your cat?) Each response was the same: an annoyed look, arms waving *NO,* followed by silence and the immediate closing of the door.

Now, what do we do? Chuck and I both looked at each other and then looked at the cat. He was still purring, not paying any attention to our conversation. So, Chuck picked him up again and carried him home with us. Rather than get back on our bikes, we chose to walk, because it was only five minutes back to our house.

When we arrived, we put him in the Kitty Cat Hospital room and gave him some food. I'm not sure whether he was more grateful for the food or the attention we were lavishing on him as he alternated between eating ravenously and walking over to us, purring profusely. What an incredibly grateful, happy cat! And there was obviously only one suitable name for him: Cyclops.

With such a friendly personality, we thought he would be easily adoptable, so within a few days, we took him to the animal shelter on base. They bathed him and had him neutered during that time, which was one less thing we felt responsible for.

I would like to say that I easily detached myself from Cyclops, knowing that Chuck and I had done a good thing, and trusted that he would be taken care of. But that wasn't the case. I constantly worried about this needy little creature and went to visit him every day.

Each day I left the shelter, it tore my heart to pieces looking at him in that cage, knowing how sweet he was, and how alone. Finally, I broke down and couldn't take the emotional stress anymore. After the 10th day, I happily brought him back home and let him out of his world of confinement to rejoin his friends.

Then we tried Plan B, which was to make posters like we did for Muffin. They read: "Free male cat, neutered, very friendly, missing an eye, great personality. His name is Cyclops." *Would anyone adopt a cat with this description?* We wanted to be honest about the eye, but secretly I somehow knew we wanted to keep him and were just going through the motions of trying to find a home.

After we hung posters all over the base, I had another scheduled band trip out of town. Chuck manned the fort once again, and when I returned, he confessed that he had gotten very attached to Cyclops. We both agreed to keep him, took all the posters down, and, well… another good-intentioned cat adoption failure. *We did it again! We're really good at this…*

Now, we were up to six cats: Big Boy, Little Boy, Pretty Girl, Spunky, Muffin, and Cyclops. But I couldn't imagine life minus any of them.

Failed adoptions had become a pattern, and what I had feared most was now a reality: I had truly become a CRAZY CAT LADY! *Even the vet was calling me that. How did this happen???*

Cyclops was our love sponge – the sweetest, most loving, and grateful cat I had ever known – except for all the others! And he had a special game he liked to play: fetch. We'd throw him either a small, store-bought plastic ball with a bell inside or a homemade ball made of scrunched-up aluminum foil. He would run as fast as he could, grab it in his mouth, retrieve it like a dog, and carry it back to us. Good boy!

His favorite cat friend was Muffin, and they loved to sleep together in one of our cat beds or curl up together on the couch. Perhaps they had known each other in that old neighborhood. He also loved his new big brother, Spunky.

Amazingly, there were no integration problems in bringing another male cat into the house, but how on earth were we going to manage with six cats? We had never intended to have more than two.

Now, we had a more serious dilemma looming on the horizon. In one more year, we would be relocating back to the U.S., and it was time to start researching our options for traveling back to the States with all these cats. What if we could only transport two, like when we first arrived in 1990?

Big Boy and Little Boy were our original family members, but how could we possibly leave the others behind? I shuddered at the thought. We had put in so much time, effort, and love with the other four, it seemed just plain cruel.

CHAPTER 15

POTTY TALK

"Mom, this is not a very polite name for a chapter. Do you really have to talk about where we do our business?"

— The Fur Family

I never gave litter boxes much thought — until we moved to Japan, and our cat population exploded.

When I was growing up on Wellington Street, we kept one litter box in the cellar — the "underground room," which was a cold, damp, unfinished basement. Dad used it for his woodworking workshop and to store hunting and fishing equipment.

That lone box was used by our cats exclusively during the time of transition when they were learning to do their business outside. It was only temporary, because the natural, outdoor environment was more than sufficient. When they were fully "potty trained," the box disappeared, and they never wanted to utilize it inside the house again.

We had a giant sandbox in the backyard that my brother Dave and I used to play in, but since it resembled a larger version of their indoor box, we were forced to keep it covered when we weren't playing, thereby helping the cats resist the temptation to use it for their own purposes.

Over the years, I've noticed that cats have become more pampered as companion animals and have evolved into using indoor facilities most of the time. The litter box now seems to be their preferred means to have some bathroom fun. I've even witnessed some of my cats *intentionally* come inside the house to use their box and immediately go back outside to play. I have no doubt that soon, they will fully embrace the porcelain throne itself!

This shift to "indoor plumbing" has generated a whole new field of marketing opportunities and umpteen questions from cat owners:

Just how many litter boxes do I really need? What kind of litter should I use? What size box? How do I dispose of the litter? Where in my house should I put my litter box(es)? Why do I need to use litter boxes anyway? Can't they just relieve themselves outside? Why are they coming INSIDE to use the box? What if my cat refuses to use the box? WHY CAN'T THEY JUST LEARN TO USE THE TOILET?

To be fair, having a litter box for your cat can also yield positive benefits, such as indicating a medical or behavioral problem. And that raises this question: *Why is my cat peeing outside the box?* As an Animal Communicator, I'm often asked to try and solve this mystery with other people's felines.

For some homes, having a litter box available for their cats 24/7 is a necessity. Many feline companions live exclusively indoors – definitely a trend that was not that common when I was growing up. For crowded urban or apartment dwellers, keeping their cats indoors is sometimes the only option. For others, there could be dangers like street traffic or wildlife.

There are many good reasons that owners choose to keep their cats inside.

I've always lived in environments where my cats could spend time both indoors and outdoors, except for when we lived in Virginia Beach with Big Boy and Little Boy and kept them almost exclusively indoors.

Whenever we moved, we chose houses in quiet neighborhoods with virtually no traffic, like at the end of a cul-de-sac or dead-end street. Although I also prefer a quiet environment for myself, the cats' safety is *always* the first concern when choosing a house. That's my preference and one of my non-negotiables!

When Chuck and I arrived in Japan with Big Boy and Little Boy, we put their box in a small alcove where the washer and dryer were situated, next to our tiny Japanese bathroom. There was literally just enough space for it to fit like a glove, and I wanted to keep the "bathroom-themed items" together.

Clumping cat litter had not been invented yet, and the only option was litter that needed to be changed at least weekly. The smell was annoying, no matter what pretty scent the companies listed on the containers as part of their slick advertising to entice you to buy their products.

Chuck had the honor of emptying the box and changing the litter, and for that, I was extremely grateful. It wasn't that I was lazy and didn't want to contribute, but the full box of litter *and* cat poop was heavy and awkward to move. I didn't know how to physically handle it well enough to keep it all from spilling onto the floor.

By 1993, when we added Pretty Girl and Spunky to the family, the world of cat litter had forever changed – in a good way – because clumping cat litter had finally arrived on the scene! Even better, it was available to purchase at the grocery store on Yokota Air Base where we did our shopping. Sometimes, overseas stores were the last to stock the latest, greatest products.

This magical litter forms a clump with whatever moisture shows up in the box and absorbs the odor. All you have to do is scoop it out with a slotted, plastic litter scooper, dispose of it in a trash bag, and *voila*: no more dirty litter box and no more foul cat odors!

What an improvement – wow! It was now safe to add as many cats as we wanted to the family. Well, that's not the reason our cat family exploded from two to eight, but it sure made it easier to manage more cats.

Today, there are even more improvements to litter, as it can be used as a monitoring device to detect potential health issues by reacting to subtle changes in the animal's urine pH. If it's outside the "normal" range, it changes color, and some litter can also detect blood.

Although I purchase commercial litter, I don't use the small, impractical-sized litter boxes available in stores. They are *way too small* for my cats (in my humble opinion), and they've never been able to use them successfully without missing their target and making messes all over the floor.

I've experimented with the boxes that have a cover and an opening for the cat to crawl through (perhaps designed to give them privacy), but the entire box gets filthy and reeks of urine that lands on the sides rather than on the litter – sometimes after just one use – and there isn't enough room for the cats to turn around.

I prefer to use large, rectangular plastic storage containers and place the lids underneath them on the floor to catch any extra litter that falls out after the cats bury their treasures. The ones I purchase are generally 4 or 5 inches tall, just enough for the cats to easily climb over.

You can also find fancy litter boxes with electronic scooping mechanisms and others that look more like a piece of furniture than a litter box, but I like my large storage containers.

There is also the ever-popular dilemma of how many boxes you should have. I've read articles that say it should be based on the number of cats that will use it. I personally think those articles are written by marketing companies that sell both litter boxes *and* litter, and not by cat owners. They make me laugh hysterically, because most of them suggest – strongly and confidently – that you should keep one more box than the number of cats you have. I can just picture myself with anywhere from nine to 11 litter boxes in the house…

In Japan, we successfully navigated life with eight cats and just one litter box. For the next 25 years, with a constant population of eight to ten cats, we continued to use only one box 95% of the time.

My advice for the number of litter boxes you should have? The minimum number you need to keep everyone happy! For me, that's usually just one.

Fast forward 30 years to my current home. When I adopted Lilli, a 12-year-old blind cat, I had one box for my declining cat population of only two cats, Pumpkin and Fuji. To help Lilli adjust to her new surroundings, I set up a temporary box for her in my small bathroom, just until she was comfortable in the house and could navigate her way to the other box in the utility room. Within two months, I took the temporary box away, thinking that one was more than enough for three cats.

But as soon as I removed Lilli's bathroom box, Fuji – my then 15-year-old matriarch calico – started bullying her in the lone utility room box. Lilli was afraid to use this box that had served so many cats and started peeing and pooping on my shower stall floor. I give her credit for at least doing her jobs in the bathroom!

I felt forced into submission by Fuji, the bossy queen bee, and succumbed to her rude behavior by putting Lilli's box back in my small bathroom.

It really killed me to do this – out of sheer principle! For 25 years, I had eight to ten cats on an ongoing basis and used only one litter box most of the time. Now, with Fuji, Lilli, and Pumpkin, I had just three cats but *two* litter boxes. *I had failed…*

I eventually asserted my authority, Fuji became more accepting of Lilli, and once again, I removed the extra box, keeping only one for three cats, which they only use when the weather is bad outside or they're just plain lazy! For my part, I just keep on scooping…

CHAPTER 16

BASHFUL AND BOBTAIL

"Mom, we're going to show you a little bit about the nature of feral cats. We're a little different than our fully domesticated brothers and sisters, because our fear factor is extremely high, and sometimes it takes forever to trust a human. But we're just as lovable! Please be patient with us."

– Bashful and Bobtail

There was a strong likelihood that other cats we befriended could be a target for the horrible scabies infestation, so I continued to be on the lookout for any signs to appear in either the cats that were "officially" ours or the stray felines in our neighborhood that occasionally meandered through our property for a snack or full-course meal.

One of those cats was a gray-and-white female tabby we named Bashful. She was the first feral cat I ever befriended, and her name typified her demeanor. We fed her outside for three years and saw her experience two pregnancies (that we knew of) during that time. She wouldn't let me get close to her, and although I was totally helpless in providing a safe place for her to have kittens, I felt that I could at least keep her well-fed enough to nourish and take care of them.

After the first litter was born, we found three very young kittens, perhaps two to three weeks old, in the wooded area across the street from our house, where we usually put a bowl of dry food. From their coloring and markings, it was easy to determine who the fathers were from the stray male cats in the neighborhood!

Unfortunately, I learned a very painful lesson from these kittens. Although we were very successful with Pretty Girl and her young ones, Bashful was different. She was not tame, and the kittens were too young to be moved. We thought we would help increase their chance for survival outdoors by taking them out of the woods and bringing them into our house, but after we interfered, Bashful wanted nothing to do with them.

Sadly, she never went near them again, and we were unable to keep them warm enough and bottle-fed to survive. One by one, they passed away over the course of two weeks. I was devastated and felt as if I had totally betrayed both Bashful and her kittens to the point where the grief was so overwhelming that I lost my appetite for over a week.

Getting Bashful spayed seemed out of the question because we weren't able to even get close enough to touch her. Therefore, the inevitable happened, and she became pregnant once again. This time though, we decided that if we should find any kittens, we would just let nature take its course and not try to "help" them.

After she gave birth, we kept on the lookout for kittens, but there were no signs of any. We thought they hadn't survived, but six months later, a beautiful tiger kitten with a hooked tail, big ears, and a booming voice made her grand appearance in the middle of the road in front of our house!

Her lungs and vocal cords must have been double the normal size for a kitten, judging by the power of her *singing* voice – she was even louder than Big Boy! Her vocalizing was nonstop, and I'm sure it woke up the entire neighborhood with the volume it projected over the airways.

This kitten was obviously trying to get our attention, and based on her size, we knew she was from Bashful's most recent litter. She was the only one we found – if, in fact, there were any others – and like her mother, she also wouldn't let us get close to her. That wasn't surprising, because she was the offspring of a feral cat and had never been touched by a human.

Her tail pointed straight upward and had a curly hook at the tip, allowing us to see closely enough to tell she was a female. *Oh, great... another unspayed female born in the wild that will grow up, get pregnant, and have MORE feral cats to roam the neighborhood.*

To add to the scenario, this kitten had signs of mange on her skin. We had to figure out a way to catch her, treat the mange, and get her spayed. We could then release her back into the wild, since we'd determined she was untamable.

Bashful was finished mothering this kitten, and had virtually no interaction with her anymore, so we felt safe about separating the two of them. By virtue of her offspring's most notable physical characteristic – the funny-looking tail – she easily earned the name "Bobtail." If we had thought of it, we could also have named her after a singer with a powerful voice, like Liza Minelli or Barbara Streisand, but the name Bobtail definitely worked and gave us something to refer to her by, although we had no plans to keep her.

Bashful had allowed us to start petting her about a month before Bobtail was born. We were able to build a bond, earn her trust, bring her inside to treat the mites, and then take her to the vet to get spayed. She spent just a few weeks recovering in our Kitty Cat Hospital room, and then we released her back outside.

Meanwhile, we continued to feed Bobtail and devised a foolproof plan to catch her: We placed an open cat carrier outside the front door of our house at feeding time and lured her inside the carrier with a can of tuna fish! Then we closed the door quickly, and *voila* – success! It took all of five minutes to complete our scheme and bring her inside the house to the now-vacant Kitty Cat Hospital.

I slowly opened the door of the cat carrier and let her walk into her temporary living quarters when she felt safe enough. I stayed with her and, little by little, she cautiously crept out of the carrier, pausing with each step. She sniffed the air in her new, unfamiliar surroundings, and when she realized I was still in the room, only inches away, she panicked and bolted to a corner, facing away from me to try and make herself invisible. *This is my big chance… I'm chomping at the bit to touch that hooked tail and see what it feels like…*

This young tiger kitten, who was now almost seven months old, had never been touched by human hands, and she was petrified! I approached her lovingly while she sat in the corner, staring at the wall with no chance to escape, and petted her all the way down her back, starting at the top of her head and ending at the tip of her tail. I did this multiple times.

I later learned, as an Animal Communicator and Energy Healer, that this technique is referred to as a *Bladder Sweep*, and it calms the nervous system of an animal, stimulating the acupressure points along the bladder meridian. In a strange way, intuitively, I'd always done this with cats, but never knew why it worked. They seem to love it, as do dogs!

I gently picked this frightened girl up in my arms and held her close to my body when she unexpectedly started to relax! In fact, her ears perked up, her eyes got bigger, and she started to purr – *loudly* – the volume almost matching that of her singing voice. I think she liked it as much as I did!

This was a new sensation for her, and as I petted that funny-looking tail, I discovered that it was full-length and simply crooked and curled up on itself at the tip. It was rather humorous, because that tip actually moved back and forth when she was happy, while the rest of her tail didn't move an inch.

As the result of this hugely successful petting episode, it was apparent that Bobtail was adoptable, so rather than return her to the wild after we got her spayed, we would try to find a home for her.

Chuck administered the dreaded sulfur bath to this little girl, and then I brought her to bed with me and put her alongside my chest area toward the outer side of the bed. She liked it so much that she slept there all night! Success! We repeated this nighttime routine for a week, then took her to get spayed.

From December through February, I committed to taming her even further. Chuck was never able to get physically close to Bobtail, which we thought was because of the bath episode, but she *never* let him near her. In fact, she wouldn't let anyone touch her except me. I later learned that it's very common for the offspring of feral cats to bond with only one person.

Of course, you can't find a permanent home for a cat that won't let you touch them (*sigh*). Consequently, that first night of placing her next to me at bedtime turned into… well… um… 19 years!

Yet another well-intentioned, potential adoption failure…

* * *

I wasn't prepared for the unexpected way Bashful's life ended, but later realized it was the Universe working out a solution to the dilemma we faced about whether to bring her back to the States with us when we returned in October 1995.

We had fed this shy girl for three years, but during that time, she never interacted with our other cats, and I was afraid she wouldn't adapt well if we brought her back with them. I was scared that she wouldn't have been able to emotionally handle the long trip, which would entail multiple flights in a cat carrier.

There would also be an adjustment period, which could be several months long, when we would have to live in different temporary living quarters – potentially all indoors – until we were finally settled into a house. Although we had made great strides in taming her, Bashful was still a feral cat.

We were allowed to travel with a maximum of eight cats under the Status of Forces Agreement (SOFA) at a cost of $80 per animal versus making our own arrangements and traveling separate from the military at a price of over $700 per animal – yikes! That choice was a no brainer, so we reserved eight spaces through the military. We could always cancel the eighth spot if we didn't need it, but couldn't add it back later.

Although including Bashful with our other cats would have given us eight, something about it just didn't *feel* right. It was my intuition speaking, but I didn't know how it would play out.

In the summer of 1995, just a few months before our scheduled flight to my next assignment at Robins AFB, Georgia, Chuck and I took one final vacation, which included nearly three weeks of incredible travel through Australia, New Zealand, and Hawaii. Our neighbors, Rhonda and Jack, graciously fed our cats, including Bashful, while we were gone.

When we arrived home, however, Bashful was nowhere to be found. Rhonda delivered the sad news that Bashful had been hit by a car a week before our return. Although they didn't see her get hit, they witnessed her struggling to pull herself across the street with the front part of her body, dragging what appeared to be her paralyzed lower body behind her. They thought it best to take her to be euthanized and didn't want to upset us on our vacation by telling us about it before we returned.

It was sad, yet a blessing in disguise, because we didn't have to make the agonizing decision of whether to take Bashful with us into a very stressful emotional situation from which she might never recover, or leave her in Japan with the uncertainty of whether she would survive or starve to death.

The clock was ticking, and now only two months remained before our departure to the U.S., but we still had space available for one more cat... just in case.

CHAPTER 17

MR. PEABODY

"Mom, there were 4,000 bicycles parked at the train station, but I found yours right away and curled up next to it, waiting for your return. I was so hungry, desperate for a home and some love. You literally saved my life. And not only that, I gained an entire family of felines who told me they had space for one more kitty to live with them forever! What a lucky guy I am!"

— Mr. Peabody

What are the odds of riding your bicycle to a train station five minutes from your house, parking it amidst at least 4,000 other bicycles, taking the train to a water park in Tokyo for the day, returning to the parking lot eight hours later with 4,000 other bikes still there, and finding an emaciated, flea-infested, ear mite-infested, filthy, white cat with black splotches that's missing an eye, rolling on its side and kneading in mid-air while purring, at YOUR bicycle?

Well, in my case, the odds were high, because that's exactly what happened on a hot and hazy July day in 1995, just two months before Chuck and I were scheduled to return to the U.S. after completing five years of overseas duty at Yokota Air Base, Japan.

And *coincidentally*, because of Bashful's death, we happened to have space for one more cat to join us on our *sayonara* flight home to the States. Reserving eight spots total, *just in case*, was strangely prophetic on our part.

After a refreshing day at the water park, we got off the train and walked toward our bikes. (It was amazing that we could even remember where we'd parked them, given the large number of bikes in that parking lot.) Chuck looked down at the scrawny feline that was rolling on the ground alongside my bike and said, "Looks like you've made a friend!"

We crouched down to get a closer look at the little guy, and it was apparent that he didn't belong to anyone except *us* now and had obviously been directed to our bikes by angels – or something else – from the spiritual dimension. There was no other explanation.

Chuck gently picked up this pathetic-looking, still-purring fellow, wrapped him in a towel we had brought to the water park, and carried him in one arm while we rode our bikes back to the house. We were home in no time, and the now delighted, content cat put up no struggle whatsoever.

The first order of business was to give him some food, then turn on the water in the bathtub and wash him. He was all too grateful for the food and didn't put up a fuss about the bath either, so Chuck was spared ruining another T-shirt. Beneath all that dirt, there actually *was* a white cat with black splotches!

The next order of business was to figure out what to call him. Cyclops already had the one-eyed cat name, so what came to mind was an old cartoon character named Peabody, who wore large glasses and had a dog named Sherman. The name "Peabody" stuck, along with the title "Mister" that gave him some dignity, which he desperately needed.

Like Cyclops, Mr. Peabody's missing eye didn't look like it was from an intentional incident like a fight, but rather from nutritional deficiencies and poor living conditions – he was homeless. I don't know how many more days Mr. Peabody would have survived had he not found us, but there couldn't have been many. Thankfully, his life had just taken a turn for the better, and we now had two one-eyed cats.

He seemed to have a sickly constitution, though, with wheezing problems that I called "Kitty Cat Asthma." I don't even know if there is such a disease because it was never diagnosed, but that's what I called it. He was given various medications over the years to try and help his breathing, but the symptoms never entirely disappeared. He just coped with it.

We also suspected that Mr. Peabody was a little bit deaf since he didn't react to loud noises like the other cats. His favorite game was "Attack of the Killer Vacuum Cleaner," in which he excelled! Each time the vacuum moved along the floor, he swatted it, jumped back, then swatted it again, unfazed by the loud noise. He did this repeatedly until we were finished vacuuming. He had no competition from the other seven cats, because they all quickly disappeared when the loud monster came out of the deep, dark jungle closet to wage war on him.

Mr. Peabody didn't have a mean bone in his body, just like the other cats we had taken in, and I felt grateful and completely blessed with this motley crew of misfit cats that now filled our house with love.

Our happy feline family consisted of Big Boy, Little Boy, Pretty Girl, Spunky, Muffin, Cyclops, Bobtail, and now Mr. Peabody. I suspect that Bashful was smiling from the other side, and quite possibly the one that guided Mr. Peabody to my bicycle that hot summer day.

It was now time to prepare for the trip back to America with our full house!

CHAPTER 18

EIGHT CATS, EIGHT CARRIERS (NO CAT LEFT BEHIND)

"We want to thank you, Mom! You did the impossible by transporting all eight of us in our individual carriers across the ocean and through multiple airports until we arrived in our new country. We were uncomfortable and scared, but did our best to endure it. Most importantly, though, you kept us together as a family, and we are so grateful!"

– The Core Eight
(Big Boy, Little Boy, Pretty Girl, Spunky, Muffin, Cyclops, Bobtail, Mr. Peabody)

How on earth are we going to do this? Eight cats?

It was time to make the final preparations for our long flight back to the States in September 1995 to my next assignment at Robins Air Force Base, Georgia, in the town of Warner Robins, two hours south of Atlanta. We had no idea where we were going to stay when we arrived or where we would live permanently. We had too many cats to even consider on-base housing.

But first things first. How do we transport the cats? We were allowed to bring all eight, but the rules required that each one have its own airline-approved carrier with a water dish. There was no doubling up. We still had the carriers for Big Boy and Little Boy but needed six more.

I was thankful and elated that we were able to bring our entire family back with us, but several of them had "emotional issues," and I would have preferred to double them up to lessen their fears. Nonetheless, we continued to make preparations.

Yokota Air Base had a thrift store, so we kept our eyes on the lookout for extra airline-approved carriers. Many Air Force personnel brought animals with them to Japan and, when they were finished with the carriers, donated them to the store.

One by one, we added to our collection until we reached the magic number of eight. Six were definitely sized for cats, and two were for slightly larger animals, probably small dogs, but that didn't matter. Big Boy and Little Boy would fit nicely in those.

After we found an airline-approved carrier for each cat, the next hurdle was coordinating with the airlines through the Air Force travel office to book our flights to Atlanta, arriving no later than September 30th, the date on my military orders.

The plan was for Chuck and myself to depart on the same day via commercial aircraft from Narita International Airport in Tokyo, unlike when I arrived in 1990, and Chuck joined me six weeks later. There were restrictions, however, because each plane could only accommodate a maximum of four animals per "pet compartment," so we would have to divide the cats into two groups and fly separately.

That meant we had to depart on different flights, timing them to arrive as close to the same time as possible in Atlanta.

Chuck's parents would meet us with their large van and drive ALL of us to Warner Robins: four adults, eight cats, eight cat carriers, and all our luggage!

We booked the flights, one of us with a layover in San Francisco, and one in Chicago, where we checked through customs before we transferred to our flights to Atlanta.

Two of the major details were now taken care of, so on to the next.

How do we get to the airport? Who could possibly have a vehicle large enough to fit all of us? The thought of having to take a train was probably the worst traveling nightmare I could imagine. Thankfully, that didn't come to pass. We were able to use one of the squadron vans (after all, this was "official travel!"), and one of my friends from the band agreed to drive us.

Next, where do we put all the cats during the week that we move out of American Village, have our household goods packed, and stay in temporary lodging on base while I out-process?

I love my Air Force family, and so many friends stepped up to offer help. Rhonda and Jack knew our cats well, so we entrusted them with the two that were the most afraid: Spunky and Bobtail. That way, they didn't have to move very far during this time of transition, and only had to be carried 50 feet through the backyard to Rhonda and Jack's house.

We farmed the other cats out to friends who lived on base, except for Pretty Girl, who we were afraid would try to escape from any house we brought her to. She was such a faithful homebody, and given her previous history of continuing to live at the old, dilapidated house where she had her kittens – waiting for the owner who never returned – we were pretty sure she'd stay close to our house if we left her there. And she did. We made sure she had enough food and water, plus she had her favorite tree in the yard to climb.

The vet suggested giving the cats a tranquilizer before the trip to ease their anxiety, but we decided against it. Once they were situated inside their carriers and finished the mournful "Help me, I'm trapped and feel like I'm going to die" pleas, they resigned themselves to their temporary confinement and fell asleep.

If I had been an Animal Communicator back then, I would have told them in advance that we were moving and they would be safe, but at the time, I didn't know how to do that – the idea that I would become an Animal Communicator didn't materialize until 25 years later.

But a timely Bible verse *did* come into the picture to give me reassurance about the move. I was led to read Psalm 121:8, which says, "The Lord will watch over your coming and going both now and forevermore." I knew in my heart that we would be protected and successfully transport this huge family of cats back to the U.S. and to our new home. I still live by the comfort of that scripture today and never worry when I travel.

As we emptied the house and completed the out-processing paperwork, along with multiple appointments, we lived geographically separated from the cats for about a week, just as we had anticipated. And then, finally, it was time to round everyone up, load the Air Force van, and drive to Narita – with one important final stop: the Yokota Air Base Chapel for an official Catholic animal blessing, complete with the sprinkling of holy water, of course!

One of the chaplains, Father. Lee, did the honors. There was much prayer to be had in preparation for this journey – it was a MAJOR undertaking!

Eight cats? Who DOES this? What were we thinking?

For me, I was thinking about the health and safety of these beautiful felines, who were so needy, faithful, and devoted to us and to one another, each with a story to tell. They were family. I loved them dearly, and there was *no way* I would ever leave any of them behind.

The van ride to Narita went without a hitch, and Chuck and I boarded our separate planes with all eight cats and carriers intact. We had now completed our final *sayonara* to a beautiful five-year adventure in the Land of the Rising Sun.

I do believe in the power of prayer, because we had the smoothest trip imaginable. All the flights were on time, nobody got sick, nobody got lost – and we all arrived in Atlanta safely, greeted by Chuck's parents and their large van. When we got to the baggage claim area, we doubled some of the cats up to use fewer carriers so they could see and be with each other, and to save space in the van.

The cats fared amazingly well. They were calm, almost as if nothing had happened, and no one tried to escape when we opened the carriers. Plus, now they could all see each other and know they were still together. They were no doubt confused after having been cooped up for so long, and were still in a submissive state. I also believe they trusted us so much that they didn't have any reason to put up a fight.

And of course, I knew we were divinely protected. I wondered sometimes if each of these cats had their own guardian angel – especially since they all had lived through so much trauma in their early lives. They were my miracle kitties.

Onto the next destination: a two-hour drive to a Days Inn in Warner Robins that allowed animals. We stayed in a suite that was larger than a standard-size hotel room (which also helped accommodate a litter box) with doors that opened to an interior hallway rather than directly outside the hotel. That minimized the chances of a cat trying to escape to satisfy their curiosity. If somebody tried to run out – which happened twice – we only had to run down the hallway to retrieve them. We stayed at the Days Inn for two weeks while we looked for something more permanent.

As military members, we were given options for housing. You had to apply to live on base, and different types of arrangements were available according to pay grade, rank, and size of family. Single airmen were offered dorm rooms, and members with dependents could apply for a house, sometimes a duplex, with the number of bedrooms allotted based on the size of the family. If there was space available that met your criteria, you could move on base immediately, and if not, you were put on a waiting list. If approved, rent and utilities were covered by the government.

Those who preferred to live off-base were given a Basic Allowance for Quarters (BAQ), and the amount varied, also based on pay grade, rank, and if they had any dependents. It also fluctuated from base to base, according to the cost of living for that specific geographical location.

Many military members purchased property, rather than rent a house or apartment. Some career fields transferred members less frequently, allowing them to stay in one location long enough – perhaps even five to ten years – before they were relocated, making it worth the investment.

We didn't qualify for base housing because we had too many cats, so that was not an option. But we didn't want to live on-base anyway – we wanted to buy a house. We searched diligently, but couldn't find one that we were particularly drawn to, so instead, we purchased a beautiful, wooded lot in town and had one built.

I only recommend doing this once in a lifetime – *ohhhhh… the stress!* Waiting and waiting and waiting for contractors to show up, the endless trips to Home Depot, the *massive* number of decisions to be made, furniture to purchase, and on and on.

We toured several houses from *Southern Living* magazine's "Parade of Homes" list in middle Georgia, which showcased fully decorated, beautiful properties in many southern towns. They held an open house at each property for about a week to show off their beauty, demonstrating what is possible with interior decorating! This included listing the suppliers where you could purchase materials like wallpaper, cabinets, and paint. It was a wonderful, convenient way to get ideas about colors, layouts, furniture, etc. The possibilities were endless, as were the number of choices to set up an entire household.

I frankly don't ever want to go through that arduous process again. And the expense! Before it was all said and done, it probably cost at least one-and-a-half times the original amount we intended to spend.

While the house was being built (oh, and it always takes longer than they tell you... It was supposed to be six months, but turned out to be more than eight), we needed to find a temporary place to live that offered a short-term lease and would allow eight cats – *good luck with that!*

After exhausting almost all options, we finally found a neighborhood (in a not-so-safe, questionable part of town) with small duplex, single-story, brick apartments – the *only* place with short-term leases allowing multiple animals.

The unit available to us was old, dark, and dingy, and the previous occupants had cleaned and disassembled a car engine in the living room -– nasty carpet, nasty smell. What a depressing change from our bright, clean, renovated house in Japan! We reluctantly signed the lease since there was no other choice, but it was only temporary, and at least it was a place for all of us to live in the meantime.

A month before we moved out, one of the duplexes down the street was burglarized. I was distraught, losing sleep from worry and panic. In all the years living in Japan, we *never* worried about safety, never locked our cars, and rarely locked our house.

Now we were living in a different place, obviously not as safe as we were used to, and my worst fear was, *"What if somebody breaks in and hurts the cats? Or kills them?"*

This was yet another time to beef up the prayers. In the midst of all the fear, one morning about a week after that break-in, I woke up unexpectedly with lyrics to a familiar praise song floating in my head: *"We are standing on holy ground, and I know that there are angels all around…"*

The song was prophetic to me, and I knew in my heart it was a heavenly message to let me know we were protected and going to be safe. The fear dissipated, and we endured the final month in that dreary little duplex until it was time to move into our new house on Laurel Oak Lane. It was worth the wait, though. The final product was beautiful!

We had accomplished the nearly impossible task of traveling safely across the world with eight cats, eight carriers, two separate planes, a hotel stay, a shoddy duplex apartment, and a final move into our new home.

I missed Japan terribly, but loved my new assignment at Robins AFB and was fortunate to be stationed with some of the same wonderful people I had served with in Japan. I looked forward to new adventures – which included learning to play the bagpipes – and was determined to keep our cat population of eight in check!

I didn't know it at the time, but this was my Core Eight group of cats, which was the start of my caring for 8-10 cats at a time for 23 consecutive years! This particular combination of felines, though, was unlike any other that I've had. I can't find words to describe the intense bond of love that existed between all of us. Was it because they each came out of traumatic circumstances? I don't know, but it was extraordinary.

There were *zero* integration problems among them when we brought a new member into the household. They all just got along. Many times, all eight slept together on the bed. I've never seen anything like it!

And it all started with the dream I'd had in Japan that directed me to help Pretty Girl, the tortoiseshell cat with an orange mustache. It was a dream I would look back on many times and marvel at the wisdom of the universe in directing these specific beings into my life who would eventually guide me into the world of animal communication and reincarnation.

But there were many more cats – and adventures – to come before I would connect all the dots to make sense of it, turning my spiritual life upside down in the process and integrating all that I learned. The Divine Creator has been very patient with me. (I'm a slow learner!)

CHAPTER 19

LAUREL OAK LANE

"We love our new house, Mom! We finally get to spread out and claim our territories. All that moving from place to place and living in small spaces has worn us out – not to mention getting a bit claustrophobic in those carriers. Please, can we stay here for awhile? And we'll make you a deal. If we don't ever have to move again, we promise to keep our hunting to ourselves and won't bring you any more presents." (hee hee…)

– The Core Eight

Our new house on Laurel Oak Lane had a huge floor-to-ceiling picture window in the great room overlooking beautiful trees in the wooded lot, which we kept *au natural* and maintenance free, rather than creating a yard. It was a gorgeous setting on a dead-end street.

As we settled into our new home, the eight feline world travelers were thrilled to be out of their short-term living conditions and spread their paws throughout the large house, claiming their territories. One of the favorite hangout spots for those that could jump (namely, Muffin) was on top of the tall, white kitchen cabinets close to the ceiling.

I was stationed with the Band of the Air Force Reserve, comprised of active-duty musicians supporting the Air Force

Reserve Command. Our mission at Robins AFB was unique. As a clarinetist, along with the other woodwind players in the band, I was going to learn how to play the bagpipes – thus began my bagpiping career! Plus, it was another instrument to learn as a doubler.

I was thrilled and determined to learn the pipes as quickly as possible, and I did! Four months and hundreds of practice hours after my first lesson, I was able to fully participate with the Air Force Reserve Pipe Band in two high-profile performances in March 1996 that were centered around St. Patrick's Day.

The first took place on the steps of the U.S. Capitol in Washington, D.C., piping for the President of the United States and the Prime Minister of Ireland at their annual luncheon hosted by the Speaker of the House.

Then, we were flown to Nashville, Tennessee, to perform on the Nashville Network's *Prime Time Country* show for their episode celebrating St. Patrick's Day. The studio even provided professional makeup artists to put the finishing touches on our already stellar appearance.

Those were incredible introductory experiences with this unique band, and many other high-profile playing opportunities came bounding our way.

On January 1, 1997, we were the *lead unit* in the five-mile Tournament of Roses Parade in Pasadena, California, along with an Air Force Marching Band composed of members representing several Air Force field bands.

1997 marked the 50th Anniversary of the U.S. Air Force as a separate branch of the Armed Forces, and this parade helped celebrate that fact, not only with the presence of our Air Force Band to start the parade, but with the most spectacular "fly-over" I ever witnessed, one of the most memorable moments of my Air Force career.

When we stepped out to begin the parade, the Air Force B-2 Spirit airplane, known as the Stealth Bomber, surprised us with an otherworldly appearance directly overhead. As its name suggests, it seemed to come out of nowhere, totally silent and invisible at first, then literally becoming visible all at once, resting directly above us, hovering at a low altitude. *Am I on Star Trek?*

That moment when the bomber suddenly became visible remains ever fresh in my mind when I walk down memory lane with my bagpiping career.

To me, it was ironic that I was learning to play the bagpipes, because when I was in high school, my mother's only cousin was in the Navy, stationed on a submarine near Scotland. When they went ashore, he purchased a kilt and all the accoutrements that went with it and gave it to me as a gift. *How random* – or so I thought!

Not having any clue as to what I would ever do with a kilt, my parents stored it safely in a cedar chest for the next 20 years! As soon as I was stationed at Robins AFB and was going to learn the pipes, I asked them to send it to me. Not surprisingly, it fit perfectly, and I still wear it to this day! *What are the chances of that happening?*

This was just one example of how random events early in life would become precursors of things to come. I've never doubted there was a Higher Intelligence in the Universe that orchestrated these "coincidences!"

I remember having a notable "spiritual moment" while standing in one of the three bedrooms of our house. Life was going well, but I was still a spiritual seeker and threw out this all-encompassing prayer to God: *Make me a saint!*

I had been reading biographies of some women saints in the Catholic church and was inspired by how they seemed to keep their peace in the midst of sometimes very difficult and adverse circumstances. They made it seem so easy!

I also recall throwing out other huge prayer requests to God before Chuck and I moved to Japan, such as *"Make me an intercessor"* and *"Make me a healer…"* And yes, *"Make me a missionary"* was thrown in there, too.

Shortly after that last one, the Air Force transferred me to Japan! Although I was not a missionary in the traditional sense of the word, I was sent to live in a foreign country. That is a perfect illustration that prayers are often answered in unexpected ways.

As the next 25 years unfolded, I regretted everything I'd asked for and wanted to take every prayer back! It seemed so easy to read stories about highly venerated, holy people and dream about "happily ever after" scenarios while I did great things for God, but as in the lives of the saints and through the example of Jesus, I would learn through the way of the cross.

Years later, I heard it said by Fr. Richard Rohr from the *Center for Action and Contemplation* that "We find God not by doing it right, but by doing it wrong." He referred to this as "falling upward."

I yearned to do something grandiose and important for God that impacted a lot of people. I had all the good intentions in the world, but in reality was quite clueless as to what I was actually throwing out to the universe in my zeal.

Chuck shared my ideals, and we embarked on the long, arduous process of adopting an older child from an orphanage in Russia – again, having all good intentions, along with no parenting experience. But this was the perfect, altruistic act and a great thing to do for God. Plus, we would be helping a child who didn't have a home!

The adoption process consisted of mounds of paperwork and documents that required notarization and state seals (which took months and months to compile) that we had to submit to the adoption agency, along with home studies where the case workers visited your home to inspect the environment the child would be living in.

Unfortunately, they didn't give any guidance on what to expect from overseas adoptions, such as the unique challenges and obstacles to overcome with these children. And as inexperienced as we were, we didn't know what questions to ask, so we entered this world of parenting somewhat blindfolded. There was no internet at the time, so valuable resources were not at our fingertips.

One year into that process, my father, who had recently been diagnosed with Type 2 diabetes, was diagnosed with lung cancer. In May of 1996, one month shy of my parents' 49th wedding anniversary, Dad coughed up some blood. It happened twice, and when the doctors took x-rays, they found the cancer, which was heavy in one lung and had mildly spread to the other.

The shock was tremendous, because he was only 72 and had quit smoking 15 years prior. For several months, he had been implementing positive lifestyle changes to improve his health and actually looked and felt the best that he had in many years.

Mom, trying to remain hopeful and optimistic, attempted to paint a better picture and prognosis than was really possible, because, at that time, Dad's chances of recovery were extremely low.

I believed in supernatural healing (and after all, I had told God I wanted to be a healer), but was in total denial. I'd never dealt with a serious illness of a close family member before, and I didn't know how to accept it.

In July, I went to Malone to visit for what would turn out to be the last time I would see Dad alive. He was starting chemo and radiation treatments, which in hindsight, from my perspective, only sped up the dying process.

I brought my bagpipes on that trip and experienced a special, tender moment at the hospital when I waited for Dad in the parking lot and played as he walked to his car following one of the treatments. I've played pipes for hundreds of funerals, but that special moment of piping for him in the parking lot supersedes any of those occasions.

I spoke with my parents on a weekly basis, but on Labor Day, less than two months after I had traveled to Malone, I felt an urge to call for an extra chat, which I now understand was an intuitive moment. That was the last time I spoke with Dad, and also when the seriousness of his illness *finally* hit me.

He had planned to mail me a package that week but was too weak to do it and had never failed to keep his word for something like that. For the first time ever, he didn't sound good.

Two days later, I traveled with the band to Maxwell Air Force Base, Alabama, and after I arrived, our squadron's secretary at Robins called and left a message for me to call my mother. I knew something bad had happened, and I panicked so much that I forgot the phone number – the number I had grown up with!

When I finally remembered the number and reached her, she told me she had taken Dad to the hospital the previous night because he was coughing uncontrollably. She expected to go back to see him in the morning, but sadly, he didn't make it through the night and had passed away. It turned out to be the only night he actually spent in the hospital during the treatments, and for that I was grateful.

None of us were with him, and I had no preparation for the grueling emotions that I felt after his death. When you talk about how the sympathetic nervous system responds to stress, the expression *"Fight, Flight, or Freeze"* is often used. I definitely *froze* and remained that way for several months.

While I was grieving, Chuck and I stopped the already long adoption process temporarily, but it would take over a year before I was emotionally stable enough to continue. By the time the adoption of our first daughter (Kristina, age five, from Ufa, Russia) took place, it was over two and a half years from when we started.

The timing, however, was perfect. My enlistment in the Air Force was finished eight days after the adoption decree was issued, and I had made the tough decision to come off Active Duty after 13 years of service to stay home with Kristina.

But first, we had to travel to Russia to bring this little girl home!

CHAPTER 20

KRISTINA'S ADOPTION

"Mom, there's a terror in the house! It's a little girl... Please help me!"

— Mr. Peabody

We traveled to Moscow in December 1997, then on to Ufa, in the Republic of Bashkortostan, along with three other couples who were also adopting, to meet the children. Kristina was living in what they called Baby Home No.2, a large house owned by a merchant at the turn of the 20th century that had been converted into an orphanage following the 1917 Bolshevik Revolution.

How did we choose this specific girl to adopt? All we had were pictures and a video to look at. Kristina's coloring and features blended in with ours, but there was one additional *sign* that showed up after we made the decision. In her photos, she was wearing a blue dress with a pink bow on her head and something appliqued on the dress.

We didn't pay close attention to that applique at first, but when I looked closer, it was a *small... black... cat!* Obviously, that was a confirmation that she was the right one for us — at least in *my* mind.

Kristina was five, although the size of a two-year-old, with a slightly distended belly from lack of proper nutrition. She had a spunky personality and a happy demeanor. She loved the small, stuffed koala bear we gave her as a gift. Ironically, it was December 24th.

The court hearing was the next day – Christmas in the United States – which turned out to be an informal meeting in the judge's office, along with the Minister of Education and our translator. Everyone had to give their approval, and the adoption was official that same day. Kristina was our Christmas child!

Chuck returned home by himself to finish some of the house preparations, while I remained in Russia for another week to wait for the remaining paperwork to be completed at the embassy.

Thankfully, our translator was still available to help me, at least on a limited basis. The stories from my week alone with Kristina would be enough for another book, but I'll share a few of the more interesting ones here.

I went to the orphanage on New Year's Eve with the translator to pick up Kristina, and the challenges began immediately, starting while waiting at the airport in Ufa for our flight to Moscow.

There were stray cats living at the airport, and many had kittens. (Of course, if this had been in the States, I would have taken them all home with me!) Suddenly, this young, five-year-old girl, who was now my daughter and who spoke no English, started throwing the stray kittens into the air and across the seats in our boarding area. "Wheee!" she gleefully laughed in Russian... *Oh, no... We have eight cats at home... What have I gotten myself into?*

Through our translator, I tried to impress upon Kristina that it's important to be kind to the cats, and she assured me she would. That remained to be seen.

While waiting for our flight, I gave my new daughter some clementines. The children at the orphanage had virtually no nutritious food, and fruit was non-existent, so she proceeded to eat four of them – the first three with the peel still on! And, of course, I made sure she had enough water and other snacks. She loved the water bottles, too, so I gave her more and more… You can guess where this is going!

While we were standing in line on the runway in the freezing cold weather, waiting to board the plane for our flight back to Moscow, where we would out-process through the embassy, Kristina kept saying what I thought was "I want some water" in Russian, so I continued giving her *more* water. *Way to go, Kathy! You learned those Russian phrases so well, and you're giving your new daughter exactly what she asked for. You passed the Parenting 101 class with flying colors!*

But now Kristina began wiggling her body and swaying back and forth. My Russian vocabulary was limited, and I didn't realize that the phrases I had learned for "I want to drink" and "I have to pee" were almost the same. I obviously learned incorrectly, but it didn't matter. I was clueless and stood there dumbfounded about what to do next.

Finally, a passenger standing next to me translated into English what this frantic little girl was saying: "I have to go to the bathroom!" First parenting lesson learned: No water – or anything else to drink – when there is no toilet in sight! When it was our turn to board, we almost flew onto the plane to go use the restroom… *whew, just in the nick of time!*

Kristina and I survived together in the hotel room in Moscow for a week, trying to find amusement any way we could. This included playing catch with water bottles and running up and down the hallways for exercise.

Every night at bedtime, I witnessed the "rocking" behavior we had heard about before our trip, where many children who live in orphanages comfort themselves by rocking their bodies to fall asleep. It was true. Kristina would enter her "zone," where she tuned me out, rocking back and forth, left and right, until she was sleeping. To this day, she still rocks back and forth as a means of comfort.

We also didn't know it at the time, but Kristina had a multitude of learning disabilities that were not conveyed to us during the adoption process. When I asked the translator to tell me what was in the medical records, she was vague and glossed over those parts. I didn't think to dig deeper to get more information at the time.

We later found out that it was a common practice for Russian officials/adoption agencies to falsify records or misrepresent the truth about medical information. Many adults who worked at the orphanages really loved the children, so they did whatever they could to get them adopted. That was just how the system worked, along with the "extra expenses" (bribes) we were expected to pay to get everyone's approval for adoption.

We thought that many of Kristina's medical issues and learning difficulties that would unfold over time would resolve eventually, but they did not. We were not given accurate information, and if we had known, we would have sought out the resources we needed much sooner.

With the knowledge we later gained from the proper translation of her medical records, I can only imagine the stress she must have experienced, starting with her birth, when she was born breach and not breathing, so the doctors had to resuscitate her. No doubt that caused some brain damage, along with the effects of alcohol during pregnancy from her birth mother, who surrendered her parental rights immediately and later died in a car accident when Kristina was two.

This little girl with a difficult start in life was kept at the hospital her entire first year until her birth father finally made arrangements for her to be sent to Baby Home No. 2 in Ufa, shortly before he died from lung cancer. She was truly an orphan and spent the next four years in the Home, with poor nutrition causing further damage to her development, until we adopted her.

During our afternoons in Moscow, waiting for the paperwork, Kristina and I walked through the streets in spite of the cold temperatures, taking in the sights and street vendors. I don't think she had seen much of the outside world during her four years at the orphanage.

Her favorite vendors were the ones selling apples, which were humongous! As we stared at one of the vendors selling them, she kept repeating (in Russian, of course), "I want an apple," over and over and over… and more insistent each time!

While we stood in line waiting to purchase one, a very kind Russian man ahead of us, who I'm convinced had pity on me after hearing her desperate pleas, bought an apple for her. I'm not sure if he was more moved by her continuous begging or my overwhelmed facial expressions, but I was very grateful for his kindness. We brought the apple to a bench next to a large, concrete building and took turns taking bites. Somehow, we survived the week together.

After completing all the final adoption paperwork, including passports and a medical check, we were ready for our flight back to Georgia. There would be no translator with us, though, so I was on my own. *How difficult could this be?*

The travel day included a very early morning van trip from the hotel to the Moscow airport, with multiple suitcases and a bottle of champagne that the driver gave to me. I had no arms left to hold Kristina's hand as we navigated through the airport. She was wild and started to run all over the place.

I was worn out before we even reached the gate, and I'm absolutely certain that God sent angels to help us. A young American couple heading in the same direction saw my plight and offered to carry some of our luggage while I managed my daughter.

Thus began our 24-hour journey on multiple planes, including a layover in Sweden, while this poor, stressed little girl slept a total of 15 minutes! (The children's Dramamine did not work!) She was totally hyper and uncontrollable, repeatedly bouncing up and down in her seat.

To make matters worse, *all* the flight attendants kept offering her chocolate and other candy to try and settle her down. Go figure! This was not an adventure for the faint of heart! It was the most difficult traveling experience I've ever lived through.

After the endless flying ordeal, we arrived in Atlanta and eventually made it through customs and immigration while Kristina proudly did somersaults on the floor as I was attempting to give the agents folders full of the important paperwork I had accumulated from the previous two weeks.

I could see Chuck in the distance, along with his parents and other members of his immediate family who had driven from parts of Tennessee and Alabama to meet us when we arrived. *Help me…* Our contingent of greeters were smiling profusely, waving stuffed animals in the air, while I – totally exhausted and worn out – could only think of one thing: *TAG – you're it!*

But we made it back safe and sound. From her lack of sleep, Kristina totally crashed on the couch from exhaustion when we finally arrived at our home in Warner Robins.

I was confident that our daughter would be kind to the cats, as she had promised through the translator. And while she is a very kind-hearted girl, her idea of "kind" was totally different from mine, although her actions were always playful. Mr. Peabody, our one-eyed Japanese train station refugee, experienced some of her "playfulness" when she hoisted him down the stairs in mid-air on more than one occasion.

Oh, no…

When I left Active Duty, I remained in the Air Force Reserves for eight more years in the Chaplain Assistant career field and eventually retired after 21 years of service. It was a later life regret that I didn't spend the full 20 years on Active Duty, but I've tried to look past that decision and recognize all the good that happened because of it.

Really, the regret was that I didn't do enough to take care of myself during those subsequent years with Kristina and the other two girls we adopted later. Neglecting myself was a huge contributing factor to the depression I gradually fell into as the years went by. *What was that prayer? Make me a saint? How's that working out for you, Kathy?*

CHAPTER 21

FROM GEORGIA BACK TO VIRGINIA BEACH

"Mom, do we really have to move again? We thought we were in our 'forever house.' I guess we'll have to adapt again. But we're 'International Travelers,' so moving to another state will be easy, and we will rise to the occasion. But in the midst of this chaos, we've got sad news: It's time for one of us to cross over the rainbow bridge. It's tough when someone leaves, but thanks to you, we're family, and we will get through the grief together."

– Big Boy, Little Boy, Pretty Girl,
Spunky, Muffin, Bobtail, Mr. Peabody

Chuck and I were adaptable, resilient people, capable of adjusting to any locale or situation we faced, and even though we enjoyed much of our three years living in middle Georgia, there were long-term considerations that shaped our decision to move back to Virginia Beach after we adopted Kristina in January 1998.

First, Warner Robins was not a typical southern town. It had been built to support the nearby Air Force base when it first opened in 1942. The town still served that purpose, but apart from my job while on Active Duty, we were not involved in anything else in the community. Even the church we attended was in a different town.

There was just something missing in Warner Robins – it didn't have the *feel* of a small town, the kind both Chuck and I were raised in. There was no quaint downtown that we envisioned returning to one day, and to us, it felt more like an urban community. Although the town's population when we moved there was 48,000 – a smaller, more comfortable size than any place we had lived together previously, and a feature we really liked – we never felt a sense of permanence. (Interestingly, the population had nearly doubled just 30 years later – definitely "urban sprawl" in my mind!)

As much as we tried to envision it as our home for many years, that never happened. Perhaps it was divine intervention that prevented us from feeling that permanence and nudged us to move farther north after Kristina's adoption.

Next, although we had built a beautiful house, it was spacious and required a tremendous amount of upkeep. The 1700 square foot daylight basement went unused, and we managed quite nicely living in the other 1700 square feet on the main floor.

I've never been one that was "married to a house," and could easily pick up and move. Chuck and I had done it many times. Although we were within a day's drive from his parents' house in middle Tennessee, we were two days away from my mom and brother Steve, who still lived in upstate New York. After my father passed away, Malone seemed even farther away, and flying was the only viable option to visit them. We wanted to return to a location that was within a shorter driving distance.

And then there was the climate. From mid-spring through the fall, we spent most of our time inside airconditioned buildings, even when we weren't at our jobs. The heat and humidity were intense during the summer months – too severe for me, with daily temperatures averaging near 100 degrees. At times, I was so miserable that even with a slight breeze, just walking outside felt like being immersed in car exhaust!

Even worse was the discomfort I felt playing bagpipes in that heat – especially if our band wore the full regalia – Whew! There was no way to avoid it, especially during the July 4th Independence Day celebrations, of which we were an integral part.

A final consideration was that we were now parents and wanted to be close to our network of church friends in Virginia Beach that we'd known since our mid-20s. It was important to us that our daughter be raised in an environment with like-minded people whose children were close to her in age.

I was always comfortable living in Virginia Beach and was quite happy with the anticipation of not only returning to a more moderate climate, but reconnecting with our group of friends. Geographically, it would situate us to within a day's drive to both Tennessee and New York.

Since my enlistment in the Air Force had ended eight days after Kristina and I returned from Russia (what a coincidence!), I'd been able to leave Active Duty immediately and transfer into the Air Force Reserves, but not as a musician. There were no Air Force Band options for me at the time, except in the National Guard, but that wasn't feasible geographically, so I joined the Chaplain Assistant career field and attended their technical training school at Maxwell AFB, Alabama, for six weeks.

Chuck and I believed that my getting off Active Duty was the best decision for all of us, and it probably was. My job in the Air Force required a lot of travel, and with Kristina's needs, for me to continue living that on-the-go lifestyle didn't seem to foster the most ideal family situation. This little girl had been without parents her entire life, and it was important for me to be present with her as a mom to build our relationship.

As with other life decisions that seemed good to me at the time but later morphed into difficulties, I still believed the verse from Romans 8:28 that "All things work together for good to them that love God, to them that are called according to His purpose."

Believing that truth after leaving Active Duty wasn't easy, but now I understand that it was another steppingstone into what my life has become today. It helped guide me to more fully discovering my soul's purpose as a healer and Animal Communicator. At the time, though, I was preoccupied with trying to navigate the throes of parenthood.

Eventually, I made peace with the fact that I was now a mother and would be for the remainder of my life. My *unwavering perseverance* once again helped me plow through some difficult years that lay ahead. Kristina was a goodhearted girl, and there were virtually no discipline problems that couldn't be solved with a "time-out." Her joyful personality brightened everyone's life she came in contact with – human, that is, not feline.

With her precocious behavior toward our cats, I was constantly on alert, monitoring their safety – especially Mr. Peabody's

– which proved to be a full-time job. And I stopped her from hitting Cyclops on more than one occasion, which tore my heart out, because he was the sweetest, most docile one of all. After what seemed like hundreds of time-outs, Kristina's behavior finally improved!

But the time spent preparing to relocate seemed to drag by for me, because I was trying to be the perfect mom to a five-year-old girl who didn't speak English, and since she was losing her Russian by not using it on a daily basis, there were four months where she was "in between" languages and hardly spoke at all.

We later found out that Kristina had speech development problems, even in her native tongue. Little did we know of the intellectual disabilities and cognitive processing disorders that also plagued her, which we wouldn't grasp for several more years.

Although I didn't recognize it as such, I was in a fit of depression, inwardly upset that I had left the job and career I loved and guilty that I felt that way! I was angry at myself but believed that "anger" was an undesirable quality – perhaps even sinful – so I hid my feelings, even from myself, and happily stuffed them away.

In listening to other women I knew, I thought I should be excited to be a mom, but it was really difficult. A few months after adopting Kristina, I was talking to one of my sisters-in-law (a mom of multiple children) over the phone about the difficulties I was experiencing, and I remember her saying, "Yes, but don't you just love it?" No, I didn't love it! And I felt guilty about that. If I'd had the awareness then that I should never compare myself to another person and had known how to reach out for help, I think it would have eased my transition into being a parent, but I thought I could just figure it out on my own! *Good thinking, Kathy...*

We planned to make the move back to Virginia within six months, taking advantage of our final Air Force relocation benefit. There were a few obstacles to overcome, but we believed we were being divinely guided in this process and trusted that God would help us work out the details. And He truly did – in a big way!

Selling our house within that time period was miraculous, because the family on the corner of our street was looking to upsize for their growing family and wanted to stay in the same neighborhood. When they looked at our house, they LOVED it and made an offer that we accepted immediately.

After the contract was finalized and the dates were scheduled for us to vacate, I had a strong sense within me that God was saying, "You saw what I did for the house, now just wait and see what I'm going to do for the other details!" They, too, were miraculous!

When we'd moved to Georgia three years earlier, Chuck started out working as a teacher in the Macon, Georgia, school district, just 30 minutes from Warner Robins. But by the end of the school year, he decided to change careers and learned a whole new set of skills in the ever-growing computer industry. He quickly landed a job as a civilian at Robins Air Force Base, working with computers. This was a great foundational step for what would eventually become his new career.

While preparing for our relocation, he was offered a job in Virginia Beach through the efforts of a good friend who worked in the IT (Information Technology) department of a company close to where we used to live, and of course, he accepted!

Other long-time friends helped us find a house on Parkland Lane, just a half mile from Chuck's new office. It was a two-story, colonial-style brick house on a dead-end street, with fruit trees and a stream flowing through the backyard, just two miles from our previous neighborhood and adjacent to a small park full of children's play equipment.

It was secluded, yet less than two miles from the Interstate. We could drive to anywhere in the Hampton Roads area, including the oceanfront, and be there within 30 minutes – city traffic permitting, of course! It was the perfect house and location for all of us and was a safe setting for the cats. What a blessing!

We had conquered all the major obstacles in moving back to Virginia Beach, but we would not be bringing all eight cats back with us.

Two months before our scheduled departure, Cyclops, the sweet, little one-eyed golden boy, who had desperately begged for attention and come home with us on Chuck's bicycle in Japan, started to lose weight. He was not a large cat by any means, and really couldn't afford to drop even a few pounds.

After numerous trips to the vet, which included steroid and vitamin B12 injections to help stimulate his appetite, nothing worked. They also couldn't come up with a diagnosis, but his health failed rapidly, and he died in our home at the end of May with no fanfare or ceremony. We had gone out to the grocery store, and when we returned, he lay motionless on the gray carpeted floor in our great room.

When we found Cyclops in Japan, we thought he was about a year old at the time, but in hindsight, he must have been older – possibly even closer to four or five. It was only five years since then, though, and he seemed too young to have serious health problems. Plus, he had never been sick a day in his life after we adopted him. It didn't make sense.

I was heartbroken, because this was the first loss of our Core Eight group of cats, the crew that had traveled with us all the way from Japan just three years earlier. Now, we would only be taking the remaining seven back to Virginia Beach. Cyclops' death left a tremendous void in our family.

In July of 1998, the movers arrived at our house on Laurel Oak Lane to pack our household goods, and Chuck and I loaded up our two blue Toyota Camrys with Kristina and our seven cats: Big Boy, Little Boy, Pretty Girl, Spunky, Muffin, Bobtail, and Mr. Peabody.

We were finally on our way back to Virginia!

It was also time to take stock of the many household items we had purchased over the years in anticipation of where they would fit in our new home on Parkland Lane.

Did I mention that I was a Crazy Cat Lady, and that sometimes, well, those women tend to accumulate a large number of feline-related items? Surely, that hadn't happened to me…

CHAPTER 22

CRAZY CAT LADY PARAPHERNALIA

> *"We hate to tell you, Mom, but you're insane! Or is this your idea of further proving that you're a Crazy Cat Lady? We thought that having a house full of live felines would be enough for you, but no… Why did you bring all this useless, fake cat junk into the house?"*
>
> – The Fur Family

It's an unspoken rule that every Crazy Cat Lady (CCL), or aspiring one, needs to have her paraphernalia. Not only her collection of *living* cats, but every item under the sun that either has a cat image on it, is shaped like a cat, or resembles a cat in any way.

There should be reminders of cats everywhere: in the house, the car, the yard, or anywhere the CCL takes up space. The collection can begin at any age and can also be a steppingstone to acquiring her live assortment. This will secure her well-earned, bona fide title of "Crazy Cat Lady."

For my readers who are not "cat people," I give you permission to skip this chapter! But if you want a good laugh from the absurdity of what I did, keep reading…

My collection included – but was not limited to – the following, starting in the kitchen:

- Two sets of placemats, one shaped like a gray-and-white cartoon cat and the other with a tabby cat sitting on a cushion.
- My favorite refrigerator magnet, shaped like Garfield, the lovable, orange cartoon cat, standing with his arms wide open, asking/exclaiming, "Have you had your hug today?"
- A square, ceramic trivet with two Italian tiger cats painted on it and the caption: *"ATTENTI AI GATTI"* (Beware of the Cat!)
- Two sets of salt and pepper shakers, one which was dual purposed as a set of white porcelain napkin holders in the shape of cats in which the bellies were the "hole" to insert the napkins.
- A Japanese "Happy Cat" – a colorful porcelain cat with its paw held upward as if to greet you. They were thought to bring good luck and graced the entrance of every restaurant in Japan. Who wouldn't want one of those?

Last but not least, what every kitchen desperately needs: not one, but *two* sets of chopstick holders purchased in Japan! One was a set of 10 cute, little, flat, tan pottery cats, whose fat bellies were flattened to set the chopsticks on. They resembled squashed "sumo cats" lying on their backs. The other set was also pottery, with small, blue-and-gray striped painted cats lounging in different positions, allowing the chopsticks to be set on their bodies. Each of the 16 pieces measured 1 ½ inches in length.

Next, the feline wardrobe, which included:

- Socks
- A fashion scarf with cats printed throughout
- Sweatshirts and T-shirts with cats wearing athletic equipment, hats, or swimwear on the front side and playfully displaying their furry hind ends on the back
- Nightshirts, one with a cat that looked half-dead declaring, "I don't do mornings," and others with giant, lovable feline faces

The best T-shirt I ever owned depicted a caricature of a frazzled woman's head, surrounded by 25 cats with the perfect advertisement for those needing a CCL Recovery Program. It read: "Cat Addicts Anonymous – I Can Stop Any Time I Want."

My jewelry included multiple fashion pins, some made of gold with various shaped cats, two pewter pins, each with three Meowy Christmas cats, and one more pin with a cat sitting at the computer with a computer mouse shaped like a real mouse…

And earrings – well, if I had pierced ears, I'm sure I'd have a collection of those, too!

For Halloween, the "Bat Cat Candle Holder" was the best centerpiece, with a black cat wearing a Batman mask, sitting in the center with spaces for four votive candles around its body.

Christmas paraphernalia included:

- Christmas cards – one with nine cats playing musical instruments that someone gave to me, which I eventually framed, because I had nine cats at the time!
- Christmas stockings with cat decorations on them
- Socks (not to be confused with the regular cat socks for other times of the year)
- Tree ornaments
- A sweater with multiple kittens playing with balls of yarn knit into the design

My most prized Christmas item was the *Jingle Cats* music CD, which showcased popular Christmas songs with cats' meows doing the "singing," pitched to match the lyrics of the songs! This one totally freaked my cats out when they heard the meowing sounds. They perked their ears up, stared, and ran off!

Other items included:

- Birthday and all-occasion cards
- The annual Cat Calendar, which goes on the wall next to the computer. My mother religiously sends those to me – I don't have to search for them!
- Throw pillows
- Bathroom toilet cleaner brushes
- Several stuffed animals, one I named after my cat Muffin (which I gave to my mother)
- Carved wooden cat statues purchased in Thailand
- Brass statues

- Brass candlestick holders
- A deck of playing cards with "Hello Kitty" pictures on the front, purchased in Japan
- Russian Stacking Dolls painted with cats

When we adopted Kristina from Russia on Christmas Day in 1997, during our stay in Moscow, we often went shopping for local Russian crafts, and that's where we found the Stacking Dolls.

Also known as Matryoshka, or Nesting Dolls, they were unique. Each one came apart in the middle section, and inside, you would find a smaller doll, and then an even smaller doll, etc. We found some with anywhere from 4-14 dolls stacked inside each other. The cat set we bought had four dolls with cat faces, each hand-painted a different color.

In addition to traditional Russian designs, we found not only the cats, but dolls with themes of anything an American tourist could want, including U.S. presidents and professional sports teams. (I absolutely had to buy the set of New York Yankees dolls!)

My favorite CCL mementos were several carved, wooden cats from Thailand. While stationed in Japan, I had the opportunity to travel to Thailand on four occasions, two with work and two for vacation.

During each trip, I was able to shop at the Night Bazaar in Chiang Mai, an open-air market lining the streets of the city, which consisted of vendor after vendor selling their goods. The Bazaar was so large that it seemed like every crafter in

Thailand, including several of the Hill Tribes, had sent their homemade treasures to sell with tourists in mind. It was a shopper's paradise – totally my kind of place! I love original *anything* that's artsy and do my best to support creative people and their work.

From my perspective as an American visiting a developing country, the prices were more than dirt cheap, and I usually felt guilty haggling over them. I would gladly have paid these folks *twice* the amount they asked, in most cases, but per their custom, they expect to negotiate, and I suspect they feel a rush of adrenaline in the process.

After I worked through the guilt of trying to pay less money for a handmade treasure that I thought was worth far more, I began my career as a haggler – and I started to enjoy it! So much so that after I found my first carved, wooden cat "statue" with a whitewashed finish and hint of pastel colors, I couldn't stop with just one, so I searched through vendor after vendor, obsessively looking for more.

All total, including the darker, wood-stained ones that I also haggled over, I wound up with nearly a dozen carved, wooden cats! These were not tiny, three-inch-tall cats, but rather 8-16 inches in height, and all depicted in different poses, so there were no duplicates. I even bought one that is perched on a ledge, peering down and staring at you, that can be displayed at the edge of a cabinet or refrigerator.

The saving grace of purchasing bulky items on band trips was that if I shipped them from a U.S. postal site, I would pay U.S. postal rates – not expensive overseas shipping costs – because

I was sending them to a U.S. Military address at Yokota Air Base, where I was stationed.

That was easy, since our duty-related trips in Thailand were sponsored either by the U.S. Consulate or U.S. Information Services. No problem! Two weeks later, all my treasures arrived safe and sound at our post office in Japan. That was a nice perk of being in the military.

The fruits of my overseas shopping exploits eventually made their way back to the U.S. with our household goods shipment when my assignment ended, and those carved cats stayed on display in the china cabinet, relegating a beautiful set of Wedgewood china to the bottom shelf, where it went unseen for many years. After all, first things first! *Really, Kathy?*

My preoccupation with cat paraphernalia extended to non-tangible items as well, including a restaurant in Japan we inadvertently stumbled onto one night while walking the streets of Tokyo with some friends. A hypnotizing aroma filled the air, and we were determined to find its source.

Following our noses, we were led to what became one of our favorite restaurants: The Four Cats! The house specialty, deep-fried garlic, was the irresistible smell that permeated the air – and it tasted even better!

The name "Four Cats" was apropos, as coincidentally, we had four cats at the time. And we were more than relieved to find out that the name of the restaurant did *not* imply that there were cats on the menu. (Well, maybe I did check to make sure we still had four cats when we got home that night…)

The absurdity of my ever-present feline addiction even expanded to storytelling with my daughter Kristina after we came back from Russia. She had just turned five when we adopted her, and as a new parent, I was trying to find things we would enjoy doing together.

Kristina and I spent multiple hours almost every day at local parks, especially ones that had swing sets. It was her favorite activity. She would swing for hours, so I decided to become a storyteller and practice using our imaginations! It would be fun!

Of course, I knew nothing about telling stories, and wasn't even sure I remembered any from childhood, but Kristina loved all the books I read to her, so I figured I could learn to tell stories, too.

I purchased a book on storytelling, which included a few childhood tales, along with pointers on how to enhance them with your delivery style. That was my starting point.

My daughter's English language skills were slowly developing, and I tried to personalize the stories with a little creativity, a lot of expression, and HOURS of repetition so she could understand them!

It was easier than I thought. In every story, our cats became the main characters: The favorites were:

1. *The Three Kitty Cat Pigs*, which always featured Big Boy, Little Boy, and Mr. Peabody. We even made this into a play and retold it as a family in a dramatization for our church fellowship group's talent show.

2. Original dinosaur tales in which the main characters were names of our cats. Kristina chose a topic, and I modified the plot each time to make it a new story.

3. An adaptation of a cute little fairy tale called *Cheese and Crackers*. Mr. Peabody was the hero that rescued a hungry baby's family members who were swallowed, one by one, by a big, fat bear on their way to the market to buy him (the baby) some cheese and crackers! This was her absolute favorite!

She never tired of listening to my storytelling, and those were some of our happiest times together during her childhood.

My cat paraphernalia days have long since passed – or have they? I completed my first 5K as a walker/jogger a couple years ago. The theme was Superheroes, and the participants were encouraged to dress as their favorite hero. Who did I choose? Catwoman, of course! *I still have my costume…*

CHAPTER 23

PARKLAND LANE

"Mom, this is one of the toughest stories to tell. I didn't want to leave you, but I got sick. Eventually, you'll realize that I couldn't be separated from you for very long and will return – even though you won't recognize me right away in my brand-new body. Best of all, I'll get to witness your becoming an Animal Communicator! Then we can finally have a real conversation, and I can help you heal from the trauma you experienced and the difficult emotions you stored from witnessing the end of my life as your No.1 cat."

– Big Boy

We moved from Georgia back to Virginia Beach in July 1998, six months after we adopted Kristina, and I transitioned from Active Duty into the Air Force Reserves. Chuck started his new job working in IT at the nearby Christian Broadcasting Network complex, less than half a mile from our new home on Parkland Lane.

I was overjoyed to be back in familiar surroundings, and we enjoyed a happy reunion with our many friends, along with the Christian fellowship group we had been a part of eight years earlier. We settled in immediately.

Our seven cats easily adjusted to their new surroundings, but Cyclops' death should have been my clue that these cats weren't going to live forever. With my ever-optimistic, Pollyanna, pie-in-the-sky dreamer personality, however, I didn't take the hint. To make matters worse, it was my beloved soulmate cat Big Boy that was the next to succumb to health problems, and I failed to see the seriousness of what was happening to him.

Big Boy was now 15 and developed cancer in his head, which affected his vision and hearing. I was so attached to this cat, though, and was of the mindset that as long as he had the will to live, I would honor that. Big Boy and I had a strong bond, and I just didn't want to let him go. His condition continued to deteriorate, but I was determined to keep him with me as long as I could.

As Big Boy's health declined, I was also wrestling with the moral implications of euthanasia when it came to my cats. I did not want to play God and be the one who determined when they would die. For me, that option was an absolute last resort. Since Big Boy's death, I've resolved that issue and try to consider the bigger picture. Now, I ask many questions, like, "Am I doing this for *me* or for the animal?"

As an Animal Communicator, I treasure the opportunities I've been blessed with to connect with animals when they are in a hospice situation, and I can ask them what *they* want. Their answers are never the same. Even before I was trained to do this, I asked my animals directly, and they *always* gave me an answer, usually through circumstances, such as disappearing for two days after I'd made an appointment with the vet and couldn't find them. They mysteriously reappeared after I canceled the appointment! This has happened multiple times. I do my best to honor their wishes.

My denial of Big Boy's illness was the cause of much guilt, because this faithful cat that I was joined to at the hip, who even though he was on pain meds and had lost his sight and hearing, had to have been uncomfortable. But I remained oblivious and continued with life as usual.

I held fast to my determination to let him live as long as he was still engaged with life and responsive to me in a positive way. He even continued to sleep on my head and purr like he had always done up until the last few days of his life. I no longer berate myself for that.

I made the best decisions I could at the time and still live by the code that as long as an animal shows signs that they want to live, I will honor that. Now, as an Animal Communicator, I can also help other people make end-of-life decisions based on their animal's wishes.

The day before Big Boy died, I carried him outside to lie in the yard, which he loved, trying to help make him as happy as possible. He slept in the sun for a few hours, and then I brought him back inside.

Caution, graphic description to follow: The next day, for the first time ever in his 15-year life, *he stopped purring and was non-responsive to me.* I looked closer at his head, and some flies had laid eggs in there which had hatched. He was infested with maggots. I didn't know what they were right away, but when we figured it out, I was mortified. We took him to the emergency vet immediately and had him put to sleep. *How could I have let this happen?*

Today, I have a greater understanding that his spirit had either already left his body or was in the process of doing so. His body was alive, but *he* was no longer there.

I berated myself for the next 20 years for how selfish and insensitive I'd been for not seeing the true scope of his illness. In a sick sort of way, I was punishing myself and consequently shut off the fullness of my emotions toward other animals.

But in spite of my own emotional pain, I still couldn't turn away a needy cat or one that obviously wanted to be part of the family. I took in many, many strays after Big Boy's death, but it took a full 20 years to overcome the guilt that I'd stored surrounding his final days.

The healing power of EFT (Emotional Freedom Technique) Tapping, a technique I learned later in my schooling to become an Animal Communicator and Energy Healer, set me free from the stored guilt that had impacted my ability to connect with other animals at a deep, emotional level.

I'm grateful to Big Boy for his tremendous devotion to me and for being the catalyst for the healing I can now help bring to others through EFT Tapping. I will describe this technique in greater detail later in the book.

A year after Big Boy's death, two more cats, whom we named Gray Kitty and Georgie, wandered into our yard. They arrived at nearly the same time, both intact male cats and roughly three or four years old.

Gray Kitty, a fluffy, gray, long-haired beauty, slept in piles of leaves that had accumulated along our backyard fence line just above the stream. He earned his name because we always referred to him as the "Gray Kitty," especially at mealtime, when the common question was: "Did you feed the Gray Kitty yet?"

One morning, when we brought his food outside, we noticed that a big chunk of flesh was missing from his cheek. Previously, we had noticed a torn ear, but this was more serious. Something had attacked him overnight.

We took him to the vet to have his face stitched back together and then let him recuperate in the garage, separated from the other cats. Naturally, the predictable happened, and Gray Kitty wormed his way into the main part of the house.

Although I was not an "official" Animal Communicator yet, I'm sure if he had spoken to me, this is what he would have said: "This is much cozier than the garage! I'm not any trouble! I'll stay out of everyone's way and be very content at the bottom of the pecking order." And he did – even to the point of refusing to eat on the floor with the other cats and only eating on the countertop by himself. (Note: I don't recommend feeding cats on the countertop!)

Georgie, a black-and-white tuxedo cat – so named because of his physical resemblance to George, the Japanese cat that we helped heal from scabies – was also a frequent outdoor visitor in our yard. He, too, looked ragged and also adopted us. We had both boys neutered, of course.

I don't know how these guys successfully infiltrated the household without disrupting the status quo, but they did. It was miraculous. Their integration with the others was so seamless that eventually, Georgie took over the role of *King Cat* and became the best feline ruler I ever had. Although Little Boy was the oldest male cat, he was not a dominant personality and acquiesced.

The feline household ran smoothly, the others felt secure under Georgie's leadership, and each one knew their place. Nobody fought. This was a once-in-a-lifetime cat that knew how to manage his kingdom!

Life had begun to stabilize with Kristina, and we began to get answers to some of her health issues, which helped improve her cognitive issues. We took her to an osteopathic doctor in Dallas, Texas, who introduced us to food sensitivities and alternative medicine, and thus began our experience with chiropractic care, craniosacral therapy, applied kinesiology, NAET (Nambudripad's Allergy Elimination Technique), NET (Neuro Emotional Technique), Chinese herbs, supplements, and acupuncture.

Traditional Western medicine did not work with Kristina. I'm forever grateful to those humble, holistic medicine practitioners, because they gave us hope that she could overcome some of her medical issues, or at least manage life better. It was an incredibly difficult time in our lives, trying to figure out her needs. And to my surprise, I discovered that holistic healthcare management would work for me, too!

When Kristina turned 11, we adopted two sisters from the Donetsk region of the Ukraine, Masha and Dasha, who were 13 and 11, respectively. Chuck, Kristina, and I traveled to the Ukraine together, and after we were given custody of the girls during the paperwork process, we spent the next three weeks together in Kiev and Donetsk finalizing the adoptions.

Masha and Dasha had been living in separate 'boarding schools' (the Ukrainian name for orphanages for older children) and hadn't seen each other in two years at the time we adopted them! We had a fantastic translator who worked closely with us every step of the way, and it turned out to be a totally opposite experience from going to Russia to adopt Kristina.

Back in the States, life was a challenge with three adolescent girls. Once again, *"What was I thinking?"* Our family life was additionally taxed because Chuck worked a lot of overtime with his IT position. He became the *go-to* person in his office for any computer issues that needed to be resolved, not only because he was very good at what he did, but also because our house was just a stone's throw away, and he could be at his office in minutes.

The seven years we lived in Virginia Beach before moving to Staunton were full of mixed blessings. The high point for me, at least in terms of being a musician, was playing flute and directing the youth choir at the Catholic church we were members of for six of those years.

I was tremendously privileged to have the role of mentoring a talented stream of youth – instrumentalists and singers. They were so gifted that we embarked on a successful recording project and made a CD! I also recorded a second one as a duo, playing flute with one of our pianists.

We provided music for literally hundreds of events, including Catholic masses, nursing homes, Christmas caroling in private homes for donations (a Filipino tradition, which was perfect, because most of the choir members came from the large Filipino population of Virginia Beach), and two large youth retreats, one in Virginia Beach and one in Nebraska. We also created our own mission trip, traveling to southwestern Virginia as an outreach to very remote parishes and nursing homes.

I loved what I did, and although I repeatedly told my choir kids how much God loved them, it was still difficult to feel that love for myself. It was a familiar pattern, so I did what was familiar: keep smiling and moving forward, always hoping for the best.

As exhilarating as the youth choir experience was, the lows of life were equally low. Parenting is truly *not* for the faint of heart, especially when you have no confidence as a parent trying to help emotionally damaged adolescent girls – one with disabilities – and you don't know the extent of their challenges.

We adopted Masha and Dasha with good intentions, like we had with Kristina's adoption, also considering that it would be great for her to have siblings. Chuck and I were drawn to adopt older children because there was a tremendous need to get them placed in families. We had so much to offer and wanted to give these girls a fresh opportunity to have a fulfilling life.

Masha and Dasha were definitely from at-risk backgrounds, with alcoholism the cause of their mother's death when they were nine and seven years old. Their past circumstances were dreadful. I won't go into detail, but if there had been an effective social services system in the region of the Ukraine they were from, the girls would have been removed from their homes at a very young age.

We didn't know what to do with the challenges that faced us and didn't know how or whom to reach out to for help. We had big hearts that wanted to make a difference in these girls' lives, giving them hope for a better future.

Although still in the Air Force Reserves, I was working in the Chaplain Assistant career field, and my life as an Air Force musician was long past. I never grieved the loss of my Air Force career or Big Boy's death, but rather stuffed the feelings. But in taking care of everyone else, I was starting to lose my own identity. Now, in hindsight, I realize that I had also dissociated from the pain. There were no emotional highs or lows. Just existence. But I kept that smile on my face.

I was not familiar with depression or its symptoms, because I had always considered myself a happy person, or at least was in denial and pretended to be. Anything short of that was certainly a weakness of character, at least in my mind. Maybe an occasional circumstance was "depressing," but that's as close as I ever got to naming it. I certainly wasn't open to the possibility that I could be depressed in a more severe way, or that I needed support. It was not in my nature to ask for help. I later found out that "anger turning inward" can contribute to depression. I sure had plenty of that stuffed inside, combined with all the guilt and sadness I was clinging to. In today's world, I would seek help immediately!

Our life in Virginia Beach was very hectic, not only because of the traffic and busy schedules with three daughters, but also with the extra hours that Chuck was away from home working, so we decided to try and find a way to slow down the pace of our lives.

We sold our large house on Parkland Lane to take advantage of the ballooning housing market and moved into a townhouse in the neighborhood where we'd lived before moving to Japan. That put us in a better financial situation with less maintenance, but moving into a smaller house didn't solve the fast-paced lifestyle, and less than a year later, we decided to make yet *another* change.

There were many things I loved about living in a beach community, but thoughts crept in again about returning to a small-town environment, like what Chuck and I had been used to in our formative years. We'd purchased a timeshare when we were newly married at Massanutten Resort in the Shenandoah Valley, a little over three hours away. We were familiar with this mountainous region of Virginia and decided to purchase an investment property at the same resort. It was a beautiful, two-story house with a finished basement, one street above the ski slopes, and we set it up to accommodate 12 people.

During the course of furnishing the house, we made several trips back and forth with a trailer, transporting items we had bought at local furniture outlets and thrift stores in Virginia Beach. After each trip, we made a mental note of the calmness we felt in the beautiful setting of the valley. The nearby Shenandoah and Blue Ridge Mountains were also a drawing card. What a contrast from the environment we were living in!

One day, when we were at Massanutten organizing the rental house, Masha and Dasha started playing outside, rolling down the hill outside the property. Kristina just observed and was afraid to join them. I realized that so much of her life was spent indoors (except for an occasional trip to the ocean or swimming pool) that she just wasn't comfortable being in the outdoors.

That was my wakeup call. *There has to be a better life.*

Yes, I was ready to make yet another change. Although it was tough to leave the youth choir and the many friends we had made, we decided to make a move to this scenic, quieter part of Virginia and try to slow down the pace of our lives.

Early Adulthood

Big Boy, the Attack Cat!

Big Boy on a leash

Big Boy sleeping on mommy's head!

Little Boy

Pretty Girl

Spunky and Pretty Girl

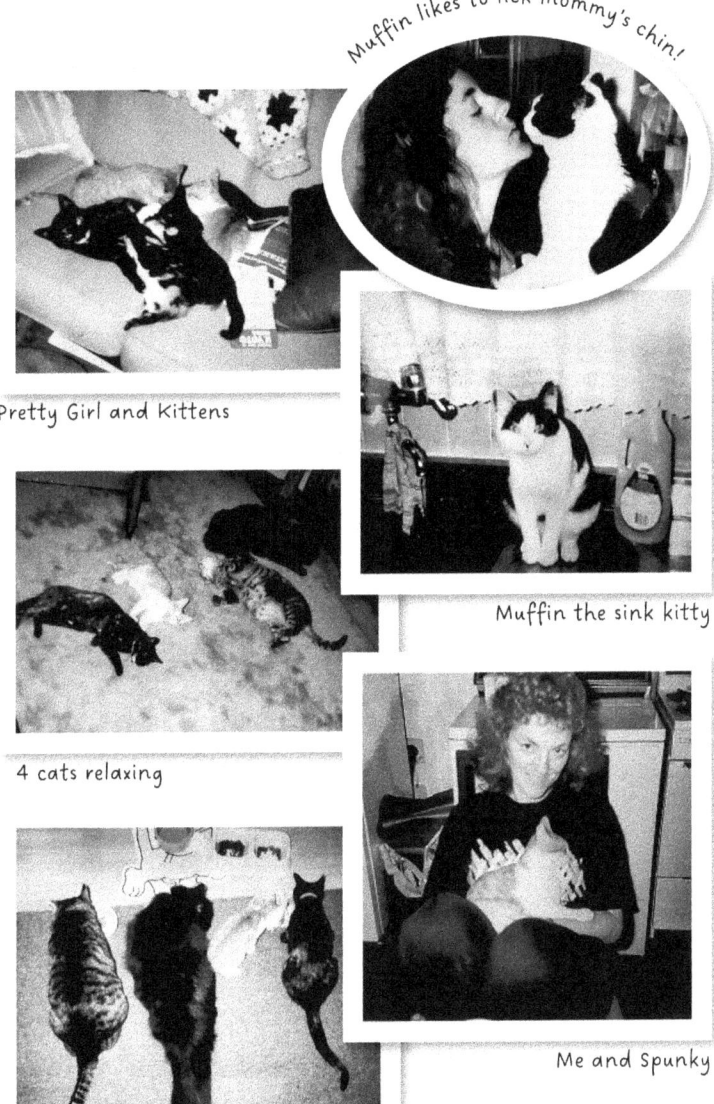

Me holding Mr. Peabody

Core Eight - Pretty Girl, Muffin, Spunky, Mr. Peabody, Bobtail, Cyclops, Little Boy, Big Boy

Mr. Peabody

Bobtail

Japan to US with 8 Cats, 8 Carriers

Basic Training - 1984

Air Force Publicity Pic - 1985

Trip to Australia for WWII
commemmorative celebrations,
wearing WWII time period
uniforms - 1994

Air Force Pipe Band - March 1996

Mom and Dad's 49th Anniversary,
June 1996. 3 months before Dad passed

Last pic with Dad -July 1996

Siblings 1996 After Dad's Funeral

Family after Dad's funeral, 1996

CHAPTER 24

THE MOVE TO STAUNTON

"I'm hanging in there as best I can, but I don't feel well. My lungs are weakening, and I'm having more trouble breathing than usual. I'm doing my best to get through the next move, but this might be it for me, Mom. Thanks for rescuing me from that train station in Japan. You've given me such a great life. I love you!"

– Mr. Peabody

On Memorial Day weekend 2005, we moved to Staunton, (pronounced "Stanton") in the Shenandoah Valley of Virginia. Like a scene from the movie *Groundhog Day*, where the same events keep repeating over and over, we once again packed up the household, this time with both a car and a van, three daughters, and *nine* cats: Little Boy, Pretty Girl, Spunky, Muffin, Bobtail, Mr. Peabody, Gray Kitty, Georgie, and Gumby – a last-minute addition.

Gumby looked like Little Boy – black with fluffy long hair. About a month before we moved, some neighbors begged us to take this stray, adult male cat they couldn't keep. Of course, we did, but he never lived with us long in Staunton. He preferred the quiet solitude of the nearby wooded area and befriended other families.

I think Gumby was one of those felines that preferred to be "an only cat" rather than part of our large crew. Too much activity seemed to overstimulate him, and he kept to himself, appearing to be a loner, but rather, just seeking a quiet life. We couldn't force him to stay with our family, but we had done our best to give him a home, and I believe we saved his life. We now lived in a much quieter neighborhood in Staunton, and he seemed content with his life as a hermit, occasionally visiting other neighbors who liked him (and no doubt fed him!). I was disappointed but never took it personally.

I was thankful that he periodically stopped by for a visit. For some reason, this fluffy black cat was enamored with the sound of bagpipes and happily strutted into our yard to say hello whenever he heard me playing them. I've never had a cat since then who willingly sought them out!

We purchased a two-story, colonial-style house on Stocker Street with a full basement. It was situated in a quiet neighborhood at the end of a dead-end street backing up to a forest, with lots of room for the cats.

There were two sheds in the backyard, one that was large enough to be equipped with electricity and had served as an art studio for the previous elderly owner. I turned that building into a sewing area and tearoom and showcased the dress-up pictures we took of my daughters and me.

Chuck took an IT job in Harrisonburg, a small city of 43,000 (and growing), located between Staunton and Massanutten, but with its layout, it felt more like a large city – not what we were looking for. We chose instead to live in nearby, historic

Staunton, only a 30-minute commute to Chuck's new job, with a smaller population of 25,000 and a restored, historic downtown.

As I reflect on the unsettledness of our life at that time, I realize that the household moves were just a symptom of other problems that would surface later. Yet, those struggles were a part of the path that ultimately led me to where I am today, and I'm eternally grateful for that.

The timing of the move coincided with a family reunion at a retreat center in southwestern Virginia for Chuck's side of the family. But a week before we left Virginia Beach, Mr. Peabody's respiratory problems worsened. Although we were medicating him with antibiotics, like we had done in the past when his breathing issues flared up, this time, he got weaker. We decided to bring him with us to the reunion and continue giving him his medication in hopes that his health would improve.

At the retreat center, we slept in cabins and were not able to keep Mr. Peabody with us overnight, so he slept in our van. He was still severely congested, and I believe he suffered a setback due to the chilly night air. The final evening, though, we were allowed to let him sleep inside the large building on the premises with the kitchen and dining areas. Although he wasn't feeling well, he was a cheerful cat, and completely won over the hearts of all the family members – totally worthy of being in the family group picture!

When we came back to Staunton, this sickly cat disappeared during our unpacking and settling in. I had noticed him sitting on the porch of the house across the street from us a few times and presumed he was still with us, even in the midst of all the commotion. But setting the house up was overwhelming, and there was just too much to keep track of.

The next day, Mr. Peabody was nowhere to be found, and I thought he had wandered off into the wooded area behind the house to die alone. About two weeks later, when we officially met Steve and Joyce (the neighbors across the street), we told them about all our cats, and that one was missing. Steve spoke up and told us about a sick, white cat that had come onto their porch, but they didn't know whom he belonged to. Thinking it was a stray, they called Animal Control to come and take him away.

Mr. Peabody was taken to the local SPCA, where they euthanized him. From their perspective, I'm sure he appeared to be too ill to rehabilitate and adopt out, and I really can't blame them for that. It was just a sad case of missed communication with neighbors we hadn't met and of living with so much stress that we were distracted from keeping close tabs on this one-eyed cat with such a beautiful soul and loving disposition.

I called the shelter, and they still had his body in their freezer area (Yes, that's a morose thought). They kindly let us bring him home to be buried, and I was devastated once again at the loss of another beloved cat but couldn't do anything to change the circumstances.

My heart grieved so much for this cat that didn't have a mean bone in his body. He had overcome so much, and we weren't even able to be with him at the end. To me, it was a sad ending to his life, and it was becoming more difficult to *just keep smiling*...

CHAPTER 25

FUJI

"Mom, you're going to think I'm a little 'wild thing' when you first see me, but I'm putting on that persona so nobody else will catch me. You'll be back at this apple orchard again in a month, and I'll let my guard down so this time you can bring me home. I'm going to play one of the most important roles in your life, although it will take several years before you figure it out. I'll give you a hint: I've been with you before in a 'bigger' cat body, and it will blow your socks off once you realize who I am. I can't wait!"

– Fuji

"Seriously, Mom, a CALICO? They're weirdos!"

– The Fur Family

The house on Stocker Street needed remodeling, but we were quite familiar with that process, and the basic floor plan was comfortable with a lot of windows. My favorite feature was the sunroom in the back of the house, which, after Chuck did all the work, included new full-length windows on all sides and two sliding glass doors. Behind our house was a forest, and the view beyond the glass sunroom was beautiful.

Interestingly, the previous owner had fed stray cats in that room, and the doors must have remained open most of the time to allow them in because the floor wreaked of urine!

Several scourings of a mixture of vinegar, water, and bleach helped eliminate the smell, but Chuck eventually installed a new tile floor to completely rid the room of the foul odor.

The house had been vacant for eight months before we bought it, and when we moved in, the woman who fed the strays during that time stopped by the house to introduce herself, telling us that she had trapped them, had them spayed and neutered, and released them somewhere else. We never saw them after we moved in, which was certainly OK, because we really didn't need any more cats – we had enough!

I sometimes wondered if I kept *collecting* cats to fill some sort of void or make up for an internal emotional deficiency, but now I realize it was something far beyond that. Every cat adoption was divinely orchestrated. In fact, as I look back on the occasional thought that popped into my head that I should open my own cat sanctuary, I realize that, in an informal way, that's exactly what I did.

So, what do you do when you have enough cats? Well… adopt some more, of course! This time, not all of them wandered into our yard. They found other creative ways to join the family.

Fuji, the calico who's pictured on the front cover of this book, would years later become the "Queen Bee," aka "Feline Matriarch," of the cat household. She was quite a remarkable cat.

For Kristina's birthday in October 2005, we decided to go apple picking as a family. There were plenty of apple orchards scattered throughout the Shenandoah Valley, just waiting for unsuspecting "fruitaholics" to enter their premises and leave with exorbitant numbers of fresh apples.

We chose a place called Dickie Brothers, way, way out in the country. After the nearly two-hour drive through the winding, mountainous terrain, we arrived at the orchard, parked our van in the gravel parking lot, grabbed several half-bushel-sized bags, and drove out to the various rows of apple trees scattered with whatever variety of apples were ripe enough to be picked. There is absolutely nothing better than a freshly picked apple – and I confess I ate at least one to "sample it" while we were still picking!

Between Chuck, Masha, Dasha, Kristina, and myself, I can confidently say we picked a fair number of apples that day! Thankfully, we had driven our van out to the fields and didn't have to hand-carry the multitude of heavy baskets we had in our possession back to the barn to pay for them.

When we returned to the parking lot with our bounty, I noticed a young calico kitten darting around the cars. I made a mental note, *"Isn't that a wild little thing?"* It was just an observation. After all, I *am* a Crazy Cat Lady, and I'm supposed to notice these things! However, my internal dialogue went like this: Stop it, *Kathy! Don't even go there... you have enough cats. Don't give her any attention, or you'll get attached. This is probably her home anyway.* So, after the initial sighting, I put all other thoughts about the kitten out of my mind.

We paid for the apples, counting it a blessing that we paid by the bag and not by the pound! It was hard to control ourselves from picking more and more when they were all so beautiful and fresh.

I relished every moment of the long drive back to Staunton, completely immersed in this perfect fall day in the Shenandoah

Valley. The mountains and the overlooking views from the Blue Ridge Parkway were heavenly, and the serenity was such a contrast to our lifestyle in Virginia Beach.

As we unpacked the apples, keeping some in our refrigerator and putting many more in one of our sheds, I thought we had enough apples to last a year. That is, until my ravenous, fruit-loving daughters ransacked the bags and devoured them like they were going out of style. They even ate the cores! A mere one month later, we were nearly out of apples.

So, on a cold Saturday morning in late November, we humbly drove back out to Dickie Brothers to get more. Masha stayed home this time because she struggled with motion sickness, and since the trip was long and on winding roads, it was just the four of us.

When we arrived at the orchard for the second time in a month, the Pick Your Own option was not available, because they had already picked the remaining apples off the trees to avoid losing them when the first winter frost hit.

There were, however, plenty of pre-picked apples available to purchase at the barn. And that was fine, because now we had a choice of several more varieties, and since they had been picked since our earlier trip in October, they were just as fresh.

While Chuck and I were looking through the large bins of various apples, Kristina and Dasha were conspiring with the orchard owner, trying to catch the wild little calico kitten we had seen a month earlier. "Mom! Mom!" Dasha exclaimed, "The man said if we can catch her, we can keep her!"

I forced a smile, but the inner conflict I'd experienced a month earlier when I first saw her once again filled my mind. I was *always* open to bringing another cat into the family, yet our house was full of them, and to even entertain the idea of adding *just one more* seemed ludicrous.

I had to think about Chuck and all the family responsibilities we already had. He had been agreeable to accepting so many cats, and as much as I would have adopted *every* homeless cat if I could, I had to consider his feelings and our mutual responsibilities.

Once again, I tried to brush it off. *We're safe... She's too wild, and that will never happen. I'm going to get more apples...*

Within five minutes, two adolescent girls, grinning from ear to ear, came proudly walking toward me with a cute little calico kitten wrapped in Kristina's arms! "Mom, we caught her! Now we can keep her!" *Oh, no... Dad's not going to like this... But I don't want to disappoint my daughters! We better go out to the parking lot and say some serious prayers so that he'll be agreeable about bringing this little girl home...*

I grabbed the kitten from Kristina and held her tight while my daughters and I walked out to the parking lot together and said some prayers that must have gone way up into the heavenlies, because they worked! Chuck miraculously consented.

The calico, now trapped in my arms, made no attempt to escape (of course, I wouldn't have let her if she'd tried!). And frankly, I think she wanted to be catnapped! Yet my inner dialogue continued: *Like we need another cat... We don't ever NEED another cat. But we've never had a calico...*

The orchard owner told us that this spirited little girl, along with her littermates, had been dumped off in their parking lot early in the summer. She was one of only two survivors from that litter, and both of them were hanging around the barn. The owner planned to let her sibling, a male, stay there as a barn cat and was all too happy to find a home for this female.

She had been too wild to catch – until that moment when Kristina picked her up. I have no doubt that she was divinely guided to allow us to catch her, because she was waiting for *us* – she was *our* cat.

We made a makeshift cat carrier out of a box and loaded her into the van along with several more bushels of apples. Here we go again: a billion apples and another feline family member!

The next order of business was to give her a name. It was obvious we needed to find one associated with apples, so we considered the various varieties to see if one would fit:

Winesap… Rome… McIntosh (that was a possibility if it was a male, but no)… Golden Delicious… Granny Smith (maybe for a senior, but no, definitely not that) … Stayman… Jonagold… Red Delicious… Fuji… *THAT'S IT!* Her name is Fuji, after the apple (not Mt. Fuji in Japan). It was the perfect name!

Little did I realize that this feisty, little calico would, throughout her life, play one of the most significant roles in my story of spiritual transformation and journey into animal reincarnation, a story that gradually unfolded over the next 15 years. She is the one that would "seal the deal," leave me with no doubts, and teach me exactly what I was supposed to learn.

CHAPTER 26

ANOTHER MAMA CAT WITH KITTENS

> *Mom, we really hate to see you go through this scenario again, having to separate a mother cat from her kittens, just like you did with Pretty Girl in Japan, but don't be so hard on yourself. You did what you thought was right, and there were so many emotions to process. In tough situations like this, it can feel like no matter what decision you make, it's wrong. And yet, there don't seem to be any other options."*
>
> – The Fur Family

Introducing Fuji to the household wasn't difficult. We set her apart in a room by herself in the basement, where I spent time just being with her. This feisty little calico kitten actually possessed a calm and sweet demeanor and settled down quickly – a total non-intruder to the established cat kingdom.

During Fuji's adjustment period in the basement, we set up a separate litter box for her, which was a good idea because I detected some diarrhea – along with worms – both in her stool and on the floor (tapeworms, a sign of fleas). If left untreated, they can become life-threatening for a cat. We took her to the vet for an initial checkup and to treat the worms. A month later, we took her back for a re-check, and she still had them.

They were no longer visible to us, and her behavior didn't seem to be affected, but we had to do another round of dewormer…

She was also getting a little older, and although not a large cat by any means, it was time to think about getting her spayed. Two more months passed, moving us into March, when we made the appointment, only to find out that she *still* had worms, although, once again, they were not visible.

They wouldn't spay her until she was free of them, so on to a *third* round of dewormer. *This is getting old.* We were totally sick of the back-and-forth visits to the vet, in addition to having to give her the medication. But we continued that protocol for her.

Fuji was totally integrated with the other cats by now, so she came and went in and out of the house as she pleased, just like the others. We generally kept pretty good track of everyone, and, *most of the time,* noticed if anyone turned up missing – except one time in early May when I realized that nobody had seen Fuji for a few days.

She eventually returned and came in through the sunroom with some of the other cats. I was relieved, but confused, because it was out of character for her to disappear like that. She was not a wanderer.

I made a mental note, though, that when she walked into the house, she appeared to be a bit distracted, flustered, and shaken up. I couldn't put my finger on it, but could sense it, and over the next few days, this thought popped into my head: *What if she was in heat and we didn't know it, and she went out and found herself a tom-cat? What if she's pregnant? Oh, no…*

That didn't seem possible, because there were no signs at all to indicate that she was in heat. We had been through that experience several years earlier with Pretty Girl and Muffin, and there were no similar symptoms with Fuji.

Still, we let some time lapse and monitored her for about a month. We didn't want or need any more cats *(famous last words – do I sound like a broken record?)*, but also didn't want to make another appointment to get her spayed, only to find out she was pregnant and have them abort the babies. For us, that was not an option.

The gestation period for a pregnant cat is 64-71 days, just slightly longer than two months, so we decided to wait it out, observing whether she looked any bigger or was putting on weight.

Fuji was still young herself – likely between 9-12 months old – and this was not an ideal situation. I had heard that it wasn't good for a female cat to get pregnant the first time they go into heat. Maybe it would be the equivalent of a pre-teen girl getting pregnant after she had her first menstrual cycle. But Fuji never looked pregnant. She looked like any other young cat that was growing up while gaining a normal amount of weight, so we dismissed that notion!

To make matters worse, we had planned a multi-week vacation in upstate New York in July, renting a house on a lake near Malone, which we referred to as a "camp." I'd always wanted to do that since I was a child.

When it came time for our trip, all five of us began the vacation at the camp together, but Chuck had to be back at work, so after a week, he and Masha returned to Virginia. I stayed at the camp with Dasha and Kristina for three more weeks, spending time with my mom, brother Steve, and his family.

Halfway through those final three weeks of vacation, Masha called and gave me the news: "You're a grandma to three beautiful grand-kittens! There a calico, a tan-and-white, and a gold-and-white."

Fuji had given birth to them on a chair in the living room in the middle of the day. Masha didn't witness their birth, but found them, all safe and sound, later in the evening. Thankfully, there were only three, because, given her small size, I don't think she could have carried any more than that.

Thinking back, this was all surreal. Perhaps Fuji really *was* gaining weight, and I purposely closed my eyes to it, living in denial that we had another mama cat that was going to have babies. The world didn't need more kittens; it just needed more responsible adults to get their cats spayed and neutered, and I had failed.

Now, what do we do? Chuck immediately said no to keeping any of them, and I couldn't blame him, because we were up to nine or ten cats at that time. We decided to help socialize these healthy newborns who would be fully adoptable when the time came.

I also think I must have had a lobotomy, because I had forgotten the pain of letting go of Pretty Girl's kittens 10 years earlier, swearing I'd never do that again. I didn't know how to handle the guilt I still carried and certainly didn't want to face it. But here I was, in the same situation, getting ready to separate yet *another* mother cat from her kittens.

In an effort to cope, I tried to remain emotionally detached from the kittens, afraid that I would love them too much and be devastated when we gave them away. And I dreaded what it was going to do to Fuji. But in my detachment, I don't believe I gave them enough love; for that, I had to rely on my daughters.

We set up a room for all of them in the basement, and Fuji was a good mom. Occasionally, she needed a break, though, and appeared by herself on the main floor. We had no idea how she escaped from her room with the kittens, especially since we kept all the doors closed.

One day, we caught this clever calico in the act! She agilely jumped onto some bookshelves first, then wriggled into the ceiling – or rather, the drop ceiling foam tiles that were not all intact, leaving an opening with a ledge to the wooden ceiling beams. Next, she walked across the beams to the adjacent laundry room, jumped down onto the washer and dryer, and made her final descent to the floor. Free at last! She definitely won the prize for ingenuity.

We placed an ad in the local newspaper to look for homes for the kittens, but when a man responded and said he was looking for a couple of barn cats, I was mortified! I couldn't bear the thought of Fuji's babies living in a barn with strangers. I let the ad expire, and didn't answer any more calls. *What do we do now? I really don't want to adopt any of them out, but my hands are tied, and there is no choice.*

Within a couple weeks after the ad expired, I was in a conversation with a friend from church who told me she was looking for a kitten for her youngest daughter. I told her about Fuji's babies, and she agreed to come over and meet them.

She ended up adopting both females, the calico and the tan-and-white one. I was relieved that they would stay together, and her daughter named them Callie and Chrissy. The remaining gold-and-white one was a male with really large feet, so we called him Boots, and he remained with us. It was difficult enough parting with the two girls.

When Callie and Chrissy left with their new family, even though I knew they would have a good home, the same horrendous feeling I had when we gave away Pretty Girl's kittens returned. I felt like I had totally betrayed Fuji, who, like Pretty Girl, wandered around the house looking for her babies. The only consolation for Fuji was that she didn't go into mourning to the extent that Pretty Girl did, and seemed to recover within a couple months.

Boots, however, lost his playmates, and was never the same after that. He lost the desire to play, acted depressed, and became a loner. He was still young, but remained that way for the rest of his life, and I don't know if it was solely from the aftereffects of the loss, or if that was just his personality.

He started spending more and more time outside – at least he loved the outdoors, and I was grateful for that. But I worried about his safety. He was super-sweet, innocent, docile, and definitely not streetwise enough to take care of himself. I didn't want to crush his spirit by making him stay inside, because he had already experienced enough loss when his sisters left the house.

This handsome gold-and-white boy didn't form a particularly close bond with anyone – even Fuji – as he got a little older, with one exception: my mother.

Mom wanted to see our new home in Staunton, so she arranged to visit both Dave's and my family on the same trip, first spending time with them in North Carolina, and then two weeks with us.

Mom loved Boots, and while she was here, formed an ultra-close bond with him. He sat with her on the couch every day when she read the newspaper and accompanied her everywhere. I'm sure she would have catnapped him and snuck him in her suitcase on the trip back to Malone if she had lived in an apartment that allowed pets. After that trip, she inquired about Boots in every conversation.

Fuji, as she grew, became attached to *me* and was ultra-sensitive to my feelings. One day, when she was about three, I had one of my worst parent days ever while in the midst of major difficulties with Masha. (I can talk about all of this now because she and I have a great relationship, but back then, when she was a 16-year-old, we were in a war zone). On that day, she reamed me out in the car over some trivial thing, and being overly sensitive, I couldn't respond and went inward. I was also driving and had to focus on the road.

When we arrived home, I retreated to my bedroom and collapsed from emotional exhaustion. I couldn't take the stress anymore and started bawling like a baby. Then, in my greatest pain, Fuji jumped onto the bed and lay down next to me.

I will always remember that special moment and was taken aback that a cat could be so intuitive. She remained sensitive to my emotions for the rest of her life, and I commonly referred to her as my "emotional support cat"!

Fuji had a few mannerisms that I marveled at. First, she could *purr on demand*, meaning that she didn't need the usual petting to start her purr generator. Sometimes, all I did was just *look* at her and she'd start to purr, or when she slept next to me, I'd wake up and hear her already purring! Maybe a happy dream?

She also had virtually *no audible voice* when it came to expressing herself. I always considered her to be an opinionated cat, but when she wanted me to do something like open a door for her, she'd look at me and move her mouth as if to speak, but nothing came out!

My favorite "Fuji quirk" of all began unexpectedly. One time, when she was about a year old, I picked her up, as usual, but this time, she kept climbing up my body until she reached my shoulders, wrapping herself around my neck. It was precious! This became her favorite place to hang out (although I had to make sure her nails were trimmed, because she held on tight as if giving me a firm handshake), and I often crouched low to the floor so she could launch herself up on my shoulders all by herself.

I'll never forget the thought that flashed through my mind the first time she climbed onto my shoulders: *Wow! I haven't had a cat up near my head like this since Big Boy!*

CHAPTER 27

LOUIE

"Mom, it's time you learned a little more about Divine Timing. It's been happening to you all your life, but you're not quite recognizing it yet for what it is! Louie is going to teach you. And by the way, he is quite the actor!"

— The Fur Family

I'm always amazed when circumstances fall into place that are so divinely orchestrated that there is no other explanation. To me, *all* my cat adoptions fit into that category, but the timing of some specific ones, like Mr. Peabody's uncanny appearance next to my bicycle at the train station in Japan, is particularly noteworthy.

Louie's adoption is another one. Although I don't have any specific details about what happened in his life before we found him, in my fantasy world, I think it might have looked something like this...

A frightened small black-and-white kitten stood cowering against a tree behind a RaceTrac gas station/convenience store near Suffolk, Virginia. Days earlier, when he'd talked about "the plan" with his Angel Commander, it seemed like a good idea, but now, frankly, he was scared to death.

Hidden from view and alone, all he had at his disposal was a walkie-talkie, waiting for instructions from his Angel Commander on when to make his move.

> *Angel Commander (AC):* Just wait right there. I know you're thirsty, and a bit famished, but you know the rules. You have to be desperate to get their attention. *Over...*
>
> *Kitten (K):* This is too hard. I miss my siblings and my mom. I don't know where anyone is. Nothing is familiar here. Why did those other people drop me off here, anyway? *Over...*
>
> *AC:* There is a bigger plan in all of this, and you're part of it. We're waiting for a white car and three women to show up to fill their gas tank. They're on their way. *Over...*
>
> *K:* I don't know if I can do it. What if they don't notice me? And how will I know it's them? *Over...*
>
> *AC:* There's an older woman who will be pumping gas. She'll see you from a distance. One of the two younger women will come out of the car and head into the convenience store. That's when you make your move. *Over...*
>
> *K:* Will you please guide me, so I don't make a mistake? *Over...*
>
> *AC:* I'll let you know when the car pulls up to the pump, and that's your cue. Our walkie-talkies won't work after that, and my job will be finished. You'll

have to trust yourself and be brave. The next set of angels will help you throughout your life, and I will step aside. *Over...*

K: I'm scared, but if it has to be this way, I'll do my best. *Over...*

AC: You don't have to worry. You were chosen to be a part of this family. You will have many cat siblings, and you will be loved immensely. OK, it's time! Head over to the trash can by the entrance to the store and look for three women in a white car. I have to leave you now, and quickly guide them into this service station. Be brave, little one! You can do this. It's been a pleasure being a part of your life. *Over and out...*

K: Angel Commander??? Wait! Oh no... I guess I'm on my own. I'm scared, but I have to do this. Here goes...

From Louie's perspective:

Walk quickly around the corner of the building next to the trash can by the front door of the store. Arch back and rub legs against the trash can, meow mournfully, look desperate and longingly at the white car that just pulled up to the gas pump as the women get out. Don't look at other people. They're not yours. Just these women in the white car... Wait for what seems like an eternity...

Oh, my gosh! Here comes one of them walking toward me now... It's one of the younger ones, and she just picked me up, and is rocking me back and forth, looking toward the older woman so she can see me... purr... purr... purr... I can't believe this is working! She's carrying me to their car. purr... purr... purr... I hope she gets me some food and water... Wait in the car... purr... purr... purr... The older woman returns with food in hand! Thank you so much. You're calling me Louie? I like that. I have a family now...

Here is *my* perspective:

In June 2007, I was asked to participate in the music ministry for the wedding of a young couple my husband and I knew from Virginia Beach. I prepared to drive down there with Masha and Kristina, and because the wedding was on a Saturday, we decided to make it a full weekend by driving there on Friday, stay at a friend's house, and come back home on Sunday. It seemed like it would be an easy 3½-hour drive if we left Staunton early enough to avoid the heavy, mid-afternoon Hampton Roads traffic and arrive in time for the evening rehearsal.

An easy, fool-proof plan – until I carried my suitcase out the front door to our white Dodge Stratus parked in front of the house at 9:00 a.m. – and noticed that one of its tires was flat. *Ugh!* That inconvenience forced me to rearrange the perfectly well-planned day I had envisioned.

Chuck came home from work during his lunch break to repair the tire, but it set us behind by four hours, and we couldn't leave Staunton until 1:00 p.m. That meant we would be heading directly into Virginia Beach's heaviest traffic of the day, and there would most likely be a several mile backup at the Hampton Roads Bridge Tunnel.

Enter Plan B: Drive on the back roads, away from the Interstate, and approach Virginia Beach from the southside, through Suffolk and Chesapeake, rather than from Hampton and Newport News. The driving time was slightly longer, but overall would be faster with less traffic. I didn't like the idea, but it seemed like the best option.

We loaded the car and headed down to the beach. A few hours later, we were off the Interstate and driving on a four-lane road as we approached Suffolk. In the flash of an instant, my eyes landed on the fuel indicator gauge in front of me, only to see that the gas tank was almost empty. My heart started racing, and when I raised my eyes back up toward the road, they immediately landed on a RaceTrac gas station with a convenience store, directly to my left.

I barely had time to react and felt almost like the car was propelled into the left turn lane, into the station's parking lot. The whole scenario probably took all of 5-10 seconds, and within moments I was standing at the gas pump, refueling my car. Masha wanted to stretch her legs and go into the convenience store to use the restroom. The rest of the story couldn't have been scripted better if it had been written for a movie!

This is literally what happened next:

- Mom (that's me) watches Masha approach the convenience store.
- Masha stops in front of the trash can next to the door.

- There is a young black-and-white kitten on the ground next to the trash can.
- Masha squats down to pet the kitty.
- Masha lovingly picks up the kitty and holds it, rocking it back and forth, looking at me from the distance.
- Masha returns to the car with the kitty.
- Mom observes the entire scene, worried because she knows there will be no other option…
- It is now our kitty.
- Mom plans how we're going to transport the kitty back to Staunton, knowing we'll be in Virginia Beach until Sunday.
- Mom briefly entertains the idea of bringing the kitten to a no-kill shelter but knows there aren't any in that area.
- Mom goes into the convenience store to buy cat food and get a bowl of water.
- Kristina and Masha stay with the kitty until Mom returns, whereupon they give food and water to the kitty.
- The kitty is more thirsty than hungry, indicating to us that he hasn't been there very long, which was a good thing.
- Kristina wants to name him Fat Louie (from the movie *Princess Diaries*), but this boy is definitely *not* fat, so we settle on the name Louie, the name of our friend who's getting married.

Yes, our actions were ridiculously predictable. And from his size, Louie appeared to be at the perfect adoptable age of about three months and had probably been dropped off at that spot either that day or the day before.

How did that happen? What were the chances? What about the flat tire that forced us to take a different route to the beach? How did I just happen to glance at my fuel gauge the exact moment we were near the turn lane and able to pull directly into the gas station? How did that kitten just happen to be there precisely when we arrived?

This was yet another example of an amazing 'divine timing cat adoption story,' which literally seemed to happen with every cat that joined our family. (Years later, Masha confessed that she had snuck out of the house with the car the night before we left for Virginia Beach and knew about the flat tire.)

The friends who housed us agreed to let us keep Louie over the weekend. They didn't have any cats at the time and weren't interested in adopting him, but even if they had been, I never would have given him up. I knew he belonged to me, and my track record of becoming attached to every cat I rescued continued. And thankfully, they gave us a cat carrier to transport him home in – a lesson learned from Goldy and Samantha long ago…

On Sunday, we drove back to Staunton, and I was ready to implement the *New Cat Integration Plan* as follows:

- Set Louie in the carrier in the living room so the other cats could see him.
- Separate Louie from them for a couple weeks.
- Keep him inside the house so he didn't wander off.

Well, my plan lasted less than 10 minutes. Kristina didn't understand, and immediately set the carrier on the living room floor and opened it, letting him out to roam freely with the other cats, eager to explore his new surroundings. Of course, he headed out the front door.

While we were still unloading the car, I saw the little black-and-white kitten happily walking on the path next to the flowerbeds, trotting toward the car. *That's Louie! How did he get out?* The curious little guy had simply walked out the front door when we opened it to carry our luggage into the house!

And the pattern of the 'existing cats welcoming a new one without a hitch' continued as well. None of the other cats were bothered, and just left Louie alone, as if they already knew him. Some of them gave him a sniff and then nonchalantly walked away. It felt like he had always been part of the family.

Being in the right place at the right time to find Louie at that gas station was a big life lesson for me in learning to "go with the flow." So much for my perfectly planned, well-thought-out weekend excursion to Virginia Beach.

I'm so thankful for the divine timing that brought this sweet little black-and-white kitten into my life. The multitude of synchronicities that kept happening again and again regarding my cats reaffirmed to me that all is well, and not to worry about how many feline fluffballs I already had – there's always room for one more.

Welcome to the family, Louie!

CHAPTER 28

THE FLOW

"Mom, to understand The Flow better, think about water in its many expressions, like a river, the ocean, and waterfalls. They all move naturally and with a current. Learn to flow like the water in these forms – don't freeze up like an iceberg and let your life become rigid!"

– Louie

What does it mean to "go with the flow"? In my life, it means that I try to cooperate with circumstances that change without getting angry or complaining. I do my best to remain calm and have a positive attitude, look for alternative choices, and also for the silver lining. When I do this, I find that results always turn out for the best, even though it might not seem that way immediately.

My first commanding officer in the Air Force used to say that "constant variables are always changing," and it took me years to figure out that it was a friendly reminder to be flexible.

Learning to "go with the flow" has become more than just a simple cliché that I use as a reminder to relax. I imagine that it's like being by a river, and all I have to do is jump in and ride the current or *flow*. Or it could be like the ocean, and I'm riding the waves.

Here is an example from my life when I literally did *not* go with the flow, and it almost didn't have a happy ending.

When I was in my 30s, Chuck and I went on a whitewater rafting trip in Tennessee that did not go as planned. We, along with several others who had signed up for the trip that day, had chosen to go through the rapids in a *funyak*, which was an inflatable kayak, rather than cruise down the river in a full-sized raft with an experienced guide.

I speculated that the rafting company didn't have enough guides to accommodate the rather large number of people who'd signed up for the trip, so they made their best "go rafting in a funyak" sales pitch to unsuspecting rafters like me, declaring, "The funyaks can't flip over and won't land on top of you. Just follow the flow of the current, and go through it. But, if on the outside chance yours *does* flip or land on top of you, especially if you're in a whirlpool" (which, they assured us, was next to impossible), "*do such and such, blah blah blah,* to get out from underneath it."

I wasn't fully paying attention to what they said, as my mind zoomed in on the part about not flipping over. Consequently, if that unlikely scenario did take place, I wouldn't have the foggiest idea how to get out of it.

The staff made their initial plea to enlist funyakers while we were standing at the launch point of the trip, where the water was as still as the Dead Sea – a *Class A* rapid, according to the rafting classification system. In addition to *Class A*, rapids are classified from *I* to *VI*, according to difficulty, with *VI* being the most challenging. *This is going to be easy – there are no other rapids anywhere in sight.*

I was totally confident that I could navigate these still waters in a funyak, so I readily agreed to this new adventure. But as we set out from the shore in calm water and paddled down the river in these inflatable kayaks, it was very clear that I was *in way over my head*, so to speak! I had no clue how to sail through the rapids, even a *Class I*, which is considered easy, with only small ripples in the water. For *Class II* and *III*? Forget it!

At the mere *sight* of that fast-moving water cascading over rocks in the distance, my heart started racing, even before I tried to paddle through it. I had lost all sensibility, while I held onto my two-sided kayaking paddle for dear life.

Closing my eyes, I tried to fight against the turbulent water, causing the first flip, where both the funyak and myself were thrust in separate directions by the force of the water flowing through the rapids. I continued to hold the paddle tightly before it could slip away, and managed to grab the funyak before it also escaped, fighting valiantly to push myself to a shallow spot where I could climb back inside.

Then it happened again… and again… for a *third* time, the force of the water flipped the funyak. I'm not sure if this was a *Class III* rapid (in my mind, it had to be at least a *Class XLIV*!), but the water was rough, and I was still shaken up and exhausted from the previous two spills. This time, the funyak flipped *on top* of me – *impossible,* they said – and I was stuck underneath in a whirlpool, unable to breathe or push it away from my head, as it was suffocating me. I was submerged underwater, starting to drown. *HELP! Why doesn't somebody pull this stupid thing off me? This is it… I can't breathe… I'm history… there's no way out.*

In my moment of distress, with all the commotion of the rapids, rafts, and other funyakers (including Chuck) navigating through this stretch of the river, I don't think that anyone even noticed me, or was aware that I was gasping for breath and almost dead. *Where are the rafting guides? Why are they continuing to let me endure this funyak fiasco? Are they indifferent?* More than likely, they had their hands full navigating their rafts. And apparently, nobody else on the trip had a problem with their funyak except me! *I guess I can take "Become a Rafting Guide" off my bucket list...*

With the strongest fist I could muster, I punched at the funyak on top of my head till it finally popped off, landing next to me. I had nearly drowned! I firmly believe there was supernatural intervention on my behalf.

I grabbed the funyak and held onto it for dear life, letting the current carry both of us to a patch of slightly calmer water. When I was finally able to breathe normally again, I was at my wits end, and would have figured out every possible way to *walk* to our destination rather than ever setting foot in that funyak again. *And whose brilliant idea was it to call it a "funyak" anyway? I am* not *having fun...*

Away from the raging current, I tried one last time to successfully navigate the funyak. But after repeated "man overboard" incidents (or in this case, "woman overboard") – even in the calm water – I loudly shouted my displeasure at the guides in rafts observing from a distance, who shouted back, "just keep trying." I know they were not experiencing my terror, and I had reached the point where I couldn't take it anymore. Plus, my physical strength was totally depleted. My stamina was gone. And I had no clue how the other funyakers made it through all those rapids unscathed!

I refused to continue on and begged them to send someone to swap places with me. Finally, one of the guides took me seriously, and instructed his raft full of happy rafters to paddle toward me.

Thankfully, another rafter answered my plea, jumped into the water, and swam toward me, excited to experience the funyak thrill for himself. I handed him my paddle to complete the changing of the guard, and with all my strength, managed to swim over to his now-vacant spot in the large raft and climbed aboard! *I'm free!*

I salvaged the remainder of the day, erasing the memory of what had happened, and finished the trip in a large raft with four other rafters and an experienced guide. Finally, I made a good decision!

Today, when I look back on what happened, I realize I had no idea what "following the flow of the current" actually meant. That seemed rather scientific and beyond my mental capacity to conceptualize. I did learn, however, what it meant to fight *against* the current, rather than allowing it to carry me through. That was why the waves kept knocking me down, with me kicking and screaming the entire time!

The bad *funyak* experience did not deter me from whitewater rafting again, though, because I still loved being in the water, and have done it several times since, but always in a large raft with a guide. I've even mustered the courage to try kayaking in *an open kayak in calm water*. In the summer, I regularly do a seven-mile paddle down the James River in Scottsville, Virginia, about an hour from where I live. The water depth is only 3-4 feet, with very small rapids – my kind of water adventure!

The first time I navigated through the few small rapids interspersed throughout the otherwise calm James River, my heart was racing, as the memory of that horrible funyak experience was still in my body. I took a deep breath and repeated words of affirmation to myself, like "You got this, Kathy!" and "You can do this!" Even though the water was not deep, I felt like I was reliving the disaster that had happened in Tennessee.

But this time, my actions led to a much happier ending. I let the river's current lead me through the water on my kayak and had my most successful water experience ever! It felt like the river was carrying me as I floated across the whitecaps. I finally understood the literal meaning of "going with the flow," which has given me a better perspective on how to allow that to happen in other areas of my life.

When I allow myself to flow through life's circumstances, like in the case of Louie's adoption, *divinely orchestrated events* happen to me all the time and become a natural part of my daily life. I truly experience life as a *living flow* of divine timing, which is a much more fulfilling way to live.

I'm also thankful that I've learned to listen to my intuition as another tool available to help navigate through difficult or changing circumstances. This has helped me make better decisions in every area of my life. When I don't listen to my intuition, and I stubbornly press on, using my human bulldozer tendencies, then I'm totally out of the flow, and the results usually aren't very good. I end up either creating more work for myself or greater problems!

In any case, whether or not I'm successful in going with the flow, what was that Bible verse again? Oh, yes! Romans 8:28: "And we know that all things work together for good to them that love God, to them who are called according to His purpose." Even in spite of me, thank goodness.

So, let's keep flowing... New adventures await!

CHAPTER 29

THE RETURNEES

"Hey, Mom! We're so happy to be back home, even though our cat mom doesn't recognize us anymore. However, the good news is that we've learned a great new cat trick that we're going to teach everyone! Wait till we show you..."

– Chrissy and Callie

As fate would have it, giving away Fuji's daughters (Chrissy and Callie) to a new home was not the end of the story. When they were three years old, their adopted family's circumstances changed, and they were not able to keep the two sisters, so they reached out and asked if we would be willing to take them back.

No brainer... Of *course,* we would take them back!

I was overjoyed at this unexpected opportunity to bring the girls back to our home! (And relieve me of the guilt I felt when I gave them away.)

When Chrissy and Callie returned, though, it wasn't a big, happy reunion with Fuji and Boots. I think I had very unrealistic expectations and sadly observed that their relational dynamics had changed. *Of course, they had! They were all three years older...*

Even though I tried to reintroduce everyone by putting all four in the basement where Fuji had raised them as kittens, I don't believe they ever fully recognized each other again.

Boots continued spending most of his time outside, and Fuji showed the first signs of what I referred to as *her opinionated self* (also known as "The Return of the Feisty Calico!"). She wanted nothing to do with the girls, hissed at them, and wanted to be left alone. Eventually, she "tolerated" them.

That didn't bother me, however, I was glad the girls had returned to us and gave them as much love as I could to make up for when they were kittens.

Chrissy and Callie integrated well with the remaining felines, and the only quirk that drove me crazy was that Chrissy had learned how to stand tall on her hind legs and vigorously – with every ounce of concentration she could muster – paw at a door incessantly to get our attention until we opened it.

That wouldn't have bothered me so much if it hadn't served as a training tool for the other cats, who quickly learned from her example and joyfully copied her behavior. I now had a house full of doorknockers!

CHAPTER 30

THREE HORSES AND A PUMPKIN

> *"We'll let the new golden cat live here – and yes, Mom, we're starting to agree with you that you can never have too many cats! But those horses better stay at the barn! They're really big!"*
>
> – The Fur Family

I always wanted a horse when I was a little girl. In fact, I fantasized about one day living on a ranch in Arizona, riding till my heart's content! That seemed like an impossibility, though, because as a child, I never had an opportunity to have one or even take lessons. My experience was limited to playing with the only doll I ever owned: Jane West and her palomino horse!

My childhood dream was relegated to one terrifying experience when I was eleven. My mother had a friend with a horse who agreed to let me ride in her large, fenced-in paddock.

I had absolutely no skills but was excited beyond belief! *How difficult could this be? You just get in the saddle and hold on, and they walk around slowly, giving you a glorious experience with immediate bonding, right?* Wrong!

This is what really happened: I climbed into the saddle of this unfamiliar beast, and when we started walking around the paddock somewhat leisurely, the horse didn't want to do that anymore.

In the blink of an eye, it bolted back to the barn at full speed, while my right knee was literally less than an inch from barbed wire as we flew by along the fence line through a gate! I was holding on for dear life and miraculously didn't fall off.

Although terrified, it didn't dissuade my interest in the equine species, and the fleeting moments of sheer terror that stayed with me later became a teaching tool when I learned the Emotional Freedom Technique (EFT, AKA *Tapping*), which uses acupressure points to (help) release emotional trauma through the physical body). I now know the power of this technique through personal experience. In that brief run through the paddock, I'd developed a fear of going fast on a horse, which I was able to heal through EFT.

As an adult, Chuck and I went on several vacation trail rides, but the horses always followed one another head to tail, never went faster than a walk, and you didn't need any riding skills.

Now, in Staunton, Virginia, as a 48-year-old adult, I was about to have my first opportunity to fulfill that childhood dream of having my own horse. Kristina was introduced to horses through the local therapeutic riding program, which she participated in through Special Olympics. Dasha started riding at Endless Trails Stable, a barn 15 minutes from our house owned by Sarah, that held weekly horse camps every summer. Becky, a friend from church, told us about the camps and had two horses herself.

Thus began our love story with these amazing creatures. If we'd had the land, we probably would have wound up with just as many horses as cats, but thankfully, we stopped at three and boarded them at Endless Trails: Nelly (whom we bought from Becky), Jake, and Wendy. I was thinking that Dasha, Kristina, and I could ride together! *What a great bonding experience to have with my daughters!*

Nelly was the first one we decided to purchase. She was a 10-yr-old chestnut mare with a white blaze on her forehead, a cross between a Tennessee Walker and a Belgian Draft. She only stood at 15 hands, just tall enough to be considered a horse and not a pony.

Nelly was awesome on the trails and used as a lesson horse for beginning riders – just about as safe as you can get. I also thought she was very talented, because she knew how to trot in two different ways: the traditional "English style" and the smooth "gait" of the Tennessee Walker. She made everyone at the barn laugh, though, because sometimes she got confused about which style she wanted to use and switched back and forth between the gait and the more traditional English trot – while you were riding her! It alternated between feeling bumpy and feeling smooth, as we moved through the trails.

Nelly also never learned how to properly canter, because her front legs would try to trot, and her back legs would try to canter – all at the same time! Her legs flailed in different directions, and it was quite entertaining. But we loved her because she was level-headed, and you never had to worry about her spooking.

Next, there was Jake, a 12-year-old chestnut gelding quarter horse who, like Nelly, also had a white blaze on his forehead. When he was two years old, a local vet transported him, along with several other horses, to Virginia from Texas. He had a brand mark of J-K on his left hind quarters, which indicated what ranch he belonged to.

Laura, a local riding instructor and trainer, occasionally used Jake as a lesson horse and was trying to find a new home for him. His owners were a retired couple, with the husband planning to ride him when he no longer worked, but who later changed his mind.

That meant that, except for being used for a few lessons here and there, Jake didn't have a job, other than being a "pasture ornament" and eating to his heart's content. Now, *that* was a job he excelled at! So much so that this happy fellow gained a considerable amount of weight and could be considered "a bit pudgy." It was time to relieve him of his pasture ornament duties and put him to work.

We headed to Laura's barn with a sizable riding ring for Dasha to give him a test ride. We were looking for a suitable horse for her to grow into as her skills increased, aspiring to eventually ride in horse shows. As she moved around the riding ring on Jake's back, she was able to easily walk, trot, canter and jump him over short rails.

Although he was overweight, we still considered buying Jake and brought him to Endless Trails on a trial basis for the up-and-coming two weeks of camps. They needed extra horses to accommodate the large number of children eager to learn about horsemanship and how to ride; plus, it helped us in our decision-making process, because we were able to spend more time getting to know him.

During the first week of camp, I wanted to try him out also, and to my surprise, he was *incredibly comfortable* – more so than any other horse I'd sat on, including Nelly, whom we had already bought. Dasha wasn't as interested after we brought him to Endless Trails, but gosh, he felt good! *What about for me?*

It didn't take long to make that decision, because one afternoon, at the end of the day, Jake came barreling toward me at full speed… *Oh, no…* came to a perfect halt about two feet away and greeted me with a happy nicker. He saw me carrying a bucket, and to him that meant something tasty!

He wanted a treat – Jake was a foodie! *Of course, he was… look at his size.* I felt a strong connection with him at that moment and knew he was my horse.

As much as Big Boy had been *that cat* I was connected with at the hip, Jake became *that horse*. In the brief two-week timespan during the trial, he and I developed a strong bond, and I was more than happy that he was the slowest horse at the barn (except when he came running for food!). And like Nelly, he was perfectly suited for trail riding.

We still wanted a third horse, one versatile enough for Dasha to ride in shows and also good on the trails. About a month later, we found a beautiful, athletic horse named Wendy, a 10-year-old bay Morgan horse.

Wendy, a sleek and fast mover, was used for foxhunting with the local Glenmore Hunt Club and was in very good shape. As Dasha's riding skills improved, she grew into Wendy's ability and loved her, and in addition to riding in shows, learned how to foxhunt and joined Glenmore as a junior rider. Since everyone in the club already knew Wendy, Dasha fit right in with the other riders.

We now had three great horses, and trail riding was the perfect activity that Kristina, Dasha, and I could do together. These beautiful equines provided much enjoyment over the years and also helped reconnect me with nature.

Endless Trails, where we boarded our horses, was situated on over 100 acres of land and adjacent to the rolling hills of the beautiful George Washington National Forest where we did all our trail rides.

We made it a point to regularly go out to the barn to help feed, ride, or sometimes just hang out with Nelly, Jake, and Wendy. It was only 10 miles from our house, so we could be there in no time.

At the summer horse camps, for several years, I volunteered to teach crafts to the campers while Dasha helped as an aide to the younger riders. In doing so, we both "earned" riding time.

One of the best summers I ever had was the year we had five week-long camps in succession, which meant being outdoors all day, every day, for five weeks – heaven on earth!

In the winter, when we weren't riding, we continued to go out and see our horses, bring treats, and help Sarah during feeding time. There were over 20 horses on the property, including rescued minis, mustangs, and seasoned veterans used for the camps and riding lessons, who enjoyed the winter break.

Sarah's office was in the barn, and to get to the feed room, you had to walk through the office to get to the aisleway where the tack room, feed room, and four stalls were located. Although the horses were in pastures 24/7, occasionally, a stall would be needed to rest an injured horse or one that needed to be off grass temporarily.

One day in January 2010, when I went out to see our guys, I noticed a fluffy gold kitten, roughly six to eight months old, resting on a chair in the office. There was a bowl of cat food on the floor, along with a water dish.

I felt really drawn to this kitten, who was sociable and alert when I walked into the room, so *naturally*, I stopped to say hello and pet it. The kitten responded with an overabundance of love at the attention! *Did I come out here to see the horses or to be with this cat?*

The room was fairly dirty, because it was not a typical office. It was in a barn filled with helmets, first aid supplies, and extra tack such as lead ropes, bits, lunging ropes, crops, and blankets to put on the horses in the winter.

Although safe from the elements, it was no place for a sociable kitten – and one with respiratory issues that seemed similar to that of Mr. Peabody. There was no heat in the room, and it was damp. This little feline definitely needed a warmer environment with lots of love and attention.

My heart sank each time I walked through that office over the next two weeks. I confess that I went out to the barn more often than usual just to spend time with this golden fluffball that I felt very drawn to.

Sarah told me it had been chased up a tree by her dogs near the barn before she rescued it. For its safety, she was looking for a permanent home. She knew I already had a house full of cats, and not wanting to impose, never asked me if I would like to adopt this one to add to the mix.

Dasha also spent time with the kitten when she went out to feed the horses and *casually* mentioned to me that it needed a home. I didn't need to be convinced, because I was already obsessed with adding it to our mix and could only see one possible solution: Bring the kitty home! (And yes, Chuck and I had some discussions prior to that happening... same old, same old.) But, like the others, it felt like this was *our kitty*...

We thought our newest family member was a girl, and with my own self-diagnosed disease of *cat gender confusion*, I didn't give it a second thought, and we chose a girl's name. But when I brought "her" to the vet for an initial checkup, the vet tech picked up this golden cutie to examine its hind end more closely, and after noticing that I had indicated "female" on the paperwork, smiled and said: "Nope, it's a boy!"

Uh oh, here we go again... We thought of as many names as we could with an orange or golden color, but only one stood out: Pumpkin! It totally suited this precocious and good-natured fellow.

Pumpkin (the boy!) was given medication for his respiratory problems (several times throughout his life), but never completely healed from the symptoms. Every winter, they returned in full force, which led me to believe he had chronic allergies.

This cat definitely lived up to his name. He loved everyone and joyfully welcomed each new feline to the household that arrived after he did. He loved to sniff people in the face when he greeted them, and I considered him our version of a Walmart Greeter!

From a financial perspective, though, it was probably better that Pumpkin was a cat and not another horse. I had to find part-time employment to help pay for the equines…

CHAPTER 31

JAKE'S DIARY

"Mama, life with you is just too much fun – and you know how I love 'horsing around'! OK, that's a bad joke, but just wait till everyone reads how I trained you!" (nicker nicker…)

– Jake

I loved Jake ever since the day of the "nicker-treats" and always felt closely bonded to him, in spite of the fact that I didn't see him every day. Looking back, I'm a little embarrassed at how little I knew about riding or owning a horse. I was given lots of advice and took lessons, but there were some skills I really needed that would have helped me, especially in those first few years.

I'll let Jake finish telling the story of our relationship from his perspective.

Horse Camp

Week 1: Getting Acquainted

That ride in the horse trailer was so bumpy. Thank God it's finished, and they're letting me out. Hmmm… This doesn't look familiar. Who are these people? I don't see my barn. What am I doing here? There are lots of woods in the distance, and a ton of short people – kids! All these kids hanging around.

Now, I'm tied to a fence post with a lot of other horses around a dirt track that looks like a riding ring. I wonder what that means. I have a bad feeling... I hope I don't have to work. What's this thing called a "Horse Camp" anyway?" Are we going to camp? Wait... OMG, they're going to make me work! That is not suitable. Where's my pasture? I LIKE grazing 24/7.

Oh, look! There's that pretty girl with the blonde hair named Dasha. She came out to ride me one day last week, making me walk, trot, canter, and jump. I also see the lady who came with her. Dasha calls her "Mom," but everyone else calls her "Kathy." She seems really nice. I noticed that she's giving me more attention than anyone else and has already figured out how much I like my food.

I remember that day when they both came to meet me, and I got to show off all my skills. I guess I impressed them so much that they brought me over here to help at this camp. I'm so athletic! But if I had known they were going to make me work, I would have faked that I was incompetent. Too late now...

Weeks 2-4: Life at Camp

This is way too much work. There's no end to it – WALK, TROT, WALK, TROT, WHOA... Some of these kids are so small, and I'm such a big guy. I'm doing my best to figure out what they want. At the end of each day's work, they give me treats, and it *is* kind of nice making new friends. I wonder if I'm ever going back home. I miss my sedentary lifestyle and all the grass.

Week 5: Camp Is Finished

It's finally quiet around here. I think I might be staying at this new place! And you know what? I'm okay with that! I've got really good new friends now. I'm in a paddock with two other geldings, both white horses named John and JJ, and a beautiful mare named Nelly who looks like me, chestnut with a white blaze on her face. I really like her. This could be pleasant.

I really can't complain about the food either, although the field they put me in seems to have shorter grass than all the other ones. I heard someone say, "Diet Paddock," but I'm not sure what they meant by that. I guess I'd better get used to it.

I kind of like Kathy. She doesn't live here, but she comes to see me a lot. She laughs at my nicker, and I love the way she holds the feed bucket. She sat on my back during the camp and said, "He's SO COMFY!" Hmmm… Could she be my new human? I think she really likes me, too!

I'm going to call her "Mama." She doesn't seem very sure of herself, though. I watched her trying to ride Nelly during the camp, and she seems *clueless* about how to handle a horse. Obviously, I'm going to have to teach her. Let the games begin! *Nicker nicker…*

Life with Mama

Week 1: The New Halter

Here come's Mama. She's carrying a brand-new, royal blue halter. I'll bet that's for me. I'm so excited! How does she know that's my favorite color? I can feel it right now that we're going to have a great relationship.

"Hey, Mama, I'm over here!" Yes, put that fashionable halter on me. I wish I had a mirror to see how mighty fine I look now, if I do say so myself. Very good…

I can smell the apple-oat cookie treats in her pocket, so I'll cooperate. Besides, the grass outside this paddock is much greener and taller than what's inside. I'll bet if I give her my best nicker, she'll take me out to graze… *Nicker nicker…* Yes!

Mission accomplished.

Week 2: A Trail Ride

Here she comes again. *Best smile.* "Hey, Mama!" *Run to greet her so she doesn't have to walk too far to get me.* Aren't I thoughtful? Wait, she's not stopping to let me graze. Where are we going? To that building where the saddles are? This won't do. I'm stopping NOW. *Jerk head down, pull lead rope far from her hands, graze on the spot.* She tries to pull my head up, but I'm too strong. Haha – not going to work.

Well, I feel a little sorry for her, so I'll let her pull my head up – for three seconds! Time to jerk my head down again, graze, pull that lead rope. This is so much fun! She's trying so hard to keep my head up and make me keep walking. I'm laughing hysterically! Maybe I can even jerk my head down forcefully enough that she'll tip over!

Oh, shoot! Now I'm tied to a fence post. But I know how to untie those quick-release knots with my mouth, so I'll just do that while she goes to get the saddle. I'll help myself to this nice patch of tall, green grass by my feet and pretend I'm still tied up. *Num-num-num...* tasty!

Mama's coming back with all that heavy stuff in her arms. I see a saddle, bridle, grooming kit, and... Uh oh, she's got the hoof pick! Maybe I'd better brace myself. What if she stabs me accidentally? I don't really mind having my feet cleaned out, but sometimes she's clumsy when she does it. I'd better stand still while she holds them, or I could get hurt. *Bracing myself as she goes from hoof to hoof... 1-2-3-4...*

Whew! That wasn't too painful. At least she's getting better at this. I guess if we get the cleaning, brushing, and saddling thing over with quickly, we can be out on the trails sooner. Then, I'll just grab whatever I can from the trees to munch on as we walk along. She'll never catch on. Now, get this saddle on me so we can be on our way!

Here we go. It looks like two of my friends and their humans are also joining us. They say I'm a slow walker, so they always put me in the back of the line once we start out, but I'm really not that slow – I'm concentrating. It's important to know which trees have tasty leaves, and I have to be able to see the clusters of grass in time to quickly bend down and gobble them up. Besides, if I go too fast, Mama might fall off. I don't know how that could ever happen, though, as my back is pretty wide – "very comfy to sit on," I've been told.

Hey, slow down, you guys! You're way too far in front of us. Hold on, Mama, we gotta catch up – *trot, trot, trot.* Made it! And she's still on my back. There we go… *nice trees, head down, nice grass… num-num-num…*

Oh no! We're heading down a hill. I can feel her body out of balance as she's moving all over the place. What on earth does she want? Walk? Trot? Canter? *Gallop?* I'M SO CONFUSED! Her body is so unsteady on my back, and all I hear is "WHOA!" Are we almost finished? This is so uncomfortable, like torture. She's so erratic, and I have no idea what she wants me to do. I'm sick of the stop and go, her yanking on the reins, pulling my mouth, bending over my neck, sitting back… yikes! Make up your mind, Mama! This is painful.

Finally, we're finished. She dismounts. *Happy nicker!* Carrot treats! I love them! *Num-num-num…*Yeah, I did a good job. Now back to the posts at the riding ring to get untacked. *Jerk my head down, grab some grass, make her pull my head up some more. Doesn't bother me – I'm stronger than she is. This is fun… more grass…*

We're finally back at the riding ring. That feels so much better without my saddle and bridle. The halter is much more comfortable. It was such hard work trying to eat grass on the trails with that bit in my mouth. I'll just stand proud and wait while she puts the tack away and brings my grain. Hurry, Mama! I'll untie that quick-release knot again if you take too long.

That was such a workout, and I'm sweaty. Now she's grooming me. That feels very soothing. I'll be my most polite self, so she'll give me some extra grain. Ahhh… Mission accomplished. Good job, Jake!

Now back to the paddock. *Head down... grab some grass... walk a few feet, pull the lead rope from her hands... repeat all the way to my paddock...* I'm doing so well! What a teacher I am!

Week 3: The Lesson

Look! There's Laura – the lady who used to make me work. I thought those days with her were over. She knows me too well and makes me behave. I don't see her much anymore. What's she doing here?

Hi, Laura! WAIT... MAMA WANTS A LESSON? Is that why you're here?

Oh, no! Mama's taking me to *her* riding ring. It's a little bit smaller than the one at Laura's, but I'll bet it's the same routine: keep going around and around while the riders try to figure out what they're doing. Lessons at your barn were SO BORING, Laura. Come on, can't we do something different and more creative at Mama's ring? No? Well, I guess you're the teacher, and Mama really needs help, so I'll just have to figure out a way to have some fun. I have a plan...

Okay, Mama! Ready? Here we go... *Round and round, round and round, round and round...* I'll fool her. Every time we go by the gate, I'll just take a detour, turn into the center of the ring, and come to a complete stop. This is going to be funny! *Wheeeee....*

Hmmm... Mama doesn't sound happy. In fact, she sounds frustrated, but it's making *me* laugh... Ah, come on, Laura, let me have some fun. Party pooper. You're always making me work and be serious. Okay, okay, I'll keep going by the gate without turning into the middle. I know the routine.

On to the next game! I think Mama's trying to practice using her weight to give me signals, but this isn't much better than that trail ride. In fact, there's not much grass to try and grab in this riding ring, so it's not better at ALL – except we're on level ground. It's too much work to keep climbing up and down the hills on those trails.

What's Mama doing now? Voice commands, too? This is so difficult for me to understand – her body says one thing, but her words say something different. That means... Yup... game time! Let's play *Opposites*. Ready, Mama? You start.

Mama: Walk on.

Me*:* That's simple*: Walk backwards three steps.*

Mama (again): Walk on!

Me: *Walk backwards three more steps.*

Okay, third time's a charm...

Mama: WALK ON.

Me: Okay, Mama! I got it! *Bigger steps backwards!*

Uh oh... Mama's frustrated and confused. Laura's laughing. She gets it – it's a game! I wish she wouldn't give away my secrets, though. She's telling Mama that I'm *playing her*, and that I know *exactly* what I'm doing. She's right! I'm such a smarty pants. *Jake the Jokester...*

Week 4: Mama Goes Solo

Here we are again in this boring riding ring. Laura's not here, though, and it looks like Mama's going to try it on her own this time. Let's see... What trick can I play today?

Think, think... Perhaps I should cut her some slack, since she is sort of an old lady. She knows I can walk, trot, canter, and jump – but that was with her daughter riding me, who obviously has more skills than she does.

Think, think... She does give me lots of attention and lots of treats. I'm training her so well. "Good job, handsome fella!" That's what she tells me all the time. Be still my heart. I *am* a handsome fella!

Done thinking. Nope. No slack! I've got the best trick ever.

Let's go for a walk around the ring. *1-2-3-4-5 steps and stop.* She's trying to get me to keep walking, but I think five steps is enough. Time for a break. Okay, five more steps: *1-2-3-4-5. Stop.* Break time. Five more steps: *1-2-3-4-5. Stop.*

Had enough, Mama? All the way around the ring? *Heehee...* Okay, *1-2-3-4-5. Stop. 1-2-3-4-5. Stop.*

I know she's doing her best to try and keep me moving, but this is so much more fun!

One lap finished. What? That's all for today? Well, I guess it did take about 45 minutes to do one lap around the ring. Yup, that's enough. What a great day! I was amazing!

Back to the fence post, so she can get this heavy saddle off my back. Treats because she loves me, even when I deliberately sabotage everything we do. Grain for dinner, and now back to my paddock.

Head down, grab some grass, walk a few steps, pull the lead rope. Head down, grab some grass, walk a few steps...

Another successful lesson! Thanks, Mama!

Week 480: The years go by...

Life has been good here. I do love my Mama. We've been through thick and thin together. When I had an ulcerated cornea and needed surgery, she took me to two different vets. She was there every day to put that yucky ointment in my eye, and to help and encourage me. Then she moved Nelly and me to another barn closer to where she lives so she could see me every day, but I didn't like it there. They separated us and made us stay in different paddocks. Geldings had to stay with geldings, and mares with mares. I didn't like that, and I was lonely.

One day, I got hurt. I had abscesses in two of my feet, and then all four of them felt like they were burning. It was so bad I couldn't even stand up. It was so hot outside, and I was lying on the ground, ready to die. I heard the vet use the words "founder" and "laminitis," and that it was serious. She said everything was swollen in my laminae, the tissue that holds the hoof walls onto my feet, and that my body was not able to process the high sugar content of the grass. There was a lack of blood flow, almost like the grass was toxic to my body and I was allergic to it. I started to wonder if I would ever recover.

They helped me stand up and brought me into a stall, where I had to stay 24/7. That was miserable because all the other horses were outside, and I was all alone. It also got kind of stinky... I cried to Mama for help.

Mama did help! She brought my favorite farrier to check on me. He's the one that makes my shoes and trims my feet. He gave me special boots to wear, and Mama came to treat my feet every day. First, she soaked them in cold water, then wrapped them with bandages, and afterwards gave me some medicine. I know she must have been tired, but I was so grateful. I hated it when she left each day after she was finished.

But then came the best day of all! When I got strong enough to stand comfortably again, Mama brought Nelly and me back to our home at the other barn – in fact, I was so happy to leave that I *ran* into the trailer. No one had to coax me.

It felt *so good* to be back home! Nelly and I had sure missed our friends John and JJ, and now we were all together again in the same paddock. Thank you, Mama!

I have some other health problems, too. I have these things called *sarcoids*, which look like giant warts. Sometimes, they're uncomfortable. They're on my hind end and my face, near my eyes. Mama puts different ointments on my body and tasty Chinese herbs in my grain. I appreciate that she always tries to make me feel good.

I'm trying my best to make Mama happy and proud of me. I think she *is*, because she still tells me I'm "the most handsome guy at the barn." I like that!

And I have to admit, she's gotten better and more confident over the years. I finally let her feel like she'd accomplished something by walking all the way around the riding ring once without stopping. Another time, I actually trotted for a few seconds, but don't tell anybody. That would ruin my reputation for being the slowest horse here!

And she's figured out how to stop me from grabbing every blade of grass I see. She looks straight ahead to where we're going, takes up the slack on the lead rope by holding it closer to my head while we walk, and grabs it more tightly before I have a chance to even *think* of lowering my head toward that grass. She means business! Now, I keep my head up when we walk together. I like this new confidence that she has. It makes me feel more secure. Plus, it makes her feel important and proud of herself, so I let her feel that way.

And thank God she's finally starting to relax on those trail rides. That helps me relax, too. It's so much more fun for both of us. She doesn't tip over anymore when we go down hills, and we're working as a team now.

I still demand my treats, though.

I love my Mama.

CHAPTER 32

SQUEAKER (KATHY'S VERSION)

"Mom, here's another lesson in Divine Timing. And speaking of lessons, you could really use one in anatomy: Girl cats DO NOT have all the same body parts as boy cats..."

– The Fur Family

In the summer of 2009, we spotted a black-and-white cat hanging around our neighbor's yard, just past our lower driveway, about 300 feet from the house. The Carters – Lois a divorcee, her two grown children, and two young grandchildren – had one very large pit bull, who always stayed in their backyard behind a chain-link fence. Occasionally, I saw a smaller dog playing with the pit bull, but the two dogs never left the fenced-in area. Lois and I didn't have much contact, mostly just waving at each other from a distance, but it seemed unusual to see a cat on their property.

I also thought it was odd that I never saw them interact with the cat, who virtually looked like a statue. Every day, it sat in the same 2 x 2 square foot of grass, alert and staring directly at our house. Still, it was on the Carters' property, and it wasn't my job to go soliciting for another cat. We certainly had enough already, maintaining our consistent level of 8-10. I exercised all the self-control I could muster by not venturing over there to ask if it belonged to them.

Chuck and I had agreed on a policy to never adopt a cat that might belong to someone else (in other words, *steal it!*) unless that person gave us permission, in which case it wouldn't be considered theft. When we took care of George back in Japan, I still remember the uncomfortable guilt – how my heart started racing, and I panicked, totally convinced that the other woman who was feeding him would one day come to my front door and accuse me of catnapping.

The same daily routine continued for about six months: *Black-and-white cat sits upright in neighbor's yard, staring at our house, and I stare back… Black-and-white cat sits upright in neighbor's yard, staring at our house, and I stare back… Black-and-white cat sits upright…*

Then, one day in early December, lo and behold, the cat had made its way into our sunroom, which had windows on all sides with two sets of sliding glass doors. Since the cat was now on our property, I didn't feel guilty feeding it, presuming it was hungry. Sure enough, it had the typical ravenous, stray cat appetite that I had seen multiple times before, and I knew in my heart immediately that this cat did not belong to the Carters.

Upon closer examination, it was an older cat with squatty legs and a shortened tail that looked as if it had been squished by a slammed door or hit by a car. The fur colors were actually black, gray, and white, nicely arranged in a large checkerboard pattern of 3 to 4 inches per square. Its personality was docile and submissive (usually a sign of interaction with humans in a previous home), rather than the aloof, fearful demeanor of a homeless feral cat. Definitely not looking for trouble, just a good meal.

After enjoying the thrill of feeding another needy feline for a few days on the porch, I thought our visitor might enjoy a tour of the house, so I happily carried it inside. I felt contentment from this submissive cat, who seemed to be loving the attention and probably would have stayed in my arms for days without the slightest wiggle to try and escape. My three cat-loving daughters totally encouraged this new relationship, and even took turns putting out food on the back porch. The interesting thing was that none of the other cats seemed to mind this docile stranger that had entered our lives – or even seemed to notice. We even gave it the name *Checkers*, based on those cute checkerboard markings.

The persistence and determination of this cat from across the street had paid off, and from this point forward, it became not only a regular guest at mealtime, but was now a permanent addition to the family! I was pretty certain Chuck wouldn't notice, as Checkers was quiet and just blended in with the others.

At first, Checkers seemed like the perfect name, but alas, that name lasted less than two weeks. Every time Checkers wanted to say something, the "meow" sounded more like a squeak. Thus, "Checkers" became "Squeaker."

In determining the gender of a cat that's already been neutered or spayed, our track record for accuracy was currently at 0%. Based on temperament and interaction with the other cats, we took our best, uneducated guess – our usual unscientific approach. But the fact that, once again, none of the other male cats reacted to or objected to Squeaker's presence led us to believe that Squeaker was a female. In fact, I'm not sure they even noticed that there was another cat in the house.

Now, for all the cats that had belonged to me during my life, I really should have taken an anatomy course. Because Squeaker, after six long years of suffering the humiliation of being called a "good girl," finally regained his God-given male identity! The truth emerged from a cat-loving appliance repairman I hired to work on my heating unit, who upon closer examination of Squeaker's private parts, set the record straight:

Squeaker... was... definitely... a... male.

There had been a few clues: urinating to mark territory (although I did have female cats who also did that) and mounting some of the other cats (even though he was fixed, that should have been my *biggest* clue). I was probably on some mental vacation when I witnessed those behaviors and totally blew them off. At least we could keep his name, as that was gender neutral.

I always marveled at the timing of Squeaker's arrival, because he showed up on our back porch literally two weeks before a huge blizzard dropped 2-3 feet of snow on the ground. This was actually the first of three major snowstorms to hit our town from mid-December to mid-January. It was definitely not a typical Shenandoah Valley winter!

The entire area was taken by surprise, as the first storm was not on track to hit us directly, and nobody was prepared. The town was shut down for days, and I'm not sure what Squeaker would have done if he hadn't found the courage to come to our house and quickly blend in with the other cats. I've always felt that he somehow could sense that storm coming and was propelled to join us – just in the nick of time.

CHAPTER 33

SQUEAKER (SQUEAKER'S VERSION)

"I'm a rather crafty cat, don't you think, Mom? And by the way, when I lived in Japan as 'George,' I tried to convince you to let me live with you, but I didn't do so well. My sales skills have greatly improved in this new body."

— Squeaker

I'm worn out... I've been roaming around this neighborhood forever, looking for a new home. That last place was crazy, and I had to get out of there. So much fighting and angry voices. Just too loud for me. But now I'm sick of roaming.

It seems quiet here at the end of this street. It's near some woods with lots of trees. There's also a big dog in the yard of the property I'm sitting on right now, but I'm feeling safe with him behind the fence. I don't want to endanger myself with him or the people who live here while I scope out the interesting sights at that big house across the driveway. I'm going to use my feline superpower to cover myself with my Cloak of Invisibility so that the only ones able to see me are those furry girls who live in that house. I'm brilliant! Be still my heart.

Oh my, just look at all those sexy goddesses... I can't believe what I'm seeing – and it's right next door! I think I've died and gone to heaven: There's not one, but *TWO* calicos, and that tan-and-white one is really hot! I *HAVE* to get a closer look. Hmmm…. Looks like there's some competition over there, though. I see a whole lot of feline fur boys. Not sure how I'm going to finagle this. I need a strategy. If only I had a cardboard sign that said: "Homeless… anything helps." But I don't have a sign, and I can't write anyway… Let's see, what else can I try?

Aha! I have it: I'm going to audition for a spot! I'll sit up nice and tall and point my head over in that direction with perfect posture and eyes that gaze longingly at their house, especially when that older lady comes out. She won't be able to resist me.

I'm getting a bit hungry… actually I'm famished. I think maybe I'll take a break and go sneak over there at night when nobody's looking to see if there might be a little extra food hanging around. From the looks of some of those boys, I can tell there's no shortage in *that* department. And while I'm there, I *might* be tempted to take a closer look at those chicks! Hehe… But then I'll have to come back over here to my invisibility spot during the day, so as not to appear like I'm imposing on them by showing up uninvited. That would give them a terribly wrong impression of me.

OK, back to my audition. Perfect posture. Eyes gazing longingly. Handsome face. I see that lady, and I need to make sure she sees me. Maybe if I keep doing this, she'll invite me to lunch…This is taking longer than I thought. Doesn't she think I'm handsome? Maybe I can talk to those calicos and ask them to put in a good word for me.

* * *

It seems like I've been here forever... *Time passes*... It's getting colder out here now, and I sure could use a fresh meal. I might have to take matters into my own paws and just GO FOR IT! That's what I'll do... OK, here goes... I can do this... *(RUN, RUN, RUN)*

Wow, they've got food for me – all I can eat! I *DID* die and go to heaven! Now, I just need to figure out a way to get into the house, because I'm freezing. I have to play it smart, act grateful yet indifferent. I don't want to make any waves or upset anyone... Maybe it's too soon...There sure are a lot of cats here, but none of them are being mean to me.

* * *

I did it! They carried me in and gave me a tour of the house. It only took a few days. Gosh, I'm good... I'll have to control myself, though, and be a gentleman around here with all these ladies. I don't want to get kicked back out. This is a really nice place. I'm finally warm. Wow... I hit the jackpot! And just in the nick of time. It's snowing – really snowing. I would have been buried alive!

I notice that everyone here has a name. I wonder what they're going to call me... I'll bet it's going to be something really dignified like Leopold or Hercules... *What? Checkers?* I'm a little disappointed, but I might be able to handle that. WAIT – they changed their minds – *SQUEAKER???* No way... they've got to be kidding me. Ugh... and to top it off, they think I'm a girl! I don't know how I'm going to deal with this... this is humiliating. I wish I could talk to them and set them straight, but when I open my mouth, all I do is *squeak*...

CHAPTER 34

IT'S TOUGH WATCHING THEM DECLINE

> *"Mom, we're all subject to the cycle of life and death. Each of us wishes we could stay with you longer, but our departures are inevitable – our bodies age and fail us. Please keep the love we have for you in your heart, even after we're gone. We promise you'll always find us there. And once you fully grasp the important lessons we're teaching you about animal reincarnation and realize that we come back to you in different cat bodies, it will lessen your grief."*
>
> – The Fur Family

Every cat that's been part of my life holds a special place in my heart, even if they've only been with me for a brief amount of time, like TC, the Tiger Cat in Japan who died from the scabies mites. But when I've had these feline family members for many years, watching them decline is excruciating.

After Cyclops, Big Boy, and Mr. Peabody were gone, I resigned myself to knowing that the remaining Core Eight kitties from the Japan years would eventually die, but in addition, the Virginia Beach boys (Georgie and Gray Kitty) were also aging.

Meanwhile, after we moved to Staunton, new felines had joined us, like Fuji and her offspring (Boots, Chrissy, and Callie),

Louie, Squeaker, and Pumpkin. Years later, there would be others.

Over the next decade, the myriad of once strong felines, who were now interspersed with younger family members, became shells of what they had been in their prime and passed away. It was confusing to keep track of how many cats we had at a given time, but there was a continuous flow of 8-10 in our house for what turned out to be 23 consecutive years – and none of their adoptions were planned, except Big Boy and Little Boy, who were with us at the start of this long adventure.

The next of the Core Eight to leave us was Pretty Girl, my beautiful tortoiseshell with an orange mustache, who'd triggered the dream that started this menagerie in Japan, lived to be 21, and died at home from natural causes. Her handsome, yet timid, gold-and-white son Spunky died six months later. He developed a cancerous tumor in his throat and could barely breathe. He also had difficulty swallowing and vomited his food, thereby losing weight quickly.

Spunky's tumor was evident two weeks after he was vaccinated, and although it remains to be seen if there was a connection between the two, the cancer ultimately took his life. He might have already had the beginnings of the tumor in his body, and no doubt the vaccines taxed his immune system even more, contributing to its spread and his rapid decline.

This handsome boy, my favorite kitten from Pretty Girl's litter, who never wanted to leave his mother's side, died on the operating table at the vet clinic. We had agreed to let the doctor euthanize him if they found more cancer in his body during the surgery to remove the tumor, and that's exactly what happened. There was nothing more we could do. Ironically, his death occurred on Chuck's and my wedding anniversary.

After Spunky passed, Muffin, then 14, my sweet girl from Japan with the bad breath, who had joined us in 1993, began to lose her appetite and her strength. She had no other health problems, and the appetite stimulants we tried didn't work. She grew weaker by the day, and eventually died peacefully at home – another heartbreaking loss.

Little Boy, at age 17, became blind, and although he was able to navigate through the house fairly well, one morning, immediately after I put flea medication on his neck, he fell to the floor and was not able to stand up by himself. There was no other option than to take him to the vet, also to be euthanized.

I believe the chemicals were too strong for Little Boy with his failing health, and since that incident, I've been hesitant to use this type of flea prevention method on any other cat. I only use it as a last resort and look for alternative ways to manage fleas if they become a problem.

Georgie, the black-and-white best King Cat ever, from Virginia Beach, had no visible health problems, but without warning, he became thinner and thinner. His spirit was strong, so I held off trying to find the cause, following my intuition that I should just let him be and let nature take its course. He was eventually the first of my cats to wander off and die by himself, which I believe was the way he wanted to transition.

Georgie's passing devastated the hierarchical feline order in the household, because he had taken over the role of King Cat in a superb manner. When Big Boy died, Little Boy became the oldest male and would normally have transitioned into that leadership position, but he was a follower, not a leader, and had readily acquiesced to Georgie's dominance, allowing him to assume that important role within months of his joining the household. With Georgie as the feline leader, each cat knew their place, and they coexisted peacefully. This boy was so respected that his mere presence gave them the assurance that they were safe.

I've yet to have another cat take over this role in such a perfect manner. At the time, I wasn't familiar with the concept of "emotional leadership" and *my* role in the feline household dynamics. I would learn about that years later from Fuji, my calico who assumed the role of Feline Matriarch (my title for her!).

I'd barely recovered from Georgie's death when Gray Kitty, the gentle, fluffy gray cat, also from Virginia Beach, got very ill, and he, too, lost a huge amount of weight. We did seek help for him, but he was never officially diagnosed, no medications worked to stimulate his appetite, and again, I saw no other choice but to bring him to the vet, like I had done for Little Boy, and have him gently put to sleep.

As I was driving to the vet clinic with Gray Kitty that morning, the comforting words of a Beatles song, "Let it Be," were resounding through the speakers of my car radio: *"When I find myself in times of trouble, Mother Mary comes to me, speaking words of wisdom, let it be, let it be..."* It was a heavenly message letting me know that the Divine had not forgotten me – or my cats! I was already grieving, but knew that I wasn't alone, and the song was exactly what I needed to hear. Yet, my grief capacity was nearly maxed out.

The last of the Core Eight to pass away was Bobtail.

CHAPTER 35

BOBTAIL'S SENIOR YEARS

"I've had an awesome life, Mom! Thank you for not giving up on me when I was a wild little thing in Japan so many years ago! Now it's time for me to leave you and go join the rest of our beautiful Core Eight, where I'll continue singing to my heart's content!"

– Bobtail

Bobtail, my curly, hook-tailed tiger cat from Japan, who was now 19 years old, claimed the master bedroom as her territory. I was saddened that she only ventured far enough away to use the litter box, but she seemed content and loved watching and cackling at the birds outside the window. She couldn't wait to jump into bed at night, curl up next to me in her favorite spot under my left armpit near my heart, and go to sleep.

When she was 17, Bobtail acquired enough courage to come downstairs and eat with the others in the kitchen. She and Spunky were the only two that stayed exclusively indoors, so it was unthinkable that she would ever venture outside. One day, though, it happened – she inadvertently escaped!

I didn't realize she was missing until she didn't show up at bedtime. She hadn't been outside since she was that young, frightened, singing kitten we'd trapped in a carrier with tuna fish 17 years earlier while living in Japan. Now, she could end up becoming a tasty meal for the wildlife that roamed in the woods behind our house after dark. I just couldn't figure out what happened. This was so unlike her.

I frantically called to her for three days, ready to give up hope, when late afternoon on the third day, I heard a familiar yet faint meow coming from beneath the shed in our backyard. It was Bobtail, but not with the big, booming voice I was accustomed to. This time, she sang with a desperate *"Please help me"* plea.

The next challenge was to coax her out of her hiding place. Underneath the shed were large holes, courtesy of the groundhog families that graced our property over the years. But they weren't large enough for me to crawl inside to get her, and she would have to muster up enough courage to come out all by herself.

I sat on the ground next to the opening where she was hiding, encouraging her while thinking she would be comforted by my voice and come to me. It didn't occur to me at the time to try the tuna fish trick again, although that might have been faster!

Over two hours later, she slowly emerged from her hiding place, trembling and looking shell-shocked. I gently lifted her into my arms and hugged her, telling her how brave she was, and brought her back inside to the familiar comfort of the bedroom. She was traumatized.

I sensed that she had reverted back to being a feral cat, but with none of the skills to live outside. She had spent three nights by herself in an unknown environment with no food or water. I'm sure that as soon as she realized she was not in the house, she ran and hid under the shed for safety and didn't stir from there. I likened this to an episode of PTSD, from which it would take her at least six months to recover.

Bobtail eventually returned to her happy, singing, beautiful self, who faithfully slept at my side for her remaining days. I knew she was getting close to the end of her life when her mental faculties started to diminish, and she let others in the house pick her up and hold her. She had no resistance left.

She began to eat less, lose weight, and then died peacefully at home. Unfortunately, I was not with her. Chuck had recently reentered the Navy Reserves, and I had accompanied him to Cincinnati on a drill weekend when Bobtail passed away. I still regret that she died alone, but believe the timing was in accordance with my lesson of long ago: *I, the Lord, deal death and give life*.

Bobtail lived a long, happy life, sang to her heart's content, and was greatly loved! She was the last of the "Core Eight" cats from Japan that had traveled with us across the globe. Big Boy, Little Boy, Pretty Girl, Spunky, Muffin, Cyclops, and Mr. Peabody had all preceded her in death.

To me, it marked the end of an era.

CHAPTER 36

LUCY AKA LUCE

"Seriously Mom, did I really look like a girl? So glad that nice appliance repairman finally set you straight – and that's the second time he's had to help you tell the difference between a boy and a girl! I'll forgive you, though, for calling me Lucy. There's actually a really big reason you chose that name, but I can't tell you now. It won't make sense until I teach you more about animal reincarnation."

- Luce

In 2012, a very dirty, mature, skinny white cat with a few black spots and a narrow, pointed face showed up in our driveway, partaking of the daily smorgasbord I provided for homeless cats and whatever other critters came by for a free meal. This was the final cat to show up while I lived on Stocker Street.

The new visitor was polite, tame, and relatively quiet. It didn't beg for food, but instead, stood on its hind legs and rubbed against my body – obviously grateful. I would have said against my *legs* rather than *body*, but this cat was so long-legged that its head reached all the way to my hips when it stood up next to me!

I have long recognized the "body rub" as a signal of either the cat marking their territory, expressing gratitude, claiming ownership – or all of the above! Predictably, within three days, this tall white one adopted us, eagerly joining the indoor crew at mealtime. This was clearly an astute cat!

I once again lost track of how large our feline family had become. And, in keeping with the uneventful, seamless integrations with a new cat, none of the other seven, eight, or nine cared when this newbie came into the house. Nobody hissed, growled, or chased anybody away. *This is not how new cats typically integrate with an established household…*

It reminded me of when Squeaker joined us, and because there were no behavioral issues with the existing males, I *presumed once again* that this new cat was a female.

I wracked my brain to try and come up with a name for this tall, lanky white cat, and the *only* name that popped into my head was Lucy. I couldn't think of *anything* else to name it. We already had a Louie, and it seemed strange to have names that sounded so similar, but that's what came to me, so that's the name we all agreed on.

It didn't take long for Lucy's filthy white fur to become soft, silky, and beautiful while the bony frame filled out. "She" soon became the largest cat I had ever had, even bigger than Big Boy! *Kathy, that in itself should have been your clue that this was a male…*

Once again, my not-so-stellar skill as an expert in feline anatomy reared its ugly head, but it wasn't until three years later, when the same appliance repairman who set me straight on Squeaker's correct gender did the same for Lucy – *ugh!*

With Squeaker, I could at least keep his more neutral name, but definitely not with this white cat. Since we already had a Louie, the best option I could think of for a rename was "Luce" (pronounced *Loose*). I wanted to keep it as familiar to *him* as possible.

I would discover a few years later that Luce's timing was significant, and he would become my first cat to give me an inkling of the possibility of animal reincarnation. I'll share that story after the move to Crestwood Drive!

CHAPTER 37

CHEATED DEATH AGAIN... AND AGAIN... AND AGAIN

> *"Mom, we're relieved that none of these accidents took you away from us permanently, and we certainly hope that you'll be more careful when you're in the water. And Jake, did you have to react in such a dramatic way? We know you panicked, but we nearly lost our mom! It was a little bit over the top!"*
>
> — The Fur Family

"Cheated Death Again" became our woodwind quintet's mantra in Japan. We proudly proclaimed it after any performance plagued by unusually difficult circumstances, such as our primitive "cultural exchange" with the Hill Tribes in northern Thailand. It was our humorous way of sharing unspoken thoughts and feelings about the performance, helping us unwind and giving ourselves pats on the back.

I never thought about the actual meaning of that expression until I started reviewing some of the close calls with death that I've experienced over the course of my life.

I've "cheated death again" many times, surviving potentially life-ending circumstances. Unlike a Near Death Experience (NDE), I didn't actually die and get resuscitated back to life with stories to tell from the other side, but the incidents were serious enough that I believe there was divine intervention to keep me alive. I'll refer to these as my "Almost Death Experiences" (ADE).

I've always loved being in the water, so it seemed only natural that my first ADE occurred while I was swimming. As a child, I took lessons every summer and had dreams about prancing around like a dolphin in the ocean someday!

My big chance came when I was 10 years old, enjoying a summer vacation with my parents and brother Dave. We had driven to Connecticut to visit my aunt and uncle and spent one beautiful, hot summer day at a cottage they owned by the ocean in nearby Rhode Island.

I was thoroughly enjoying the seagulls, fresh air, beach, sand, *and* the ocean. It was invigorating to feel the waves splashing all over my body! I wasn't afraid of them, but nobody explained to me about the undertow and the current, or how quickly it could whisk you away – and whisk me away it did!

I was swimming by myself, roughly 20 feet from my family, having a wonderful time soaking up the sun and *going with the flow!* The *flow,* however, became faster and faster, while I could feel myself drifting farther and farther away from everyone. Twenty feet turned into 30 – then 40 – as the current continued to pull me into deeper water. Familiar faces were fading into the distance, and nobody noticed where I had gone. *I better get back to the shore. This doesn't feel comfortable…*

Alarm bells were sounding in my head, but I could barely move toward shallow water as the current kept pulling me farther into the ocean. I mustered all the strength I could, furiously flailing my arms, kicking my feet endlessly, and alternating between the breaststroke and crawl. My heart continued to pound faster and faster as I was gasping for breath, all the while trying to keep my head above water.

I don't know how long I battled with the current, but I fully believe there were angels or other celestial beings who either pulled me back into shallow water or gave me superhuman strength to propel myself back. I made it safely ashore, but never did tell anyone how close I came to drowning. I couldn't believe it myself and quickly put that memory aside.

ADE number two occurred nearly 15 years later, while on Christmas break from Graduate School at Michigan State University. I was enduring the discomfort of four impacted and infected wisdom teeth, which were becoming progressively more and more painful. At a dentist's recommendation, my parents and I decided to have the teeth removed before I entered the Air Force, so we made an appointment near Malone with a local oral surgeon.

This was in 1984, back when there was an abundance of "wisdom teeth removal horror stories" flying left and right. I don't think I'd met *anyone* who had a good experience of getting them taken out, and the anticipation of that day practically paralyzed me. I don't like medical procedures anyway, or anything involving my blood, so I'm sure I was emotionally predisposed to having a bad experience.

My mother drove me to the office where the procedure would take place, and it sounded like it would be fairly easy, according to the staff. They would give me a good dose of nitrous oxide (aka laughing gas) through a mask, which would cause me to relax, and then they would begin to extract my teeth.

The only problem was that as soon as I started inhaling the gas, I was *neither laughing nor relaxing*. I had a terrible reaction to the nitrous oxide: My body went into shock, and my pulse dropped to a mere 20 beats per minute!

When the staff finally noticed, they grabbed blankets to put on top of me for warmth and elevated my legs. I nearly died, and they told my mother that they would *not* be removing my teeth that day! I think the experience shook her up more than it did me, as throughout the commotion, I was peacefully drifting into la la land.

Nearly 40 years later, I found out that many members of my family have a MTHFR Genetic Mutation which affects how our bodies process folic acid. One of the indicators of this condition is an adverse reaction to nitrous oxide! *Who would've thought?*

My most recent and hopefully *final* ADE happened while sitting on the back of my horse Jake. I was 51 years old and in the process of recovering from *Adhesive Capsulitis,* commonly known as 'frozen shoulder,' a condition characterized by stiffness and severe pain in the shoulder joint. The shoulder capsule thickens and becomes stiff and tight. Thick bands of tissue called adhesions develop and then begin to fuse together.

I was unable to lift my right arm and, thinking I had torn something inside, completely stopped using it until it was diagnosed. Ironically, lack of movement was actually causing it to become even more stuck, or "frozen." Every time I tried to raise my arm, it was incredibly painful, and that's why I had stopped moving it in the first place – a vicious circle! I eventually went to physical therapy three times per week to try and "unfuse" the adhesions. That and the Chinese deep tissue massage technique called Tuina eventually helped me regain full use of my shoulder.

In late March 2011, my daughter Dasha and I decided to treat our pastor's wife, Donna, and her daughter Bonnie to a trail ride, using all three of our horses. Because of my shoulder, I decided not to ride that day, and Dasha led them by herself. It was a beautiful Sunday afternoon, and they couldn't wait!

The horse barn property is adjacent to the George Washington National Forest, where all the beautifully wooded, hilly trails are located. I opened the gate and accompanied the three riders back into the woods, helped them mount the horses, and then waited for them to finish a leisurely 45-minute ride.

When they returned, I met them in the woods, and Donna, who was riding Jake and who knew how much I loved him, asked if I wanted to sit on him before we took the horses back to the riding ring area and untacked them. My shoulder was recovering well, and I had actually gone on an easy 30-minute trail ride the previous week, so I had a measure of confidence that I would be safe.

Jake seemed happy to see me with his familiar nicker greeting, so I said, "Sure!" Donna dismounted him, I put on her helmet, and she helped hoist me off the ground while I put my foot in the stirrup and sank into his saddle. It was one of my happy places!

While we were still in the woods, Jake and I slowly walked the short distance of 30 feet to the red, metal gate where we usually dismounted. Then we would unlock the gate, and hand-walk the horses through a paddock to the riding ring, where we untacked them.

This time however, I made a very bad choice, not heeding the advice of my much smarter, horse-savvy daughter to dismount. Instead, I chose to ride Jake an extra 50 yards back to the riding ring, like I had done hundreds of times before. *What could go wrong – besides everything?*

There were other horses temporarily living in that paddock that we needed to walk past en route to the riding ring. Jake knew them from living at the barn, but they were not part of his herd.

As we approached the ring, I could sense that he was agitated and could feel his legs beneath me wanting to kick out at those horses when they walked toward us. Thankfully, he didn't, but I became very anxious during those last 20 steps leading up to the ring.

Then, in an instant, while I was positioning myself to dismount, Jake BOLTED – from a standstill to a canter in less than three seconds! I flew off his back immediately, over his right shoulder, doing a partial flip and landing on both my head and right shoulder (the frozen one) at the same time! *This was my horse Jake, the slowest horse at the barn...* Thank goodness I was wearing a helmet – something I will do for the rest of my life while on the back of a horse.

Something had apparently spooked him from behind – possibly the person who had closed the gate and was now running back to join us. I didn't black out but was very sore and slow to get up off the ground.

I had a flashback to the accident that had happened four years earlier at almost the exact same spot at the barn, at the end of the day of my daughters' first horse camp. I was run over by an 18-year-old Appaloosa named Misty who'd misjudged the distance between us and bolled me over from behind.

I don't think Misty was even aware that she'd made body contact with me, but she slammed into my back and right shoulder as she ran by, knocking me into a culvert, where I landed in loose gravel just inches away from large rocks and drainage pipes. Both my camera and I literally went flying!

If I had landed one foot farther, my head would have slammed into the large boulders in the culvert, cracking it open and causing a *real* death experience… *Whew!*

I had remained unconscious for several minutes, while my friends gently moved me out of the culvert and called an ambulance to cart me off to the emergency room 40 minutes away. Thank God there were no injuries other than a cracked rib and a broken camera!

This time, though, with Jake, because I was fully conscious, I figured it was just a bad fall and nothing too serious that wouldn't heal over time.

Four days after my flip, I attended one of my weekly band practices and noticed that the sheet music was a little blurrier than usual. I was wearing reading glasses, but still had difficulty seeing it clearly. *What's this all about?*

I did a little bit of research on *concussions* – a possibility that had never entered my mind. After all, my head wasn't throbbing with pain – it felt more like an intermittent, dull headache. I had also been taking some over-the-counter medications for the frozen shoulder pain after my physical therapy sessions, and those took care of the dull headaches as well.

I definitely could relate to what I read about "Post Concussive Syndrome," as it described me to a tee. Apparently, the symptoms – which for me were the blurred vision and dull headache – would disappear after about two weeks. I closely monitored myself, and after two weeks, sure enough, the symptoms disappeared. For me, that was great news. *End of story.*

Four weeks after that discovery (six weeks after the accident), on Easter Sunday 2011, something still didn't seem right physically, but there were logical explanations. We had stayed awake for the all-night Easter Vigil services at the Russian Orthodox Church we attended after we'd participated in a 40-day vegan Lenten fast, concluding with the Vigil, followed by a "break-the-fast" potluck breakfast.

It was our first time attending the Vigil, which concluded at 3:00 a.m., and then I ate several foods I hadn't eaten in weeks, with virtually no sleep. We didn't arrive home until after 5:00 a.m., and because I felt a little uncomfortable in the stomach, I didn't eat much else for the rest of the day. *My explanation: Obviously, the jumpy stomach came from eating all that food in the middle of the night.*

But still, I was noticeably unfocused and more tired than usual. *My explanation: Lack of sleep the night before.* I wasn't too concerned.

Moving into the evening, I became nauseous, with no food coming up. I have no recall of what happened overnight. Chuck said that I had alternating complaints of being hot and cold, but when he took my temperature, there was no fever. Things just weren't adding up.

It was now 4:00 a.m., and although I was oblivious to all that had transpired overnight, Chuck's level of concern rose dramatically, and he insisted that we go to the emergency room. I have only tiny snippets of memory from my brief stay there.

I remember that the hospital staff checked me in, put me in a wheelchair as I drifted in and out of sleep, and pushed me down a hallway to a room where they did a CT scan on my head. When they got the results, they drew a picture to show me that "your center line is off by 5 centimeters." *What does that mean?*

It meant that I had a subdural hematoma (bleeding on the brain triggered by the flip off Jake) and was slowly slipping into a coma with impending death on the horizon.

From the ER, they rushed me by ambulance to the University of Virginia (UVA) Medical Center, an hour away in Charlottesville, where a wonderful doctor performed emergency surgery on my head, drilling two holes on the right side of my temple to let the blood out. (I now refer to those sealed up holes as "my craters"!)

According to Chuck, I was very talkative in the ambulance, telling the medics I was going to *Lexington* – not Charlottesville, but I have absolutely no memory of that ride or what took place over the next several hours until I woke up from the surgery that afternoon at 4:00 p.m.

I was hooked up with IVs in my wrists and a breathing tube in my throat to help me breathe while I was unconscious. I thought I was going to suffocate, so I tried unsuccessfully with my wrists full of needles to grab the breathing tube and pull it out. Seeing that I was awake with my body squirming and trying to breathe, the nurses took the tube out for me – *whew!* That was the most uncomfortable part of the entire day!

Meanwhile, Chuck and one of the pastors and his wife from the Orthodox church were sitting in my room with me, repeating, "You're at UVA and you're safe." *What am I doing at UVA?*

I had no memory of what had happened that entire day, but now have great empathy for anyone suffering from amnesia… In reality, I was within 24 hours of dying, and if Chuck had not taken me to the ER, I would have continued to slip into a coma and fallen asleep – permanently.

Even more miraculous was the fact that he was supposed to have been deployed overseas with the Navy Reserves at that time, but his orders were canceled (actually, on my birthday in March) and rescheduled for a later date.

If he had been deployed, I would never have taken myself to the ER and would have just drifted into a deep and fatal sleep. My daughters would have eventually found me lying motionless in bed – deader than a doornail!

Thankfully, that wasn't the scenario. I had truly *Cheated Death Again* and recovered from this latest ADE with only minimal health issues and no brain damage. For about nine months, I experienced difficulty focusing, retrieving names of people I knew, and finding appropriate words to use in carrying on intelligent conversations. *Wait, maybe I've always had trouble with that! Hee hee...*

Today, those symptoms rarely rear their ugly head, and only on very hot, humid days do I have trouble focusing – nothing that a little bit of air conditioning won't cure!

After that near-fatal injury, I was panic-stricken at even the *thought* of ever getting back on a horse. I could never fall off again. It was risky, and if I did, the outcome might be even worse. But within the horse community, I was always told that if you fall off a horse, you *must* get back on– you can't let the horse win. I was a fighter, so I was determined to do that.

I wasn't angry at Jake, and never blamed him for the accident. I could have made different choices that would have been much safer and led to different results. But he was a horse, and at the end of the day, a horse is still a horse: Horses can spook!

I had previously taken some riding lessons at the therapeutic stable where Kristina rode. About three months after the brain surgery, I decided to face my fears and continue with those lessons.

I was able to ride a beautiful black Morgan horse named Target, a veteran therapeutic horse, in a controlled setting. I was scared but did it anyway, and gradually learned how to relax again while in the saddle.

By early fall, I mustered up enough courage to get back on Jake. I went on a brief 10-minute trail ride with my friend Judi and her horse John, one of Jake's pasture mates. We mounted them in the woods on a short, flat trail next to some rolling hills. This was a stretch of woods that served as the warm-up area for our longer rides.

Wild animals abound in the George Washington National Forest, and we are always on the lookout when we go on a trail ride. We don't often see anything, other than a squirrel or two, and for that brief ride, I was hyper-focused on things like my riding position, remaining calm, and moving slowly. I was riding solely for the opportunity to regain some confidence.

Suddenly, there was a rustling noise in the bushes directly above where we were walking, less than 20 feet away. *Gasp…* It was a deer!

I flinched when I saw it, because it was a total surprise, and so did Jake – but *he held his ground* and didn't move an inch. My boy had taken care of me! I slowly regained my trust in both him and myself, and overcame my fear of getting back on a horse. I was free to enjoy riding again.

I was totally grateful for the outcome of this serious brush with death – and all the others – but it did pose some serious questions:

Why am I still here? What is my life's purpose? Do I have an unfulfilled mission?

CHAPTER 38

MY SPIRITUAL QUEST

"Mom, while you're in the midst of this spiritual search, we're going to take a nap and let Divine Love work in your heart in a deeper way. We might even hibernate! But when we wake up, we're going to pull all of this together and give you some life-changing 'aha' moments!"

– The Fur Family

My Spiritual Quest has been dotted along the way with numerous steps on the path, eventually leading to becoming an Animal Communicator and Energy Healer – and being open to the possibility of reincarnation in both humans and animals. It was not a linear path, but one filled with seemingly unrelated events.

This non-linear spiritual path completely challenged my linear way of thinking. It was no longer like doing a math equation with all the steps in the proper sequence, following the rules, and then getting the correct answer. Rather, it's more like making a pot of chili: Put a bunch of different ingredients in a pot with some spices, turn the heat on, and the final result will taste nothing like the individual ingredients you started with!

Please bear with me as I share some stories from my life that don't involve animals, but later fit together like scattered puzzle pieces and influenced my spiritual journey. Many years and many cats later, I would come to understand what seemed at the time like random events. But for now, here are some of my major steppingstones...

One afternoon, when I was a teenager driving past the local bowling alley, I became unnerved while listening to a radio program that talked about Charles Darwin's theory of evolution. It only played for a few minutes, but it shook me to my core. I had never heard my religious beliefs challenged, and I didn't know how to react. That was really the issue: In those days, if something challenged my belief system, and either proved it wrong or introduced a different way of thinking, then what could I trust to be true?

It took many more years, life experiences, challenges, disappointments, and much humility to bring me to the point of fully surrendering my will to the Divine, where I was able to open my heart and allow God to teach me directly about spiritual matters, apart from my church experiences or hearsay. I'm thankful that my unwavering perseverance propelled me forward.

I continued to be a regular churchgoer throughout the turbulent college years, and then into my Air Force career. I even attended daily mass for over 20 years! I really wanted more of *something* but didn't know what it was.

Even after I had that spiritual awakening experience in my early 20s, before I met Chuck, I still seemed to be stuck in a one-sided relationship, begging God for what I wanted, and expecting Him to deliver. Once again, God felt distant. Although I regularly told others how much God loved *them*, I was still afraid of the "Getcha" God who was going to *get me* and punish me if I messed up. And so, I continued to live my life in fear of making mistakes.

I understand now that through my church upbringing and education, I had absorbed a "separation consciousness" mindset, believing I am separate from the Creator and the creation. I no longer accept that, and the shifts I have made in consciousness the past few years have healed the deep emptiness I experienced for decades. But until that happened, I continued on my seeking path.

Part of that journey included using my musical skills. During my high school years, I enjoyed playing my instruments in church on occasion. I loved the more modern, folk style of music in the 1970s, when guitars became a familiar sight in many church services. Later, when I first heard the more contemporary Christian music, I fully embraced it!

While stationed in Japan, I played my instruments in the church choir at the Yokota Air Base Chapel, and eventually became the choir director before we moved back to the U.S. I loved it and thought I had found my calling! But that was just another marker along the way.

I used to have very interesting conversations about life with one of my musical colleagues, Forrest, who was a spiritual but non-religious person. He seemed to have insights about the inner life that I couldn't understand. I was too immersed in the church and theology – all the "heady" stuff.

I didn't really understand what Forrest was talking about most of the time, but it didn't matter, because something deep inside my heart seemed to resonate with the things he was saying. We talked for long periods of time on our band trips with the Air Force during the three years that our assignments overlapped.

At that time, I had never heard the word "empath," and Forrest never used that term, but if he had, I would have recognized myself immediately – *that's what I am!* Often, I would walk into the squadron at work and sense the emotional climate of that space. I knew exactly what people were feeling. It really bothered me and was exhausting.

Forrest would say, "You're picking up everybody else's stuff!" I tried talking with our parish priest about it but got no insights or answers. I did my best to turn this sensitivity off, but in doing so, I unknowingly started to shut down both my intuition and empathic skills. I had no idea that these were the very skills I would later need as an Animal Communicator and Energy Healer, and that they were actually a gift.

Today, I have learned how to "reign in" and create energetic boundaries to protect myself when I am around other people, especially in a group setting. I'm better able to hold my own energy – and the emotions that are connected to it – without absorbing everyone else's!

A year before Chuck and I moved back to the States, Forrest spoke to me in a very serious tone during one of our conversations with words that jarred me for the next 20 years. He said, "One day you and Chuck are going to split up." *What? You're crazy. How could that ever happen?*

I put that thought out of my head as best I could and attributed it to the devil. Chuck and I were doing all the "right" spiritual practices and sharing life together the way many couples do. We maintained a house, paid the bills, traveled on vacations, ate at restaurants with friends, went to church together, etc. We always got along very well, and the notion that we would ever split up was no more plausible in my mind than the Easter Bunny being real.

Around that time, I was exploring documented miracles/mystical accounts of alleged apparitions of the Blessed Virgin Mary taking place in the 1980s in both Medjugorje, Yugoslavia, and Akita, Japan. I was very drawn to those types of phenomena and went on life-changing pilgrimages to both places.

When we moved back to Virginia Beach in 1998, I became a Youth Music Minister for six years, mentoring and teaching a tremendous group of young people. We even made a CD – I had such talented youth to work with!

In 2005, our family moved to Staunton, Virginia, where I started a youth choir at the Catholic church, but the experience was not so good. The kids were great, but I felt no support from the parish administration and was eventually forced to resign after five years of frustration.

The stress became so great that we changed churches and attended a small Russian Orthodox Church in the area, where we met wonderful folks and experienced beautiful liturgy. But that church relocated to a different city farther away, and after a year, we stopped attending.

I experienced some mysticism in Charismatic Prayer meetings, and at an occasional conference, but that didn't happen consistently, and the challenge was that after the conferences were finished, there was no place for me to follow-up and to grow, so my life went back to what it was: feeling out of place in various churches I attended and trying to satisfy my spiritual cravings for *more* – but coming up empty.

There was a yearly conference I attended in Virginia Beach that impacted me more than anything else, where I experienced some very powerful manifestations of the Holy Spirit. It was called "Catch the Fire" (CTF), held at the Christian Broadcasting Network (CBN), a half mile from our house, in the same complex of buildings where Chuck worked in the Information Technology Department.

The CTF conferences came out of a revival that started in the early 1980s in Toronto, Ontario, at the Toronto Airport Christian Fellowship (TACF) church. The immense outpouring of God the Father's love at these gatherings, in sometimes strange and unusual ways, turned into a global ministry, with Catch the Fire Conferences happening all around the world.

I first attended one with some friends for only one evening in February 2002, just out of curiosity to see what strange "manifestations" of the Spirit happened there. But the timing was perfect for me to experience a profound healing.

Three months earlier, our house had been broken into. Chuck was at a church meeting, while Kristina and I attended a homeschool music concert together. When we returned home from the concert, I slowly pulled into our driveway on Parkland Lane and noticed that the house was very dark. Something didn't *feel* right. When we opened the front door to walk in, a man carrying a gun came down our stairs toward us. He told us that he was with the police, to go upstairs, and that they had the wrong house.

I knew he was *not* a policeman, and I was never more scared in my entire life! I'm sure that my heart left my body for several minutes. Kristina and I ran upstairs as fast as possible, grabbed the cordless phone, and hid in the bathroom with the door locked while I frantically called 911 to notify the police. The 10 minutes we waited for them to arrive seemed like an eternity, and my heart never stopped racing. We probably prayed a thousand "Hail Marys" together while we lay crouched on the floor. Kristina was a trooper, and I did my best to keep her safe, reassuring her that help was on the way.

Meanwhile, in a bedroom down the hall, a friend who rented a room from us, Tim, was lying face down on his bed – thankfully unharmed – but the story could have had a different ending.

When the police arrived, searched the house, and secured our safety, Tim told us that two men had broken in, and the first one left before Kristina and I arrived. The second one, who was walking down the stairs when we came in the front door, had just left Tim's room, where he had been held face down at gunpoint.

The police deduced that the break-in was centered around illegal drugs, and that the perpetrators really did have the wrong house. The intruders were never apprehended, but I no longer felt safe in my own home.

Fast forward to the CTF conference, where I basked in an atmosphere of pure joy! The evening consisted of worshipful, contemporary Christian music, followed by multiple speakers who shared testimonies of the love of Jesus Christ, and the powerful healing work that was transpiring throughout the world through this revival.

Before I left to go home, prayer teams were scattered about the large conference room, extending their arms to pray individually over whomever wanted the "Father's Blessing," as they called it. *Yes, I want that blessing! Bring it on...* As they prayed over me with extended arms, I fell down onto the floor, gently positioned by the men standing behind me who caught me as I fell. My heart was overcome with pure love.

I lay there peacefully for several minutes alongside hundreds of other people in the room who were also soaking in this immense love, then rose slowly from the floor to go home. *This feels so peaceful...*

I wasn't expecting anything specific to happen after my "carpet time" that evening, but by the third day, I suddenly realized *I was no longer afraid to be in my house! God had healed my heart, and the fear was totally gone!* I knew without a doubt that it was a direct result of my experience. What a miracle!

That healing was so profound that I went back to the next conference one year later for three nights instead of one. I wanted more! This time, human "fire tunnels" were formed on the last day, with two lines of prayer team members facing opposite each other with outstretched arms, leaving enough space for everyone else to walk underneath.

The team members gleefully shouted, *"More, Lord... More Love... More Power... More Fire..."* over each of us as we *attempted* to remain standing while we walked through the tunnels. "Attempted" is the key word, as the power of the Holy Spirit was so intense that most of us going through the tunnel wound up stumbling down to the floor, unable to get up for several minutes, and had to be whisked away to an empty spot to make room for other stumblers!

Of course, I wanted more, and when I fell over, an incredible surge of *LAUGHTER* enveloped me like I had never experienced before or since – laughing steadily, without being able to stop, for at least half an hour. I was filled with so much joy, and I'm sure I released a volume of stuck emotions. I had just experienced a profound form of inner healing!

I was pretty much addicted to the CTF Conferences, and in 2004, I attended the entire week. This was when the most profound series of visions of my life to date happened. I would call them "intuitive visions," and the first and most piercing one happened when I was once again lying on the floor during "carpet time."

In my mind's eye, I saw myself lying on the ground amidst the rubble of a city building being demolished by large cranes and construction equipment. In the scene, I couldn't lift myself up, and I saw smoke from the rubble rising all around. I asked God what it meant, and *very* distinctly, but not audibly, heard these words: *"I'm going to demolish you so I can rebuild you!"* It was one of the first instances in my life where I *knew* that the message came from the Divine.

I had never experienced what I would call a "vision" before, and to have one with such a serious message puzzled me, but I knew it was clearly from God, and during each of the next three CTF conferences, I had a different vision with the same theme.

Among them was one in which I was hovering over my body and saw a layer of skin peel off me like a snake. God was taking the "old skin" off to replace it with "new skin." While unnerving, these visions were at the same time consistent in their message. *Something was going to die so that something new could come about.*

We had just moved to Staunton, Virginia, in the Shenandoah Valley, and that first vision of being demolished was ever-present in my mind. When a new and difficult situation arose in my life, I wondered, "*Is this what He meant?*"

Having adopted Masha and Dasha prior to the move, we now had three teenage daughters to raise. Life was not easy. In addition to Kristina having more learning disabilities than we knew how to manage, now we were dealing with a host of new issues, such as cutting, stealing our car, running off with boyfriends, jail, police at our house regularly, and an unplanned teenage pregnancy, to name a few.

I felt like I had zero parenting skills and was a total failure. Given the girls' early childhood in the Ukraine, I understand now why many of those behaviors happened, but at the time, I was clueless.

Bit by bit, my life continued to unravel, including my marriage, culminating with Chuck and I getting a divorce in 2014 after 27 years of marriage. *How could my friend Forrest have predicted that so many years earlier?* I believed I was living the Book of Job from the Bible. *Seriously, God? Is this what you had in mind? I sure feel like I've been demolished. Everything has gone awry…*

I had hit my bottom…The only good thing about hitting bottom is that there's nowhere to go but *up!*

CHAPTER 39

CRESTWOOD DRIVE

"A fresh start, Mom! Thanks for making this move a short one – just a mile, as the crow flies. But some of us won't be staying with you much longer, as a result of the move. Please know that you didn't do anything wrong. In Boot's case, he had a different mission to fulfill."

– The Fur Family
(now Fuji, Pumpkin, Squeaker,
Chrissy, Luce, Louie)

Chuck and I were officially divorced on October 11, 2014, after 27 years of marriage. Just for the record, I wouldn't wish anyone to experience going through the travails of a divorce or its aftermath, especially after so many years together. And even though ours was not spiteful or financially devastating, it took a toll on my emotional state.

In 2012, Chuck was sent to Africa with the Navy Reserves on a remote assignment for 12 months, which ultimately triggered our breakup. Ironically, he only received that assignment because the previous, shorter one to Kuwait had been canceled. If he had gone to Kuwait, I would have died from the brain injury and subdural hematoma I suffered when I fell off my horse Jake.

Chuck actually saved my life, because I never would have taken myself to the hospital and would have died in my bed. Looking back, it seems like an eerie tradeoff between saving my life and losing my marriage. Somewhere deep within myself, I knew God's hand was in this.

Although it was a majorly stressful, low point in my life and more difficult to endure and persevere through than anything I had ever experienced. I know without a doubt that I wouldn't be doing *anything* I'm doing today if we had not split up. I certainly didn't recognize it at the time, but I needed massive amounts of inner healing and space to grow, both personally and spiritually. For that, I'm eternally grateful.

After Chuck's deployment to Africa, he returned to Staunton but moved into an apartment locally while we struggled over the next year, trying to salvage our marriage. It wasn't meant to be, however, and we moved forward with the divorce proceedings. He accepted a job out of state, but I remained in Virginia. Masha and Dasha moved out, so that left Kristina, me, and our menagerie of nine cats living at Stocker Street.

The feline household consisted of Fuji, Boots, Callie, Chrissy, Squeaker, Pumpkin, Louie, Luce, and a muted calico stray Dasha had found roaming the streets that she named Alice. Dasha recognized her as one of the feral cats she helped feed behind a local grocery store. Although this new calico was sweet and friendly, she was a wanderer and needed her space.

My primary focus now was to sell the house and buy a smaller, more manageable one.

I had a high mortgage to pay, and it was too much to maintain – not to mention the utility costs. I felt like I was its slave and, after all the turmoil I had gone through, was ready to make a complete change.

For the next year and a half, I had the house remodeled, doing whatever it took to find a buyer. That included a massive decluttering effort, selling, donating, and throwing away *so much stuff*. By the time I'd cleared out all the excess, the house actually looked great – almost enticing me to stay, but NO! It was still too much work.

After eight months of keeping the house meticulously clean to show prospective buyers, I was ecstatic when a lovely, retired military couple fell in love with it and made us a great offer. Meanwhile, I found the perfect, smaller three-bedroom house just a mile away on Crestwood Drive. Moving out of Stocker Street with a giant U-Haul was one of the happiest days of my life – a fresh start was on the horizon!

My new house was near the top of a quarter-mile-long hill, which dead-ended into the same wooded forest that extended as far as the Stocker Street house and also circled around behind my backyard. I had a quarter-acre, fenced-in lot laden with gorgeous, large oak trees.

My front yard sloped, giving the illusion of a split-level house. The exterior was constructed with gray vinyl siding on the ground level and red brick enclosing a remodeled daylight basement at the lower level. The living space had an open feel, with plenty of windows for sunlight. I loved it immediately!

I claimed the basement as my "Girl Cave," Kristina took the largest bedroom on the main floor, and the other two bedrooms became my music room and office. The living space was half the size of the Stocker Street house, and so much more manageable!

The best feature of all was that my new home was fully remodeled with a new roof, and I only had to add a few minor enhancements, like having a bedroom closet built in the basement. For the first time in my adult life, I moved into a house that didn't need to be remodeled. *Hallelujah! I've done enough remodeling for three lifetimes!*

This wonderful, small house even had a cat door already installed that led from the main floor to the basement. *How perfect! I wonder if the seller knows I'm a CCL.* Seeing how convenient the little cat door was, I took the opportunity to have three more installed, maximizing the flow of traffic for the cats and minimizing my work of opening and closing doors and windows! *Life is REALLY good now!*

I was unsure about how my felines would adjust to the move, though. This was an entirely different crew than the world-traveling, Japanese family we returned to the States with in 1995. I had a feeling there might be some problems – and there were. It was probably due to the house having less space for nine cats to sort out their territories, but I knew I'd had no other choice than to unload the Stocker Street house.

I was still overwhelmed from the stress of the divorce, getting my daughters situated, and by the move itself, as everything needed to be put in place. Eventually, the dust would settle, but for the time being, I felt out of control.

I tried my best to keep all the cats indoors until they acclimated to their new surroundings, but Alice left immediately. It really didn't surprise me, though, because she never seemed content and eventually was adopted by an older man down the street.

Two weeks after the move, Boots and Callie (two of Fuji's offspring), slipped out of the house and left. I had never experienced this in my previous moves and felt powerless to stop it. I thought everyone felt comfortable in the new neighborhood, but I was mistaken and realized that those two were probably trying to find their way back "home" to Stocker Street.

I remained in touch with several former neighbors who kept an eye out for the two siblings. Callie never showed up, and I, sadly, never saw her again. Boots had a better internal GPS than his sister. He reappeared at the old house a week later – a bit confused, because there was nothing familiar to him on the old property, neither cat nor human. He loved his outdoor territory, though, which was primarily in the yard or up a tree at the house on the corner of the street next to ours.

I drove back to the old neighborhood, called for him in front of that corner house, and there he was! He seemed ecstatic and ran over to me immediately with a happy, familiar cry that completely warmed my heart. I scooped him up in my arms, put him in the car, and drove back home to Crestwood Drive.

Boots stayed for about a week, resting and eating – and then, one morning, he was gone again. I never knew exactly how long it took him to make these treks back to the old neighborhood, but I suspect he took the direct path through the woods, and it was at least two or three days. Once again, I phoned the old neighbors and asked them to be on "Boots Patrol."

This scenario happened four more times. *This cat has an incredible GPS!* I finally had to accept the fact that Boots was never going to stay at Crestwood Drive. Fortunately, one of the Stocker Street neighbors was willing to feed him, albeit keep him outside. I was very grateful, yet sad at the same time, and continued to visit regularly, bringing cat food and other items to help support his upkeep.

I really missed this handsome gold-and-white boy, who always came running to greet me when I called his name. It grieved my heart tremendously to know that he would never live with me again and never adjust to the new surroundings. I felt there was no other option but to let him live in his old territory. I couldn't keep him inside the new house, forcing him to be an indoor cat – that was totally against his nature, and I wanted to honor who he was.

A year and a half after Boots left, I called the family who was feeding him to see whether he needed anything, but they told me they hadn't seen any sign of him recently, and he wasn't coming by for food anymore. He had disappeared.

My instinct told me that something – maybe a fox – had probably killed him. When he was a young cat, I was concerned about how much time he spent outside and that he was too gentle and naïve to be streetwise. I think that was a premonition of things to come. I felt helpless but knew that Boots had lived the remainder of his life the way he chose – to be outside in his familiar territory.

Without Boots, Callie, and Alice, the cat household of nine was now reduced to a meager six, and it seemed so quiet.

Middle Adulthood

Holding Boots

Feeding Time!

Siblings - Boyerfest 2010

Me with Karen at our Boyerfest in Florida, 6 months before she died Summer 2010

Squeaker and me

Squeaker in the Box!

Me holding Luce AKA Lucy due to my gender confusion!

Squeaker and Louie

Luce waiting for his food

Pumpkin, Chrissy Helping me at the computer!

Jake's Computer Sabotage Pic!

Me and Nelly on a trail ride

Me with Jake, forcing him to do a photo op!

CHAPTER 40

I AM A TRAILBLAZER

"Keep following the light, Mom – we're rooting for you!"

— The Fur Family

In 2021, I had a dream that I was hiking through the woods alone in the pitch dark with only the flashlight from my cell phone guiding my steps. I left my daughter Kristina at our house and meandered through the woods, up and down winding hills, moving through territory that I was not familiar with. I could only see what was immediately in front of me, guided by the light from my phone. I finally reached my destination: a small church where the trail ended. After I arrived, I went back to get Kristina and bring her with me.

The meaning of the dream jumped out at me immediately, as I remembered its vivid details. I was being guided by the light of Divine Love on my spiritual journey. I was alone at first, leaving my family and loved ones behind. I was to be a trailblazer, hiking into unknown territory and needing the light to help me forge the way.

When I reached the destination of my spiritual journey, I would then return to share this path with others (family, friends, loved ones, strangers) who would follow the trail after me.

My destination thus far includes experiencing an entirely new realm of spirituality. I now have an understanding in my heart that I am loved unconditionally by the forces of Divine Love (whom I now refer to as

"God" – not the religious, punishing one of my upbringing), and I am part of a collective consciousness that shares in that divinity. I have the capacity to love all of creation with that same love. I'm no longer isolated and in search of the Creator. The Divine Love has been within me all along, waiting for me to "wake up."

My search, which has led to an understanding of reincarnation, the quantum field, communication with all life, and energy healing has just scratched the surface! Jesus said in John 8:32, "You will know the truth, and the truth will set you free." I have been set free and now understand this scripture and others at a whole new level.

My role is to travel this path before my family and those closest to me. I'm not afraid of where it will lead, or the challenges along the way. I am compelled to press forward. God has my back!

I am a trailblazer.

CHAPTER 41

UPWARD BOUND

"Keep searching, Mom, and question everything! The answers will come to you."

– The Fur Family

In February 2014, when I hit my bottom, the furthest thing from my mind was the "vision" I'd had at the Catch the Fire Conferences nine years earlier of being demolished and rebuilt. I was in a bad place emotionally and spiritually, and what sustained me was my responsibility to my daughters, Kristina and Dasha, who still lived with me, along with my first grandson, Daniel, and our cats. Chuck had moved out of state for a different job while the divorce was being finalized, and I was left managing the house.

One positive thing I did for myself was not neglecting my physical state, as I probably walked thousands of laps around the 1.3-mile loop at the local park over the next year, most of them with a man named John whom I had known from church years ago, who had been through a divorce. He was instrumental in helping me pick up the emotional pieces of my life and navigate the beginning stages of separation. John was a sounding board for my woes, gave me wise counsel regarding detachment, and helped me try to establish boundaries for myself.

I even attended daily mass with him *twice a day* for several months, trying to figure out how to cope with change: the life I had known for most of my adult years was disintegrating before my very eyes. I tried to keep busy every moment of the day, was angry at myself that this had happened and frustrated that I couldn't fix it.

When Chuck and I were married, my perspective as a committed Catholic was that divorce was never an option. I had acquired the belief that it was shameful and a disgrace – I would never allow that to happen to me.

In spite of all my religious attempts to connect with God, I still felt isolated from Him and continued to hope that if I did even *more* spiritual things, the connection I craved would somehow magically materialize. Nothing eased the spiritual pain, and my mind spun in circles day after day, trying to figure it out. I also didn't want to be alone, so I continued to fill my time with whatever activities I could find.

Eventually, I realized I could no longer keep up this pace and sought professional help, contacting a therapist (who was also a Russian Orthodox priest, even though I was not attending Orthodox services at the time). He suggested I check out two 12-step recovery groups in addition to our weekly therapy sessions.

While most people associate 12-step programs with addiction, for me, they addressed the emotional, relational, and spiritual issues I couldn't resolve myself. I admit that I had preconceived notions about these groups and expected to walk into meetings where everyone was depressed and complained about their problems, but it was the exact opposite.

As soon as I entered my first meeting, I noticed a calmness that filled the room, and most of the participants exuded a joy that I didn't know existed. They were welcoming and told me to keep coming back!

During the sharing time, everyone took turns focusing on their experience, strength, and hope, applying the tools of the program (i.e., Steps, Traditions, Slogans, Literature) to their lives. They were finding solutions to their struggles, not sinking down into a bed of quicksand suffocating them. My willingness to work this unique recovery process gave me hope that I would get well.

The therapist also wanted me to start incorporating what Orthodox Christians call "The Jesus Prayer" into a daily prayer practice, which is simply this: "Lord Jesus Christ, Son of God, have mercy on me, a sinner." I did my best, repeatedly reciting this prayer for 30 minutes a day. I was still a good rule-follower!

The Jesus Prayer may work for some people, but for me, the only thing it did was further drive home my belief that I was a worthless human being and a failure.

I stopped the therapy but continued with the 12-step groups. This was the turning point in my transformational journey, and I finally began to navigate through the emotional turmoil in my life and begin the true healing process that needed to take place. I'm grateful for having a wonderful sponsor that I met with weekly, outside the meetings, and who helped me work the 12 Steps at a deeper level. Over the years, I have testified at many meetings that this recovery process saved my life.

The 12-step recovery groups are considered spiritual, but non-religious. At the meetings, other members referred to God using terms I had never heard, such as "Higher Power," "HP," or "The God of my understanding."

The beauty is that nobody will tell you what or who your Higher Power should be. That is up to the individual. But acknowledging that something greater than yourself exists is crucial to recovery.

For me, a large part of healing involved reconstructing my image of a Higher Power, which I slowly realized was defined by years of religious churchgoing, approaching God as a penitent person loaded with shame and guilt, believing that any moment, I was going to be condemned to hell if I didn't do things perfectly.

Now, for the first time in my life, *I, Kathy,* could define who my Higher Power was! *Really? I have the freedom to do that, and nobody is going to condemn or judge me if my thinking is different than theirs? Unbelievable!*

I could also call that Higher Power any name that worked for *me*. I didn't have to copy anyone else's Higher Power or follow any particular church or religious tradition. I only had to believe there was something greater than myself to whose care I could surrender my will and my life.

I had lived my spiritual life, up to that point, relying on the belief system of the institutions I had participated in and what I had absorbed from them, never really questioning their relevance, validity, or the impact they were having on my life. I just believed what I was taught.

Despite 30 years of intense religious effort on my part (even attending daily mass for 20 years!), I felt so separated from God and out of place – on the outside looking in – at every church I attended.

A part of me from childhood still craved the "mystical," not exactly like my favorite show *I Dream of Jeannie*, but a place where healings and miracles happened. Deep inside, I still believed it existed, but I was missing the mark. *How could I have grown up in a church with a vast history of mysticism, yet found that it was unattainable?*

The God I had come to believe in was a mean, condemning God who loved everyone but me. Following the divorce, and when John and I were no longer walking together or going to daily mass, every time I walked into the Catholic church, I felt depressed and hated myself. I finally realized this wasn't serving me and had to leave.

I began attending a Pentecostal church in town with contemporary music and a less structured worship style, which I liked. But my negative programming and poor self-image still followed me. Eventually, I had to step away from that, too.

Thanks to my recovery groups, I cried out with what I consider to be my first genuine prayer ever, from the depths of my heart: *"God, who are You, and do You love me?"*

What freedom I felt! If I had been able to hear God answer me at that moment, it probably would have sounded something like this: *"So, you're finally ready to know who I am? Well, hold on tight because we're about to go on the ride of your life! Hop on board!"*

I was finally open to discovering for myself who this "Creator of the Universe" was – and to find out whether He loved me or not. I wanted more answers, wanted to form my own opinions from my own experiences, and wanted to come to my own conclusions. I was becoming an independent thinker! *Took you long enough, Kathy...*

I began devouring books, starting with one that my brother Steve recommended called *The Secret Life of Plants*. We had been talking about two cuttings he'd made from a huge pathos plant with the intention of giving them as gifts. One was for someone special, and he noticed that it was growing at a faster rate than the other, even though their growing conditions and soil were identical.

That led to his remembering this book, which he had read in college in the 1970s. I thought it was an interesting title but didn't see how it applied to his plants, and in no way did I connect it with my search for God. But I felt compelled to order a copy and read it.

The book described in detail various experiments with plants that scientifically documented "emotions" coming from them, as well as an energy field around them. This included Kirlian photography which, according to Wikipedia, is named after Semyon Kirlian, who in 1939 accidentally discovered that if an object on a photographic plate is exposed to a high-voltage source, an aura appears around the image. Another name for this is "electrography." Some photographs of plants reveal that when part of a leaf is broken off, its aura still shows around the entire leaf!

I attribute my introduction to the world of energy associated with living matter to what I learned from this book, and the best part was that it was explained in a way that I could understand. I had difficulty in high school comprehending most of the content in my science classes, although I was great at memorizing whatever was needed to pass an exam. Applying science to real life? Not a chance!

I was utterly amazed at what I learned about plants and their emotions, and as I read the experiments, I began to perceive nature in a completely different way. I confess that I have become a tree hugger, talk to my houseplants and everything growing in the yard, and even apologize to my grass before having it mowed. I was starting to experience a oneness with all of creation and didn't even realize it.

I continued my search for a Higher Power that I could relate to and became fascinated with accounts of Near Death Experiences (NDEs). I had read a few books over the years, all from a Christian perspective, but now I was coming across this topic from other sources.

In the fall of 2017, a friend told me about Dr. Eben Alexander, a neurosurgeon who had an NDE and was writing of his experiences, but from a more scientific approach and an exploration of consciousness.

Near the end of one of his books, he made a fleeting comment, with no discussion or follow-up, that there were documented cases of reincarnation at the University of Virginia (UVA) of children who had memories of a past life, most of which disappeared after they turned five or six years old.

I found out that over the last 50 years, extensive and groundbreaking research had been done by Dr. Ian Stevenson at UVA's Division of Perceptual Studies, who, along with other faculty, collected 2,500 of these cases.

Dr. Stevenson researched multiple accounts of children reporting memories of previous lives and authored 300 papers and 14 books on reincarnation. His masterwork was published in 1997, a two-volume work entitled *Reincarnation and Biology: A Contribution to the Etiology of Birthmarks and Birth Defects*.

Dr. Jim B. Tucker is continuing the research of Ian Stevenson at the University of Virginia and in 2021 published a book combining two of his own works, *Life Before Life* and *Return to Life*, titled *Before: Children's Memories of Previous Lives*.

Eben Alexander's fleeting statement about documented cases of reincarnation had sparked my curiosity and was about to change the course of my life.

I didn't know anything about this strange topic – at least, at that time, it was strange to me – but I was aware that American psychic Edgar Cayce's Association for Research and Enlightenment Center (A.R.E.) in Virginia Beach might have information where I could learn more.

I had heard of the A.R.E. in the mid-1980s through a visiting clarinetist from another Air Force band while I was stationed at Langley AFB, Virginia, a mere 30 minutes from Virginia Beach. She had volunteered to augment our clarinet section for an upcoming tour specifically because she wanted to visit the A.R.E.

I was assigned to be her roommate on the band tour, and as we got to know each other, she talked freely about reincarnation, her beliefs and experiences. To me, at the time, this girl was totally *looney tunes*!

The impression I had from the Christian community in the Virginia Beach area where I lived was that the Edgar Cayce Center was "New Age" and dangerous to my spiritual life. I didn't know what the term "New Age" meant or have any firsthand knowledge about it. I only knew what I'd heard from other people that I respected from my own church traditions.

Today, I understand that term in an entirely different way, from a scientific and astrological perspective. In my experience, I have found many Christians to be scared of things they don't understand, and instead of having an open mind to explore and learn more, they run away. I can say this because I was one of them. Giving myself permission to think differently has changed my life, enriching it and leading to growth in ways I never knew possible.

So, I listened to this visiting clarinetist talk, but inside, I laughed everything away. Now, close to 30 years later, I became intrigued with the idea of reincarnation and wanted to know more.

A few of my friends from the 12-step groups believed in this concept, and some had even experienced "past life regressions," as they are called, but they never tried to convince me of their beliefs and rarely initiated conversations about it. It was refreshing to have friends who sought after a greater understanding of their spirituality yet maintained enough personal boundaries to let me do the same.

I still thought the entire topic of reincarnation was weird, and since it wasn't accepted within my Christian background, I dismissed it as an impossibility. Or was it?

I became more intrigued, especially because there was documented research that might shed some light. Something inside kept tugging at me to learn more. After all, I was on a quest to get answers to my previous question: *"God, who are You, and do You love me?"* Now that I was an independent thinker, maybe I should pursue this concept for myself and form my own opinion…

CHAPTER 42

PAST LIFE REGRESSION #1

"Mom, as we pause for a bit while you learn about reincarnation, we just want to warn you that your life is about to explode – in a good way!"

– The Fur Family

After I finished the book by Eben Alexander that briefly mentioned research pertaining to reincarnation in children, I scheduled a timeshare exchange in Virginia Beach between Christmas and New Year's. Since I was now an "independent thinker," I wanted to check out Edgar Cayce's A.R.E. (Association for Research and Enlightenment) Center myself.

The only thing I knew about the A.R.E. was that it had something to do with reincarnation, and that you could make an appointment to do a Past Life Regression (PLR) at their spa. A friend had told me (to my surprise) that Mr. Cayce had been a devout Christian and a Sunday School teacher, but I knew nothing else about him.

When I walked in the front door of the main building, to the right of the Help Desk hung a large picture of Edgar, calling him "The Father of Holistic Health." *What???* I was shocked! I knew even less than I thought about this man. To me, this validated the healing path I was on, because I had been incorporating holistic health and natural medicinal remedies for at least 20 years, since adopting Kristina.

Edgar Cayce (1877-1945) was known as America's "Sleeping Prophet," because all his 14,000 psychic readings occurred when he was in a deep meditative state (as if asleep) – so deep that he didn't remember anything he said when he returned to a waking state. A stenographer was present to record every word.

Over 9,000 of Cayce's readings pertained to health! This wasn't just a fly-by-night, crazy person. He worked with many different doctors to help implement the remedies he received during the readings. That blew my mind, so much so that I thought I should pay attention to the more spiritual aspect of his mission. I no longer had any hesitation about having a PLR and made an appointment for one the next day. I wanted more answers to the unspoken questions in my head.

According to www.outlanderpastlives.com, Past Life Regression is a gentle form of hypnotherapy that takes you back through time to your previous lives or incarnations by accessing memories and experiences that are normally hidden in the subconscious mind.

It can help you to:

- Understand why you feel a deep connection with certain places
- Explore your past life and current soulmate experiences
- Identify physical ailments that may be remnants of past life experiences

- Explore unresolved emotions which have carried through into this lifetime, creating fears or beliefs that you have been unable to explain
- Acknowledge and embrace the key lessons learned through past lives

Essentially, PLR is a way to obtain information about a previous lifetime that could give you insights into your current life. The facilitator (usually a hypnotherapist) will guide you into a deep state of relaxation to help you access lower brainwave levels of consciousness, such as alpha and theta.

During these slower brainwave states, you are able to relax enough to receive information through pictures, words, feelings, a "knowing," or impressions. In contrast, most of our waking hours are spent in the beta level of consciousness, with faster brain waves.

As part of the 12-step recovery process, I had begun to implement a daily meditation practice and was learning how to relax, so when it came time for the regression, it was easy to be calm and focus on what the hypnotherapist was asking me to do. She was a soft-spoken, middle-aged woman named Betty, whose colorful clothing reminded me of the Caribbean Islands, and who helped me feel at ease, turning off the lights while I lay on my back on a comfortable massage table with my eyes closed.

I was excited to begin, yet fearful at the same time. *What if I do it wrong? What if I don't "get anything?" And if I do, what if I'm making it up? What will it feel like? Will I experience any uncomfortable emotions?* My head was spinning in circles!

At the same time, I felt excited to think that the potential existed of my soul having lived at another time in history, and that I could learn something from this experience that would give me insights into my current life.

Before we started, Betty asked me what I would like to find out from the regression, to help her know what direction to pursue in asking me questions. Once we began, I couldn't think of anything specific, so she read off a list of ideas, and I chose "to love and be loved."

As Betty guided me with her voice into a relaxed state, I was conscious of everything around me, yet in control of my thoughts and actions. I was free to let my mind wander and see what it could perceive. I didn't realize it at the time, but when you are resting in a hypnotic state, you can talk and still remain in those altered levels of consciousness. In future regressions, I would speak when asked questions about what I was seeing, but for this one, I lay there in silence.

That was an aspect of hypnosis that I didn't understand at the time. I had always assumed it was a state of mind where you had no control over yourself and were forced to do whatever the person hypnotizing you asked you to do, like the stereotypical television portrayals of hypnosis. I definitely put that myth behind me!

From conversations with friends who had done PLRs, I was aware that in a previous lifetime, you could be either gender. That was an awkward concept for me to grasp at first, but I tried to remain open. It actually made sense from my biblical perspective that after we die, we are neither male nor female, yet even that was strange to me at first, because, as a child, I had associated my soul as synonymous with my gender.

Although I didn't speak during the session, the scenes I saw were permanently etched in my mind, and I relayed them to Betty as soon as we finished:

- I saw myself as a man in his early 40s wearing a cap from the World War II era. I saw concrete buildings and had a "knowing" that I was in Germany.
- I understood that my name was Ephraim, and I was Jewish. I saw a machine that looked like it was spitting out copies of papers and knew that I was a newspaper editor.
- When Betty guided me to a happy scene, I saw myself getting married to a thin, pretty woman with long, straight black hair. I saw both of our faces, and we were having a Jewish wedding ceremony with lots of dancing.
- As I was guided to learn how my life ended, I saw that I was in a concentration camp and would die there. I didn't see detailed surroundings, yet my soul felt as if it was inside this man's body. I thought about the woman I had married, and that we never had the chance to fully live our lives together. Although I didn't feel the intense emotions that would have accompanied such a death, my impression was that I felt hopeless and that my life had ended too soon.
- Finally, Betty asked who greeted me as I left that lifetime, and I saw 10-15 people I understood to be family members, cheering and welcoming me, pulling me upward. The Blessed Virgin Mary was also present.

Time seemed to pass quickly while I was in the regression, because, in my mind's eye, we changed scenes quickly, but the entire session took nearly two hours! And what I experienced was *not at all* what I was expecting, although I did tell myself to remain open to all possibilities.

I didn't know anything about the "whys" of reincarnation – and actually, a more accurate term might be that we "incarnate again" or "have another incarnation," since we don't come back in the same body. I had not heard of the concept of karma, other than the quip, "What goes around comes around!" And I'd heard the theory that perhaps, between lifetimes, we choose what we want to work on for our soul's growth in the next one. I would learn more about all of this as the years passed.

One thing that made sense immediately, though, was why I have some of the "quirks" that are a deep part of who I am, but that I would never even *think* to verbalize to anyone else. These came into my mind without hesitation:

- I have a strong compulsion to edit and correct everything I come across in written form – including handwritten letters I receive! I'm the poster child for the "grammar police!" I notice every type of editorial error, incorrect spelling, and bad grammar in sight, and not only do I love to write, but I'm constantly re-wording and editing my own work!
- I've never been able to watch movies or portrayals of the Holocaust, beginning in high school when we were forced to sit through actual footage of atrocities committed against the Jews in World War II. Something inside my heart felt like it had died as I sat there in disbelief.

- When I was in college, I went with my boyfriend Jeff to see the movie *Sophie's Choice,* starring Meryl Streep, about a Jewish woman forced to decide which of her two children would live, and then it followed her life of anguish at a concentration camp. The movie just about did me in. After forcing myself to sit through it, I could never again read any articles about the Holocaust or watch another movie or video about it. My chest would get heavy, and it plunged me into a terrible depressed state.
- I've never been "fond" of Germany or its people and always had a cold emotional feeling toward that country, even when I passed through it while stopping there for just one day on a church pilgrimage en route to Bosnia.
- A year after the regression, I happened to stumble onto an article about the Jewish tradition of reading their scriptures from right to left/back to front. To me, this was an amazing insight! For years, I ALWAYS read magazines from back to front, and when I write, I start at the back of an empty notebook and work toward the front. I still do this, even as I'm writing this book in my spiral-bound notebook with an ink pen!

These details might not seem like enough significant information to validate reincarnation or having a previous life, but to me, they were of major importance. My quirks were too odd and deeply ingrained in me. I know without a doubt that I could *never* fabricate a story like this; it was too far-fetched.

One thing I've learned about intuition is that how we receive information is uniquely different for every person, and that goes for how we interpret it as well. What might have tremendous meaning to *me* may not have the same meaning for someone else – much like trying to walk in another person's shoes!

One result of my past life regression was that I believe I carried over resentments to this lifetime from that Holocaust experience and needed to let them go. I've done my best to forgive any soul that might have harmed me, along with the collective evil done by the German Nazis.

A couple years later, I would do another regression called "Life Between Lives," where I was able to forgive the suffering inflicted during that lifetime more completely and was given a greater gift of compassion toward humanity for that terrible time in our history.

Another outcome of my first PLR was that it completely satisfied my curiosity about the whole field of reincarnation, because I experienced it *firsthand* rather than just taking somebody else's word for it. Now, I was totally absorbed in trying to discover things for myself.

While in Virginia Beach, I joined the A.R.E., and in doing so received a copy of a biography of Edgar Cayce called *There Is a River* by Thomas Sugrue, who lived with the Cayce family for several months and wrote the book with firsthand knowledge from Edgar himself. I immediately trusted this as a viable source of information.

When I read the book, I was once again pleasantly surprised at the content, which depicted Edgar as a humble man who only wished to do good and help other people. Sugrue described Edgar's psychic readings, which focused primarily on health but also delved into topics like ancient world history, including

Egypt and the Pyramids, and the lost continent of Atlantis. I was totally intrigued and wanted to learn even *more*!

Reincarnation was introduced in the later readings, which shocked Edgar – a deeply Christian man – along with everyone else. Frankly, he didn't see it coming! Like myself, this was not part of the religious tradition he had grown up with. These past-life experiences showed up in the life readings he gave for people.

Membership in the A.R.E. includes a subscription to their quarterly publication, *Venture Inward,* along with flyers for upcoming events and seminars, like the annual Member's Congress held in June and an Animal Communication Conference by world-renowned Animal Communicator Joan Ranquet. *Hmmm… I wonder what that's all about… Hold on, Kathy, you're just getting started – more adventures await!*

I was so excited that there weren't enough hours in the day to contain me or to allow time for everything I wanted to do! I couldn't wait to see more unfold as the days and months passed.

CHAPTER 43

IS ANIMAL REINCARNATION POSSIBLE?

> *"To answer this question, Mom, we're going to refer you to the Edgar Cayce Library."*
>
> – The Fur Family

Shifting my worldview to include reincarnation as one of my core beliefs really changed

EVERYTHING – how I perceived God, myself, others, the world, and all living things, just to name a few!

What about animals? Have any of my cats or horses been with me before? How could I ever prove something so esoteric? I would never even consider such an undertaking. I was on a personal mission to explore the possibilities for my own life to build upon my ever-growing sense of spirituality and purpose.

The answers to my prayer, "God, who are You, and do You love me?" were still evolving and leading to one thrilling adventure and personal discovery after another.

It took a few days to process what I had experienced during the first past life regression. After I settled down, I felt compelled to research the possibility of animals reincarnating, so I decided to look through the Cayce library on the second floor of the A.R.E. to see if this topic was addressed.

I started to search alphabetically through the cataloged readings in the file cabinets placed near the elevator, with "A" for Animals. It didn't take long to find what I wanted, because the first thing my eyes landed on was a reading that Cayce gave to a family regarding their pet dog!

In Reading 268-3, on February 15, 1933, Edgar Cayce was asked by a woman about her dog, Mona. His answer referred to a previous life she'd had in Rome when the early Christians were persecuted:

30. (Q) Where and how have I been associated with the following:

31. (Q) My little dog, Mona?
   (A) In the same experience.

32. (Q) In the Roman?
   (A) The Roman.

33. (Q) Was she a dog then?
   (A) A lion!

In another Reading, #276-6, it was reported that a 16-year-old girl had known Peggy, her dog, in Egypt.

In my heart, I believed animal reincarnation was possible, but seeing it in writing in the Cayce readings solidified it for me. The fact that I had immediately found the information I was looking for added to the synchronicities that were now happening to me all the time!

A steady stream of these Divine setups would unfold over the next three years, which, when put together, powerfully demonstrated to me the omnipotent wisdom, intelligence, and magnificence of the Creative Forces/God/Divine Love/A Power Greater than Myself – whatever term you want to use.

I'm convinced that *God couldn't wait to reveal this to me!* It was a Divine conspiracy that included my cats, who had been waiting with bated breath for me to figure it out. Every feline had positioned themselves in my life at exactly the right time, in exactly the right place – like a surprise birthday party! With a thunderous roar, they had planned this over eons of time, and their resounding "*SURPRISE!*", in unison, echoed through all of space to finally pierce my open heart!

It was humorous to me as I envisioned all these furry felines planning in advance how they were going to enter my life, no doubt competing for who would be the most pitiful and decrepit looking so that I couldn't possibly turn them away. It was a constant flow of down-and-out strays, and just when things settled down with one, another showed up.

While I mulled over this discovery, I waited until after the second past life regression to start a more active exploration with my own animals. I was still digesting the implications for my life in this new reality. *Everyone I know is going to think I've gone totally crazy! But I don't care – I have to follow the spiritual path that's in front of me.*

Let the adventures continue!

CHAPTER 44

DEMOLISHED AND REBUILT

"Mom, you're doing great by taking the risk to experience something you never expected or knew was possible. We're almost ready to show you that we've been with you before, but first you need to digest all this!"

– The Fur Family

Experiencing that first Past Life Regression, which showed that I lived as a Jew during WW II and was killed in a concentration camp, was both a shock and a relief. I was ecstatic to get some answers firsthand about reincarnation, but what I 'saw' in my mind's eye at the subconscious level was the *last* thing I was expecting.

In fact, as we were getting ready to start the session, Betty, the hypnotherapist, jokingly said, "Maybe you'll find that you were a Renaissance woman who played musical instruments!" That would have been comforting and enjoyable!

But to see myself as a victim of the Holocaust was surreal. I couldn't have made that up in a million years. The scenes were detailed, including the facial features of both myself and the woman I married.

To go along with what I learned from the Bible – that our souls are neither male nor female after we die – my circle of friends who were familiar with reincarnation introduced me to the phrase, "We are "spiritual beings having a human experience." It made total sense, and even more so as I learned from a scientific understanding of "consciousness" that there's a part of us that exists apart from our human bodies.

In a book called *Coming Back: The Science of Reincarnation,* based on the teachings of A.C. Bhaktivedanta Swami Prabhupada, a spiritual leader from India, I came across the term "transmigration" – the teaching that the soul moves from one body to the next after we die. Although I don't accept everything this teacher reveals, I like that concept.

If you want to get technical, transmigration actually happens in our current bodies. As adults, we do not exist in the same body we had as an infant! Our cells regenerate every seven years, so we've existed in many bodies over the course of our current lifetime.

These were weird concepts for me to grasp at first, but the fact that I had opened my mind to thinking differently was exciting! There is a vast amount of knowledge in the world, and I was thrilled to be exposed to new ways of thinking!

After that first PLR, I knew I had opened the door to a different understanding of spirituality, and I couldn't wait to learn more. I was embarking on a new journey and felt totally at peace within myself – possibly for the first time in my life – as if I had been given a gift.

Another unusual thing happened within a week of the first regression, something I would later call a "synchronicity" – an alignment of circumstances that are divinely orchestrated.

By the way, synchronicities have become a way of life for me now. Think of the phrase "to be in sync!" That sums it up, and they're so much fun!

Three days after the regression, I received an email from a Jewish woman I had never heard of, Sara Rigler. I was not on any mailing list from her and have no idea how she included me in her correspondence, but she was searching for people who had lived a past life during the Holocaust for a book she was writing. *Seriously???*

The timing was irrefutable, and there's no way it was a fluke. I was astonished, first to receive her email, and then to have read it without deleting it. I felt compelled to answer and share my story of the regression I had just experienced while the details were fresh in my mind.

I sent off my response and never expected to hear anything more from Sara, because I was still processing the experience and felt like I hadn't provided enough details for my account to be included in the book. I also wasn't sure if anyone would believe my story except for people like my friends who had done a PLR. In hindsight, I realized that Sara's email was an astonishing synchronicity, and I was a perfect match for what she wanted.

Well, she received over 400 responses, and two years later published the book in 2021– even including my brief story. The book is titled *I've Been Here Before: When Souls of the Holocaust Return*.

It's an intense work, and I was humbled when I read the horrific accounts that people remembered, either through nightmares or past life regressions. My account, though, was devoid of the intense emotions many of the other contributors experienced. I wouldn't have been able to handle the regression if it had been any different, and would have had to stop.

So what do I do with all this information? How do I reconcile my new knowledge and experience with the Christian faith I was raised in?

Let me first make a disclaimer: I'm not here to try and talk anybody into *anything!* I'm strictly sharing my own faith journey and the steps along the way. I believe that the Divine Creator works uniquely in each soul and will give that soul what it needs to grow if it is willing and open to receive. It's not a matter of faith being a "cookie cutter" experience for the masses!

It also dawned on me that just as it had been foretold to me at the Catch the Fire Conferences years before, I had truly been "demolished" on many levels and was now being "rebuilt." I felt propelled to keep learning and experiencing more of this newfound spiritual freedom.

Noteworthy to me was that I read from several different sources that in the Third Century, Tertullian, an early Christian author from Carthage in the Roman province of Africa, was instrumental in removing passages from the Bible that directly referenced reincarnation. Could this be true?

It's not for me to say, but there are several texts that remained, which, if read from a different perspective than what Western Christianity has taught us to believe (and even in that sphere, there are so many denominations and interpretations of the Bible that it can become totally confusing), reference reincarnation.

Looking back, there were several biblical passages that never "sat right" with me, according to what I was taught. Stories like in the third chapter of the Gospel of John, when Jesus was talking to Nicodemus, saying that you must be born again to inherit the kingdom of God. Nicodemus's response was, "How can a man come out of his mother's womb again?" What if it meant an actual rebirth in another lifetime? And what if the purpose is for our soul's growth?

And what about in the Book of Malachi 4:5-6, where it says that Elijah must return before the Messiah can come? Jesus references this later in Matthew 17:12, when he says that Elijah has come already, and they knew him not… He was referring to John the Baptist, whom they had killed.

So, was John the Baptist another incarnation of the prophet Elijah? I'd always heard that it was the *spirit* (zeal) of Elijah that John exhibited, but what if that's not what the passage means, but rather that he was the same soul?

Another story that never made sense to me until I looked at it with different eyes is from John 9:1-12 about the man born blind. Jesus' disciples asked him, "Who had sinned, this man or his parents, that he was born blind?" His answer was, "Neither this man nor his parents sinned… but this happened so that the works of God might be displayed in him." Later in the story, Jesus healed him.

What always puzzled me was why the disciples asked if he was born blind because he had sinned. How could a man who was not yet born have done something sinful that caused him to be born blind? In my mind, Jesus' followers had to have believed in the idea of having a previous life.

That brings to mind the whole concept of "karma," which we jokingly refer to when we say: "What goes around comes around!" But that's a topic for another day, dealt with in books written by people who are more familiar and experienced with this teaching. I am not an expert.

These are just a few Bible stories whose meanings I've wrestled with. I don't have to know all the answers, and I don't feel qualified to share anything more than my own experiences and reflections on them in terms of how they impact my life.

I was fascinated about the possibility that reincarnation could be true, and, for me, it also explained some other ideas I wondered about. For example, why do we sometimes "click" with certain people we've never met before, almost as if we already know them? I have heard that we travel in "soul groups," and at the soul level, we recognize each other and have had relationships together in other lifetimes.

And lastly, what about children who have extraordinary talent at a young age – like five-year-old pianists who can perform Mozart concertos perfectly? As a lifelong musician, that is *impossible*, and to me, it has to be a carryover from a previous life.

The topic of reincarnation seems to have no boundaries. There is so much to learn and experience, and perhaps it explains why we even exist on Earth!

In my discoveries and new ways of thinking, I mulled over the idea of the reincarnation of animals but tucked it under my hat for several months. I was still in awe over that first past life regression, trying to process it along with the implications it might have for my life now. And I trusted that when the time was right, more would be revealed. That was my pattern of learning.

Meanwhile, I continued to work on my emotional recovery through the 12-step programs, which I believe is the way Christianity should be taught! Here are some of the shifts I've made:

- I've learned how to forgive myself, rather than continuing to condemn myself for every little thing that's not perfect.
- I've learned how to let go of resentments, which are like giving yourself poison and expecting the other person to die.
- I've learned how to set boundaries to make my life more manageable, thereby reining in my little "empathic self's" tendency to take on everybody else's emotions and problems.
- I've learned that I am not in control of the universe, but that there is a power greater than myself that does have it fully under control.
- I've had my own spiritual awakening as the result of working the steps: I'm not responsible for everyone else's progress.

And incidentally, throughout this process, my spiritual awakening revealed that the *loving* Creator of the Universe has been with me all along. It was *me* who was in the way of receiving that love.

I no longer live with a separation consciousness from God. I'm made in His image and likeness, and that means I have the Divine spark within me, like a solar flare shooting out from the sun! I am *not* the sun, but I partake of its nature.

What incredible implications that has for my life as I move forward – and what freedom!

CHAPTER 45

LUCE'S END OF LIFE

"Mom, I'm so grateful for the few short years we had together. Although some memories of our relationship might seem trivial, like why you named me Lucy and why I deliberately hung around you and Wally, they are vital to your learning these new life lessons. Nothing is ever just a coincidence. And thank you for letting me show you when I was ready to cross over. I loved the freedom to experience the fresh outside air just a little bit longer."

– Luce

Shortly after I moved to Crestwood Drive, I became acquainted with a wonderful man named Wally, an electrician who was instrumental in my soul growth for the next six years. Although life's circumstances and geographical limitations haven't yet aligned for us to be together permanently, we had an incredible, deep bond, and he was my biggest cheerleader for this spiritual journey. We talked for hours about our inner lives, and he was the best listener I'd ever met.

Whenever he came to my house, Luce – the tall, lanky, now-beautiful white cat I mistook for a female when he came to me on Stocker Street as a skinny, filthy stray – *always* showed up. Like the other cats, he was both indoor/outdoor, but when Wally and I were together in my house, Luce appeared – from seemingly out of nowhere – and proceeded to jump on whatever piece of furniture we were occupying. He would find a cozy spot next to us, curl up in a ball, and fall asleep – a very contented cat! None of the other five remaining cats ever graced us with their presence – only Luce. This predictable routine continued for the remaining two years of his life.

Two months before Luce passed away, I noticed that he was losing weight. He was such a large cat that it wasn't readily observable, but the decline likely started months before that, and now it was happening more quickly.

I paid closer attention to his size after I went out of town for a week. When I returned home, the weight loss was dramatic, and he was about half his original "big self" weight. He would come to his food plate as if hungry and then walk away. I made an appointment with the vet immediately.

From my experience over the years with other cats, when their weight loss finally becomes noticeable, more often than not, it's too late for recovery, and whatever illness has crept in will eventually lead to their death, usually sooner than later.

For a cat to survive in the wild, it must not appear to be vulnerable to a predator, because its life will be at risk. For that reason, cats will hide their physical infirmities until they are no longer able to conceal them, and by the time they're noticeable, the sickness has become severe and often irreversible.

As a cat parent, this has been beyond frustrating, leading to huge amounts of guilt and causing me to second-guess almost every end-of-life decision I've made over the years. Each time, my mind replays the same scenario, which looks like this:

- *How did I miss seeing the signs?*
- *Why didn't I do something sooner?*
- *I let them suffer too long…*
- *If only I had known they were seriously ill...*

Then, when my cat dies, *more* guilt creeps in over whatever end-of-life decision I made on their behalf:

- *They suffered too long, and it was my fault.*
- *They will never forgive me.*
- *I should have had them put to sleep before it got this bad.*
- *I should have let them die at home.*
- *I'll never forgive myself.*
- *If only I had done something more.*
- *I wish I'd known what my cat had wanted.*

It's this final thought that sticks in my mind. What *did* my cat want? Even before I was an Animal Communicator, I tried my best to look for any sign the animal might give me to show what they wanted. Sometimes, the answer would come through my intuition, but often, it was circumstantial, like when Louie (the black-and-white kitten that found us at the gas station) "vanished" when it was time to leave for the scheduled appointment for him to be euthanized. I canceled it, and a few hours later, he reappeared. That was my sign to let him die at home.

Louie lived another week and even continued with his hunting escapades. The day he died, I had gone to work while he lay resting on the living room floor, believing he would probably not make it through the day. Then, when I came home later in the afternoon, he was still on the floor, and at the *exact moment* I walked in the door, his body shook as his spirit left, and he was gone. He had waited for me to return. It was bittersweet, and while painful to lose yet another cat, I realized that Louie had once again taught me about Divine timing: first when he waited for us at that gas station to be adopted, and now at the end of his life.

Now, as an Animal Communicator, I'm so grateful to be able to help others with their animals and to try and find answers to all those end-of-life questions and emotions that can debilitate us for years.

Luce's vet visit did not have a happy outcome. He tested positive for both Feline Leukemia and Feline FIV (a viral infection). There was no hope for recovery, and it was just a matter of time before his immune system totally collapsed, and his physical body would be nothing but skin and bones.

The vet thought it might only take a couple weeks. My options were to have him euthanized that day or wait a little longer. His behavior was normal, except for not eating. He was still drinking water. And while at the clinic, he was rubbing against my legs and purring. He definitely wasn't ready to go, and I wasn't ready to let him.

When we came back home, I said to him, "Let me know when you're ready." I wasn't sure how that was going to happen, but I felt in my heart that somehow it would. Although I was not yet an Animal Communicator, I still believed in the animal-to-human connection, and if we try to be in tune with our animals, they will give us the answers.

The difficulty "hearing" them, however, often happens when our own emotions – namely, fear, doubt, and anxiety – take over. They can cloud our ability to follow that intuition.

On the flip side, I've done my best to ask this question of all my animals when they are dying: "Have you given up on yourself and lost the will to live?" The answer is often the determining factor to guide me in what I should do. If they still want to be here, I'll let them, and try to make them as comfortable as possible.

Two more weeks passed, and Luce continued to lose weight but was still drinking water. I knew his days were numbered, but I kept trying to encourage him and offered food anyway.

Then I noticed he was unsteady when he walked down the stairs. I worried about his safety but was still waiting for a clear sign that he was ready.

He continued to go outside regularly, like he always did, and created a new favorite sleeping spot amidst a beautiful patch of orange mushrooms that seemed to spring up overnight, unlike any I had ever seen before.

I could sense his death was imminent, but something significant happened during the last week of his life. On Wally's next visit, this faithful cat immediately walked over to him and rubbed against his legs. I made the comment, "It looks like he wanted to see you one last time." What a bittersweet moment.

I didn't realize it at the time, but my comment to Wally was an intuitive hit. Luce *did* want to see him one last time – he had *waited* to die. The reasons became clearer after my second past life regression.

After Wally left, Luce was gone for two days. The guilt set in. *I didn't see the signs, and he went off to die by himself. I waited too long.* Then this resilient cat came back, and though I breathed a sigh of relief, my heart was filled with panic and indecision – two emotional states I had lived with before on multiple occasions. I felt paralyzed and couldn't do anything but wait.

My tall, white, handsome furry boy went outside one final time, and this time was gone for nearly three days. I was convinced once again that he had gone off to die by himself.

When similar scenarios happened in the past with other cats, I felt like a coward, wanting to be released from the outcome and circumstances of the cats' final days and justifying it by saying, "Well, they wanted to go off and die by themselves."

While I believe this is sometimes true, I also recognized that I didn't want to experience my own pain while watching them die and wanted to avoid taking on the responsibility of deciding when that would happen. I felt conflicted.

It reminded me of the scabies-infested Tiger Cat in Japan who died the morning I had scheduled a vet appointment, and the Bible verse that happened to be read at mass that day: "I, the Lord, deal death and give life." I learned a huge lesson about loving every animal as much as I can while they are with me.

After Luce disappeared those final two nights, I gave up all hope of finding him again. Then, lo and behold, in the middle of the night on the third day, I awoke to use the bathroom at 3:30 a.m., and Luce was lying on my bathroom floor, curled up in a ball, sleeping.

This was the sign I'd been waiting for, and I knew it was time – he had returned to let me know he was ready. What a major stretch of faith that was for me, waiting it out and living with the agony of not *knowing*.

I called the vet clinic as soon as they opened and brought him in that morning to be put to sleep. While we were by ourselves in the waiting room, I believe his spirit was already transitioning to the other side. He no longer responded to my voice and had the distant look in his eyes I was accustomed to seeing when they are "there, but not there." He died peacefully while I held him, with tears in my eyes.

Luce was only with me for five years, but his sweetness and docile personality still remain. I was happy that the scrawny, filthy white cat with a few black spots and long legs had wandered onto our property without fanfare, joining the feline crew almost unnoticed, to be loved for the final years of his life. He died with dignity when he was ready.

CHAPTER 46

PAST LIFE REGRESSION #2

"Okay, Mom, are you ready? I told you my short life with you was important – even though you gave me a girl's name. (I'm still laughing about that!) I was such a handsome guy, too! I wish we'd had more time together this lifetime, but it wasn't our first time together, and I hope it's not our last!"

– Luce

After my first Past Life Regression, I was ravenous to learn everything I could about reincarnation and the Cayce material, including the Ancient Mysteries and holistic healing. My limited view of the world had begun to open up, and I was now a sponge, absorbing everything I put in front of me. My years of spiritual seeking and hitting dead ends was over; my search for answers now came to life.

I once heard a comment at a 12-step meeting that seemed to describe me perfectly: "When the student is ready, the teacher will appear." I was more than ready and couldn't wait to explore this new view of the world and gain more clarity about the meaning and purpose of my life.

Synchronicities became part of my daily awareness, and six months after the first PLR when I attended the Members Congress at the A.R.E., they seemed to multiply and have babies! I could write another book to share all the divinely orchestrated events and insights that happened during that annual event.

Most significant was my second Past Life Regression. Now that I knew the protocol, so to speak, I wanted to experience another one. And this time, I had questions:

1. Had Wally, the electrician that I had a deep connection with, and I been together in any previous lifetimes?
2. What is my relationship with animals?
3. Did I live in Atlantis in a previous lifetime? The Cayce readings talk extensively about the lost continent of Atlantis, and I remember that, as a child, when I first heard the name, something stirred inside me. Now I was *really* intrigued.

I scheduled another appointment with Betty, the same regression hypnotherapist as before, and opted again to go with the intention of "To love and be loved," trusting that she knew what she was doing by asking me to set a specific intention, even though it was still a new concept to me. Later, through my studies to become an Animal Communicator and Energy Healer, I would learn that setting intention is of *utmost* importance in directing where the energy goes or is applied and can largely determine the outcome of your endeavors.

In this regression, I was willing to talk out loud when asked questions, but only when I needed a prompt to help if I was stuck, confused, or needed clarity.

As I relaxed once again into a deep, meditative, slower brain wave state of consciousness, I viewed another lifetime, and the first thing I saw was a narrow river, slightly wider than a stream, with a wooden rowboat parked on the shore. There was nothing else near it except woods.

Then the scene moved to a wooden house that I perceived to be built in the mid-1800s. I understood that I was living somewhere in Virginia during the Civil War. I was a large-boned woman named Lucy, somewhat tall, with long, black hair. When asked what my occupation was, I knew immediately that I was a seamstress.

There was a husky, bearded man holding a rifle standing near the house. I perceived that we were married. Like the first PLR, I saw clear facial features of both of us. There was a dog in the scene, but I didn't see details.

I had a "knowing" that the man I was married to at that time was Wally in this current lifetime. He looked different, just as I looked different, but I had that understanding. This was such an important detail to me that I wanted to make extra sure I wasn't *making it up* or forcing it through *wishful thinking*, so I asked Betty to help me with more understanding of what my relationship was to this husky, bearded man.

Using her own intuitive skills, Betty saw an image of "a man holding a ball of light" and that he was a love interest, not a father or brother figure. She had no idea that Wally was an electrician, but it made perfect sense to me and solidified my first gut reaction of knowing we were married in that lifetime.

I continued to relax in this meditative state, and Betty asked me to move my awareness to a happy scene. I saw a group of people dancing in lines (myself included), similar to the

Virginia Reel that I had learned in high school. I had the awareness that one of the musicians I play with in a local dance band was among them.

I then moved my awareness to a sad time and saw that my husband was shot in the back and killed by Union soldiers at our house. I felt no emotions during any of these scenes, but only the awareness that they were happening, and I was viewing them.

The scene at the end of my life showed that I was older, with long gray hair, lying in a bed with a younger woman holding my hand. I didn't recognize who she was and didn't associate her with anyone I knew in this lifetime. I died peacefully from an illness.

Betty asked me some other questions, including "What was your soul group's purpose?" I had been told that souls travel together through multiple lifetimes to help each other in their growth, and that a soul group could consist of thousands of people.

As I pondered that question, the only answer that came to mind was that we were here "to help the animals." I didn't share that with Betty until we were finished, because I was doubtful about its importance at the level of an entire soul group. She reaffirmed that helping animals was definitely a purpose!

"Coincidentally," a few months later, when I attended the Animal Communication Conference at the A.R.E., and my teacher, Joan Ranquet, repeated the exact same phrase about her soul's purpose, I knew I had found my tribe!

After I finished viewing the Civil War lifetime, Betty guided me to another location, directing me to a room surrounded with glass cylinders that stood 1 to 2 feet tall and about 3 inches wide, similar to glass vases without bottoms.

She asked me to choose one, pick it up and look through it. So, I did with my mind's eye, and I saw the coastline of an ocean along a sandy beach. In the scene were large dinosaur-like animals, and I immediately had a Knowing that I was in Atlantis. It was a brief scene, and then I put the cylinder back in its place.

Then she wanted me to ask my soul group to come and help me. When I did, the room (which had the lights turned off) began to get very bright until it was full of white light. My eyes were closed the entire time, and I thought maybe Betty had turned the lights on, but she hadn't. As we ended the regression, the bright light slowly faded, and when I opened my eyes, the room was just as it was when we started – nearly two hours earlier – with the lights turned off.

I had received the answers to the questions I'd posed before we started the PLR, and I knew without a doubt that Wally and I had been together before, I had an important role with animals, and I had lived in Atlantis.

Like the first regression, when I finished and came out of hypnosis, I questioned myself, *"Am I making this up?"* Once again, the details were too far-fetched for me to come up with on my own while in that meditative state. I know without a doubt that the images came into my mind without my searching for them.

Another similarity to the first PLR was that the scenes were vividly etched in my mind, and there were some quirks in this lifetime that I wouldn't dream of sharing with anyone else; but to me it made perfect sense that they were "carryovers" from the Civil War lifetime. I believe I am a composite of all my previous lifetimes, and that some of them are having more of an influence on me in this current one than others.

For example, when I was a teenager, I learned how to sew in 4H Club and was virtually unstoppable at the sewing machine. I was a sewing fiend, and in addition to day-to-day items, made all my formal dresses for band concerts and dances, costumes for Halloween, and many clothing gifts for others.

I was even determined to figure out how to make a quilt, so I designed one and constructed it all by myself. I was obsessed with sewing until my mid-20s, when I lost interest. That was a leftover trait that eventually disappeared, but nonetheless, for me it was a strong connection to that lifetime as a seamstress during the Civil War.

Wally is an avid Civil War history buff whose favorite hobby is metal detecting for relics. He has a great love and loyalty to the state of Virginia, and his connection to that era is indisputable.

Two other details from that regression blew my mind when I made the connections. The first hit me like a ton of bricks later that day while I was driving. I had known immediately that my name was Lucy and remembered that my cat Lucy/Luce appeared in the room *every* time Wally was at my house, determined to be with us wherever we were. I had made the passing comment to Wally in jest about Luce waiting to see him one last time before he died, thinking it was sweet that he was rubbing against him and walking in and out of his legs.

Why was it that I literally couldn't think of anything else to call him except "Lucy" when I was searching for a name? *THAT CAT WAS WITH US BEFORE! Was this far-fetched?* To anyone else, maybe, but not to me. It was an intuitive hit, sent to me in my unique way of receiving information.

I knew in my heart – without any hesitation – that we had known this cat in a previous life. The name Lucy didn't make sense when I named him (thinking it was a female), but I believe I was inspired to choose it, so that later I would understand the connection with Wally and put two and two together.

I don't know if Luce had been a cat, dog, or different animal – or even the dog that I saw in the regression, which is a strong possibility – but that didn't matter. I also believe without a doubt that Luce knew and remembered both of us at the soul level.

The other detail I marveled at, and thought was an *interesting coincidence,* was that in each PLR, both women I saw had detailed features and long, black hair. I thought it was odd that of all the possible features women could have, *they both had really long, black hair…*

I didn't think about the implications of this until at least a year later, when I recalled a comment Wally made to me early in our relationship when I asked him what features he liked in a woman, and he said "long, black hair." (I certainly didn't fit that preference in this lifetime, but it was never important in our relationship.)

I made the connection with the long hair immediately with the Civil War regression, but knowing that we were also together in the Nazi Germany lifetime that I learned about in my first past life regression shocked me! These were the two most recent lifetimes prior to this one, and it certainly explained our deep bond. Again, it was another specific, intuitive hit that nobody else would understand.

During the first PLR, I didn't have the wherewithal to find out if anyone in this current lifetime was also present in previous ones. I was just enthralled with the *possibility* of reincarnation and wanted to have my own experience of a regression without preconceived ideas of what would happen.

Now, I was beginning to tune in to that subtle inner voice that had lain dormant for so many years: My Intuition. I had shut it down so completely that even the thought of using skills other than logic and reason to navigate through the world and make decisions was inconceivable.

So, what was next on my all-out learning agenda? The four-day Animal Communication seminar was a mere three months away. This student was definitely ready!

CHAPTER 47

JAKE'S UNEXPECTED DEATH

> *"Mama, this was a tough time for us. I hated to leave you so soon, especially because I knew you weren't ready for me to go, but you'll understand later that the timing was perfect. You were set to embark on the next phase of your life, and my role was changing. I'm still here, though, helping you from across the veil with your new mission. And I'm still your 'handsome fella'!"*
>
> – Jake (wink wink…)

After the second past life regression that revealed I had lived during the Civil War, I was excited and invigorated, because the insight I'd gained gave me the extra "oomph" and confidence I needed to continue on this new path of spiritual growth. Part of that insight was that one of my soul's purposes in this lifetime is to help animals.

I had signed up for a four-day Animal Communication course at Edgar Cayce's A.R.E. Center and had no clue as to what I would learn or experience, but I knew it involved talking with animals, and I wanted to know more! *Maybe becoming a Doctor Doolittle wasn't just a fantasy!* I planned to leave my house at 8:30 a.m. to arrive in time for the first session.

To prepare myself for the three-and-a-half-hour drive the next morning. I decided to be a couch potato with my cats and relax while watching Netflix. But my Zen moments were interrupted by an unexpected phone call from the barn where I boarded my horses, Jake and Nelly. It wasn't good.

Jake, my 24-year-old chestnut gelding was lying down in his paddock, and they couldn't get him up. He had colicked. In a horse, this occurs when there are problems in the gastrointestinal track, and it's very painful. There are over 70 different types of intestinal problems in horses that can cause colic symptoms, which range from mild to severe (life-threatening). Ideally, you want to detect it early, and it's vitally important to get the horse standing up and moving around.

They called the vet and asked me to come out immediately, so I bolted from the couch, – leaving cats scattered all over the room – and drove out to the barn as fast as I could. The barn was nine miles away, but my speed that night made it seem more like five.

The vet managed to get Jake up just before I arrived, but he was obviously in a distressed state and mentally distant, like he was in his own world.

Whenever I went to the barn, Jake always came running to greet me with his characteristic happy nicker, anxiously awaiting his treats. This time he barely responded. I walked him back and forth on the unpaved driveway near his paddock, while the vet tried various techniques to help untangle his insides. This included inserting a long tube into his body through the throat and neck.

I walked him to an enclosed part of the barn to separate him from the other horses and monitor his symptoms. After a couple hours, he finally had a bowel movement and seemed to be improving.

I made the decision to come back home after staying with him for nearly three hours, because I was conscious of the long drive I had to make the next morning through heavy traffic. It was important to be rested and alert. I knew without a doubt I was supposed to attend this conference.

When I left the barn, Jake was walking around, had a couple more small stool movements, and seemed stable enough to make it through the night. So, I said my goodbyes and drove back home. The owner of the barn's adult daughter, Hannah, agreed to stay and check on him periodically.

When morning came, there were no texts or voicemails on my phone, so I assumed all was okay at the barn. I loaded my car, and as I was getting ready to start the engine, the phone rang. I assumed it was a follow-up call to say that Jake was doing fine, but instead it was the dreaded call that every animal owner fears: Jake had passed.

Hannah had stayed with him until midnight and then checked on him again at 4:00 a.m., and he seemed stable. But when she returned at 8:00, he was lying on the ground and no longer breathing.

I was stunned. *How could this have happened? And why on earth did it happen the morning I was leaving town to attend, of all things, an Animal Communication Conference?*

Even though I didn't understand that the course of my life was about to change, I had a gut feeling that this was Divine timing, and that somehow there was a connection between Jake's death and my new direction in life.

I started my car, pulled out of the driveway, and cried all the way to Virginia Beach.

CHAPTER 48

I KNOW WHAT I WANT TO BE WHEN I GROW UP

"You're getting it, Mom: Becoming an Animal Communicator is your next step! We can't wait to see how much fun you're going to have when you figure out what's REALLY on our minds (heehee…). This is going to be SO exhilarating and a lot less work for us. Oh, and you're going to receive a bunch of healing in the process. Woo-hoo!"

– The Fur Family

When I arrived at Edgar Cayce's A.R.E. Center in Virginia Beach for the first session of the Animal Communication Conference, I slowly scanned the L-shaped room looking for a vacant seat among the other 30 attendees.

I spotted one at the far-left corner in the front row and quietly walked over there to sit down. *Perfect. Nobody will notice me, and I will be able to clearly see and hear the teacher without any distractions.*

Joan Ranquet, world-renowned Animal Communicator and Energy Healer, stood on the small, elevated stage in front of the auditorium and asked us to briefly introduce ourselves, sharing where we were from and our reasons for attending.

In a flash, her eyes landed on *me*, as she smiled and said, "Let's start with you!" *Oh, no…*

I wasn't ready. I didn't have time to prepare an introduction, and all I could blubber was that my horse had passed away that morning. I was met with much empathy from her and everyone else, but I sure didn't want to be in the spotlight. *What have I gotten myself into?*

I survived that uncomfortable moment and listened to everyone else share their stories – I would become very good friends with some of them as we spent the next four days together.

Joan began by explaining telepathy, the mental transference of pictures, words, and feelings from one being to another. It is the foundation of learning how to communicate directly with an animal and the technique we would begin to develop and practice. This concept opened a world that I never knew existed – I could hardly contain my excitement!

I always perceived telepathy to be like those occasional "mind reading" moments when I would call my mom, and she would say, "Isn't that funny? I knew it was you!" I never thought of it as a skill that could be developed by everyone, but rather as something limited to the few people who were born that way.

But I learned from Joan that this was the way humans used to communicate before language was developed. We use telepathy when we are babies, but as we learn how to speak with words, the skill falls by the wayside, much like building a muscle at the gym – if we don't keep it strong, it weakens.

But all is not lost! We can strengthen our telepathic muscles again and learn to communicate with animals in this way! *Okay, I'm intrigued! You've got my attention now!*

We were working with energy, which is not bound by time or space. Consequently, you don't have to be present with an animal to communicate with it. You are connecting with it remotely – inside its energy field.

We practiced the technique using photos of Joan's animals that she projected on an overhead screen, which were tools to help us zero in on a particular animal and connect with its energy field. At that point, we were actually communicating with the animal in real time, through intention, beyond the boundaries of time and space.

Although today I do remote sessions with my eyes closed, the image I hold in my mind from a photo helps me focus and direct my intention to the animal who needs healing. With further training and more practice, I've been able to do remote sessions without a photo, but it's not my preference.

Additionally, connecting with an animal in a meditative state is important, because being in a slower brain wave state (alpha or theta at the subconscious level) helps us tune in more clearly to our intuition and be better able to receive pictures, words, and feelings.

I didn't see this analogy during the conference, but it's the same with people – you don't have to be present with another person to communicate with them directly! With technology, energy is flowing through either a telephone line, the internet, or a wireless network. Using telepathy allows us to bypass the technology and communicate from within, directly, using our God-given bodies and souls. *This is awesome! I feel like I've entered The Twilight Zone!*

After the second day of class, I wanted to try this new skill with my other horse, Nelly, who had just lost her pasture mate and best friend Jake. She was without him now for the first time in several years.

That evening, I experienced a heart-to-heart connection with my beautiful, 22-year-old chestnut mare, the first horse we had bought 12 years earlier. I marveled at this process as the words flowed from my heart to hers, and I told her, "You did your job well as Jake's companion." I had never perceived her in that way before, but *I knew that I knew* that I had connected with her.

On days three and four, we were introduced to an energy healing modality called Emotional Freedom Technique (EFT), also known as "Tapping." It involves literally tapping with your fingers on or over various acupressure points on the face, head, and chest to release stored emotions from the body.

Joan first demonstrated this technique to the class, instructing us to tap on ourselves while she led us from one acupressure point to the next. Then she used it on a dog named Bandit that one of the students had brought in, who was having a problem with his mouth.

Bandit was a rescue and had been previously abused on the head by his former owner's groomer. Consequently, he wouldn't let his new owner or anyone else come close to his face to help him.

This EFT demonstration on Bandit was even more remarkable to me than tapping on ourselves, because it was impossible to *touch* the dog to do it. Joan and his owner tapped in the air near

Bandit's face and head, visualizing the points and entering the dog's energy field through intention. The class also tapped in the air from a farther distance, directing our attention toward Bandit and into his energy field.

In less than a minute into the tapping, Bandit totally relaxed, yawned, dropped his head, and actually lay down on the floor, sprawled out in front of the entire room. I couldn't believe what I was seeing! *I have to learn how to do this!*

I felt like I was finally home! I knew I was on the right path, and at 58 years of age, I had finally figured out what I wanted to be when I grew up: an Animal Communicator!

* * *

At the Edgar Cayce Center, they often have a psychic available on the weekends, and you can schedule a reading. Some psychics are also mediums, a person with the ability to communicate with humans and animals who have passed on, which was the case that day. I thought that might be an interesting thing to do, just out of curiosity, so I decided to book an appointment and ask the medium if she could connect with Big Boy and find out if he was going to come back to me again in another incarnation. "What the heck?" I figured.

Even though I was attending this conference to learn about Animal Communication, I was still enthralled with the idea that, just like people, animals could be with us over multiple lifetimes. I had really never gotten past Big Boy's death, even though it had been nearly 20 years since he'd passed. It was a really deep wound.

The readings were conducted in a small corner of the bookstore sectioned off with curtains. I sat across a small table from the woman doing the reading, showed her a photo of Big Boy, and told her what I wanted to find out. I also wanted her to try and connect with my father, who had died in 1996.

After she finished, I thought the 20-minute session was a waste of time and money, where Big Boy was concerned. She stumbled over her words, unable to get any information except a little bit about what his character was like. I didn't need to know what he was like – I already knew! She spent 15 of the 20 minutes talking in circles. *Why did I spend my money on this?*

Then she moved on to try and connect with my father, and that was completely the opposite experience. It was beautiful and brought me to tears. I actually felt my father's presence, and she relayed a message that I knew was totally from him. Wow!

What was the deal with Big Boy? Why didn't she get anything? I mulled this over in my head, and months later it occurred to me that she was not allowed (from the Divine Forces) to have access to the information I'd asked for. I believed there was an important lesson for me to learn that I had to find out for myself. That was part of *my* journey, and eventually the question of Big Boy returning to me was answered in a very profound way. But more on that later.

When I arrived home after the conference, there were two things I did immediately:

First, I went out to the barn to see Nelly and tried to use what I could remember of the Tapping skills I had learned (rudimentary though they were) on her.

I did my best, trying to work her through the emotions of losing Jake, and although it wasn't what I would consider a technically stellar Tapping session, my intentions were solid, and within a minute, Nelly's head dropped, and she was licking and chewing the way horses do when they relax and submit. I was shocked! I wasn't expecting that reaction – actually, I'm not sure what I was expecting, but I knew it was going to work!

My relationship with Nelly changed and deepened as the result of both when I communicated with her telepathically from Virginia Beach and later used Tapping on her at the barn. She had always lived in the shadow of Jake and his demanding personality, and now it was her turn to be the center of attention. I could feel the difference in my heart.

Next, I enrolled in Joan Ranquet's School, Communication with all Life University, (CWALU) in the Animal Mastery Program. I didn't want to learn just *one* skill – I wanted all of it! I wanted to learn *everything* about Animal Communication!

Additionally, I would learn a lot more about working with energy and would facilitate healing through using both EFT Tapping and another modality called The Scalar Wave that targets physical issues. This was the technique I would later use with Squeaker, when he had urinary tract infections. His follow-up bloodwork confirmed that they had definitely improved.

I, too, could become an Animal Communicator – and an Energy Healer – *and I did!*

For the next 18 months, I attended weekly Zoom classes, practicing Animal Communication, EFT Tapping, and learning The Scalar Wave technique, and traveled to California for two nine-day intensive training sessions at Joan's ranchette with other students, expounding upon these techniques and much more.

I completed a large number of case studies to get hands-on experience in each of these modalities: Animal Communication, EFT Tapping, and The Scalar Wave. After I graduated from the school in July 2020, I enrolled in the Teacher Trainer program to receive more mentoring from Joan and help teach some of the weekly classes.

I was grateful for my lifelong trait of "unwavering perseverance." Two years later, at the ripe young age of 60, I was embarking on a new career – yes, I talk to animals! I wouldn't have it any other way.

CHAPTER 49

DOES THIS STUFF REALLY WORK?

> *"Mom, there are so many animals that need your help! Have confidence in what you do! WE certainly believe in you. You just need some practice in getting used to hearing us in a different way."*
>
> – The Fur Family

As a musician, I can easily measure success by how accurately I play the correct notes and rhythms of a song. Of course, there are other elements of music that are subjective, like expression, phrasing, and dynamics, but at least part of a performance is measurable. With intuitive work, there is no tangible way to do this. I have to rely on intuition, developing my telepathic muscle enough to gain confidence and trust that the information I'm receiving is accurate.

As I learned to communicate with animals, there were ample opportunities to practice, practice, practice and develop that muscle. Not only did I have 18 months of weekly classes, but to graduate I had to have a bazillion case studies in each of the three modalities – Communication, EFT Tapping, and the Scalar Wave. Even so, there are times when I still wonder, "Am I just making this stuff up? Does it really work?"

One of my early case studies was with a horse named Blue, a black, two-year-old gelding that Cindy, a friend from high school, had rescued a year earlier.

Blue had been en route from Alabama to a slaughterhouse in Canada with numerous other horses in a crowded truck. Apparently, they were supposed to be "inspected" before they crossed the border, and luckily for Blue, the man inspecting them saw potential for this young horse and separated him from the others. For the remaining horses that weren't so lucky, they would sadly suffer an agonizing, inhumane death at the hands of the "meat men," as I have heard the slaughterhouse workers called.

Although these killing facilities have been outlawed in the United States, that hasn't stopped the transport of horses across the border, slaughtered primarily to provide meat to European and Asian countries. They are brought to slaughter in every possible condition – old, young, sick, healthy, injured, and even pregnant. According to the Humane Society, more than 50 percent of horses sold at rural auctions go to slaughter after being bought by "kill buyers."

Sorry to be so direct about the reality of this abuse, but the mistreatment of animals is a difficult subject for me to even mention. My experience of having companion horses has been enlightening and beautiful, and their incredible spirit, intelligence, and faithful service to humanity shouldn't lead to such a horrendous death.

The inspector gave Blue to a woman who lived nearby the place where he was unloaded. Nothing was known about his early life, but from his acting out, he had likely been severely mistreated, not to mention being freaked out from the stress of traveling such a long distance. They had to heavily sedate him so he could be gelded, do bloodwork, and have some teeth pulled.

The woman who agreed to keep Blue was deathly afraid of him and couldn't take on the responsibility of such an emotionally damaged horse. Through the horse rescue circles, Cindy was notified and was willing to come and get him. When she picked him up, she found him in a stall by himself. They'd left his halter and lead rope with him, but it took over an hour plus a 50-foot lunge line to finally load him into her trailer.

Blue was completely traumatized, and although it had been over a year since he was rescued, he still didn't trust anyone – human or horse – except one other gelding that he'd bonded with.

When I arrived to meet them, I went into the paddock with Cindy to greet all five of her horses. Blue positioned himself alongside his friend in the back of the herd. We gave them treats, then walked back out while I figured out my "plan" to communicate with this scared, young horse. Since he wouldn't let me approach him, I definitely couldn't do it while inside his paddock, so I pulled up a lawn chair and sat down about 20 feet away from it, facing the herd.

Most of my training took place remotely, so when it came time to start my case studies, I didn't have a lot of experience doing sessions with animals in person. It was now up to me to take what I had learned from class and practice with animals both ways – remotely and in person.

Blue was one of my first, and I admit it felt awkward! It's a different dynamic than connecting with an animal through a photo because of the distractions in a live setting. It's *vital* to develop a good meditation practice to be able to shut out those distractions and hear the animal.

I was nervous, and doubts started to creep in. *What if this doesn't work? What if I don't connect with him? What if I'm just making it up?* But I kept my focus as I sat in the chair, faced the paddock, got quiet, closed my eyes, and connected with Blue in the same manner I had done in the weekly classes, tuning in to pictures, words, and feelings.

After I quieted myself, I opened my eyes and was astonished at what I saw: Blue had come out of the herd and walked over to the fence in front of me, staring at me with his ears up – a sign that he was alert and listening! *Oh, my God!*

Cindy was watching from a distance and thought Blue had come to the fence to look at her husband, who was doing yard work, but he was nowhere in sight. Blue had clearly stepped out of the herd to pay attention to *me*!

I was caught off guard! I was dumbfounded and not sure what to do in this live setting – especially with Blue staring directly at me!! *Should I close my eyes? Would he think I was rude if I wasn't looking directly at him?*

Really, we were connecting with our hearts, and it didn't matter whether my eyes were open or not. I moved past that awkward moment and closed them again, allowing me to ignore outside distractions and hear better telepathically.

I focused within my heart to listen and had a beautiful session with this young gelding, letting him "get a load off his chest," including how he had felt when he was alone in that stall after the horrendous ride crammed in with other horses. He also wanted me to relay his gratitude and appreciation to Cindy. It was one of the most magical Communication moments I've ever had, and tremendously meaningful to all of us.

I also did some EFT Tapping on Blue in his energy field, but a few feet away. Since he didn't trust me enough to stand close, I was unable to tap on him directly. Then, three days later, I did a Scalar Wave energy healing session on him remotely.

As a result of all three modalities, Blue calmed down and Cindy was able to touch him in areas where he previously hadn't let her. She continued diligently working with him and eventually achieved her goal of finding him a forever home where he is now thriving! What an amazing experience, one which I'll never forget.

* * *

Another monumental case study which boosted my confidence was with a beautiful grayish-blue, long-haired cat named Vincent, who lived clear across the globe in Australia. His human mom, Kim, had contacted CWALU looking for help, and I was assigned to work with them. This handsome boy was pooping all over the house —except in his litter box – and Kim was at her wits' end.

Vincent was less than three years old and had a very rough start to his life. Kim was his third owner, and she suspected that he might have been either abused or neglected in a previous living situation. Plus, he had only lived at the second home for a few months.

He was transported by plane to meet Kim, but during the flight, his water dish had tipped over, drenching him and causing more trauma. The reason she contacted CWALU was to try and address the pooping issue.

We set up several appointments, again integrating all three techniques: Communication, EFT Tapping, and The Scalar Wave. Over the course of a few months, I worked on Vincent remotely in multiple sessions and also did Tapping with Kim to help alleviate all the emotional stress she was experiencing.

Through a telepathic Communication session with Vincent, I was able to dig deep into his emotional trauma, trying to find out when it originated. Eventually, he revealed that the combination of all the changes that had taken place in his life up to that point had caused him to feel unsettled. He didn't know what was going to happen next or if he would be uprooted again, and didn't feel safe. The bad experience on the plane ride had topped it off. That helped me know how to direct the Tapping sessions.

The result? A much calmer cat who stopped pooping outside the box! Even Kim's friends noticed the difference and remarked at how much calmer he was.

What a testimonial for me about the effectiveness of EFT Tapping, working in conjunction with the Communication modality. I like to think that Vincent became the poster child for the work I do!

* * *

The most profound Scalar Wave energy healing session I've ever done was for a cat named Meanie, whom I refer to as "Meanie the Miracle Cat." In typical synchronistic fashion, I met his human, Ruth, at my house the night before his accident when I hosted a group of women who were interested in learning more about Animal Communication.

The next afternoon, Ruth called me in a total panic. She had accidentally run over Meanie with her car as she was backing out of her driveway! She didn't tell me specifics at the time, but just that he was lying on her porch in a ball – not moving, but still alive.

In her despairing state, she asked if I could do an emergency Scalar Wave session on him, and thankfully, the timing worked for me to do it immediately.

I've never worked with a more *intense intention* than when I worked remotely on this cat! I moved the energy through his body using all the skills I could muster. I had no inkling as to what the result would be, but I knew it would help in some way.

Ruth came to my house the next day to report that Meanie had gone off by himself and was nowhere to be found. She didn't even have a chance to take him to the emergency vet. She presumed he had gone off to die by himself. When I heard this, I was disappointed and felt sad for Meanie. My heart also ached for Ruth and the anguish she was going through, but I knew I had done the best I could.

Three days later, Ruth called and said that Meanie had shown up at her house that morning, and one of her daughters asked, "Mom, that looks like the cat you hit the other day. Could that be him?" It was indeed Meanie, and to her shock, he showed *no signs* of having been in an accident!

That's when she told me that after she hit him, he had blood coming out of his eyes and all over his face. Now, he looked totally normal.

It blew my socks off! I knew the Scalar Wave worked, but Meanie's recovery was above and beyond my wildest expectations. Ruth felt the same way and even commented that perhaps she should change his name to "Lazarus"!

* * *

Sometimes, Communication alone can make a huge difference to an animal, like my experience with a 12-year-old black lab named Luna that had been surrendered to a local dog rescue just a week earlier.

Sarah, a volunteer dog walker at the rescue, was very drawn to this girl and noticed that she might have some health issues. So, she brought her home as a foster to try and help.

Within a few days, Luna began urinating in the house, even though she knew how to use the doggie door to go outside. She seemed unable to control herself. Sarah contacted me to see if I could help with this behavior issue because they were at a desperation point, and if it continued, they would have to return her to the shelter.

I communicated with Luna remotely and asked her several things, such as what would help her adjust, did she like massages, riding in the car, treats, and baths. And of course, I asked about the peeing issue.

Luna definitely had a lot to say: She was shell-shocked and had lost her bearings. She was totally confused about what was going on in her life and didn't know what to expect next. Everything familiar had been taken away, and this had caused so much stress that she felt disoriented, resulting in her losing control over her bladder.

It made total sense. Sarah started implementing some of the things that Luna liked immediately, such as giving her a blanket to lie on and a soft ball to carry around. Luna was also specific about what areas of her body she liked to have rubbed and what areas were sensitive, which was helpful to both of them.

The next day, Sarah reported that Luna *had not had any accidents in the house since our session*, and that she seemed calmer and more relaxed! The change was so dramatic after just our Communication that it wasn't even necessary to do any Tapping with her!

Sometimes an animal just needs to get a load off its shoulders, like we do when we need someone to confide in. The very act of *letting it out* can make all the difference in the world. (And I'm happy to report that Luna became a "foster failure," and Sarah kept her!)

Going back to my original question, "Does this stuff really work?" Well, the answer is a whopping, big YES! It sure does! *Who woulda thought?*

CHAPTER 50

SQUEAKER THE WISE GUY

"Mom, you were so easy to manipulate! Sometimes a cat just has to have fun. On a serious note, thank you for all the care you gave me, especially during the last stages of my life. I loved being on the receiving end of the energy healing you were learning. I started to feel young again!"

– Squeaker

Squeaker was one of the gentlest, most tolerant male cats I've ever had. He loved to lie in the grass and, well, not really do anything! He was just content to be right where he was, living a stress-free life interrupted only by occasional bouts of playfulness from Pumpkin, our fluffy orange, precocious, ragdoll cat who liked to tackle him just for the fun of it! Thankfully, it was mostly in jest. Otherwise, there would have been broken bones and cat fur all over the yard, leaving two bald cats sulking all by themselves in the grass.

When Pumpkin played tackle, he slowly crept up to Squeaker and swiped at him just long enough to get his attention, then backed away. Squeaker didn't react the first five or six times until finally he'd had enough and fully engaged the tackle. The first time I witnessed this, I was horrified, as my unspoken rules for the cat household included "No fighting, and nobody gets hurt." I even gave them my *Look of Death*, along with my less-than-congenial tone of voice – until I realized they were just playing and totally behaving within the rules. Yet, as annoyed as Squeaker was by Pumpkin, they became the best of friends and played this game often.

Squeaker saw himself as a "very wise cat," and, in fact used those specific words to describe himself to two of my fellow Animal Communication classmates. After I enrolled in Communication with all Life University (CWALU), part of our studies included practicing telepathic communication with each other's animals. Our beginning skills included learning the animal's essence and favorite things directly from the animal itself. This way, the animal's owner could validate our results, helping us build confidence in our telepathic skill development.

Squeaker relayed his essence to both my classmates at separate times, using those exact words, which not only gave me a greater respect for Squeaker and his wisdom, but also a huge amount of confidence in the skills I was learning as an Animal Communicator. But while both students nailed it, I almost died laughing! I agreed that Squeaker was wise, but I personally thought he was more of a "wise guy," as he proved on two separate occasions.

The first one occurred when I moved into the smaller house on Crestwood Drive following my divorce. I placed the computer desk against the left wall of the living room as you walk in the front door, taking up most of the wall space. This is where I sat almost every night to attend an online class, do household bookkeeping, or just unwind while browsing the internet for music videos.

Squeaker had a hefty appetite, and every time I was within 10 feet of the kitchen, he wanted to eat. Since the house was small, pretty much anywhere on the main floor was near the kitchen, and the computer desk was totally within food range, from Squeaker's perspective.

One evening, I was sitting at my desk for an online class, and Squeaker magically appeared near my legs, trying to get my attention. He loved to sit upright with one front paw touching whatever he was next to, and the other one "pawing" at me repeatedly, most often wanting me to pick him up and put him on my lap. As he aged, he didn't have the ability to jump up on my lap anymore. In fact, I put stepping stools in front of most of my furniture so that he and the older cats would be able to climb them and successfully reach their intended destination.

On this night, I did the usual routine of bending over to pick him up. This time, however, he evaded my grasp and walked away. He did this three or four times. I was getting more and more annoyed as I was really trying to focus on my class. *What's wrong with this cat?* From his point of view, however, it was very simple: What *he* was trying to do just wasn't working, and *I* was just not getting the message.

He then changed his strategy and went to "Plan B." He nonchalantly walked over to the front door and waited there, positioning himself for me to open it and let him outside. I thought, "Oh, he wants to go out!" So I emerged from my comfy, black faux-leather computer chair, and walked about 2 feet toward the door to let him out. He waited till I was completely away from my chair, and then made a beeline for the kitchen, making sure I was following him by turning his head around to check. He had duped me! He wanted food, and the only way he could get me to go to the kitchen and feed him was to trick me into getting out of my chair and faking that he wanted to go out!

The second occasion took place in one of the back bedrooms where the TV was located, as well as a daybed which served as both a guest bed and a couch. One of my favorite ways to unwind at the end of the day was to lie on the daybed and watch either Netflix or a baseball game with my Major League Baseball (MLB) subscription.

One evening, I was very comfortably sprawled out on the daybed with the television on, and again Squeaker tried to get my attention to go into the kitchen and feed his bottomless pit. *BUT I JUST DIDN'T FEEL LIKE IT!* No other reason than that, really. I thoroughly enjoyed my relaxing time, and didn't like being interrupted. This evening was no exception. *He can wait…*

Once again, having no success at getting my attention, Squeaker pulled out his bag of tricks and came up with another ploy. I glanced over at him, and saw that he was sitting on top of some magazines in the shelf below the television. I looked away, and then quickly looked back at him in a double take, thinking, *He looks like he's going to pee…* And he not only LOOKED like he was going to pee, but that's exactly what he did! I FLEW off the daybed and grabbed him, scolded him, and sent him to "kitty cat time-out," which meant he was banished outside the house. Then I tried to clean up the mess in the cabinet as best I could, totally furious.

Squeaker, however, wanted to have the last word. Once outside, he immediately hurried to the back of the house and easily came back inside through the lower cat door he could reach; then he came marching back upstairs, heading straight to the bedroom, where I was still cleaning up his mess. He sat by the door – on the OUTSIDE – looking at me. I give him credit for having the presence of mind to *not* try and come into the room again. However, he waited with a demanding look as if to say, "*Well, I'm waiting… Aren't you going to feed me?*" This was a little less than funny at the time, but now I can look back and laugh, marveling at his ingenuity.

Squeaker really did make me laugh, and as cats go, he didn't have a mean bone in his body. He tried his best to communicate with me in the "non-telepathic way," before I became an Animal Communicator. He lost his hearing during the last few years of his life, and when he wanted to lead me somewhere, he'd start walking – you guessed it – mostly to the food bowl in the kitchen, but occasionally to the door to be let out. Knowing that I often got distracted trying to do too many things at once, he would turn around, look to make sure I was still there, and keep walking.

His efforts at communicating were especially noticeable when something was wrong. Over the years, I've rarely had issues with cats urinating outside the litter box, and when they did, it was often the result of a physical problem that required veterinary attention.

In January 2019, nine months before Squeaker passed away, I had begun to notice some liquid in one of the square-shaped, colored Tupperware plates from which the cats ate on the kitchen floor. I was thinking "liquid vomit" at first, as there was no noticeable smell to it, but when I poured it out, it had that "urine color," and I knew that's exactly what it was. This happened several mornings in a row.

I suspected Squeaker right away, although I didn't catch him in the act at first. It turned out that he had a urinary tract infection (UTI) and needed medication. He also had thyroid issues and was at the very beginning stages of kidney disease. This required that I put a medicated cream on alternating ears to bring the thyroid levels back to normal, and that I change his diet. At the time, I thought Squeaker was only about fourteen to fifteen years old, but the vet seemed to think he was more like twenty. This certainly explained why he was not only extraordinarily wise, but also why he seemed to be having an onslaught of health challenges.

I was applying the cream to his ears every day and continuing to treat the UTI, which turned into either one long infection that never went away, or three separate ones, and we were on our third round of antibiotics. This was a four-month-long merry-go-round. Finally, the vet suggested they send Squeaker's blood work to an outside lab to determine the specific strain of bacteria that was present, so he could prescribe the correct antibiotic to treat it.

During this time, I was learning the Scalar Wave Energy Healing modality that I now use regularly as an Animal Communicator and Energy Healer. It can be broken down into two main parts, and is administered within the animal's energy field, either in person or remotely. I frequently perform Scalar Wave Healing, as well as the Animal Communication sessions, remotely. From the quiet of my home, I'm able to get into a deep meditative state (usually the alpha level of consciousness) and put myself in the animal's energy field – no matter what the distance between us – through *intention* and visualization.

One of the amazing discoveries for me was that energy is not bound by time or space, enabling me to work in a different location from the animal I'm helping. This concept wasn't difficult for me to grasp, as with my cell phone I can easily and instantly connect with someone clear across the globe. Energy Healing is like having my own wireless internet connection. In fact, one of my favorite case studies was the beautiful cat named Vincent who lived in Australia – halfway around the world!

Here's how a Scalar Wave Energy session works, whether I do it remotely or in person. First, by setting my intention to heal, I use my hands to feel and connect with the universal healing energy outside the animal; then, I run this energy into and through the animal's body, up and down the "chakras." The purpose is to balance these ethereal disks of spinning energy that correspond to certain nerve bundles and major organs in both human and animal bodies. There are seven main chakras that run along the spine, and each has a corresponding color exactly like, and in the same order as, the colors of a rainbow.

When I work on an animal in person, sometimes I have to start from a distance if the animal won't let me get close. If I'm across the room, I visualize my hands hovering over its body as I move the energy. If the animal is calm enough so that I'm able to sit next to it, I hover my hands directly over its body without touching it. To someone watching me, I probably look either like a crazy person or a dropout from a sign language class because of the way I use my arms and hands. They are usually moving around in silly positions in mid-air, shifting the energy around; I would definitely *not* want to be caught doing this on camera!

Next, with *intention* and using my hands, I bring the bioscalar energy, which I envision as white light, into the center of the body from three different directions. I start with (1) the top of the head and bottom of the feet, then move to (2) the left and right sides, and finish with (3) the top and underside of the body. This energy meets inside the middle of the body as it flows in from each opposing direction. The waves then cancel each other out, stop oscillating, and create a single standing wave. I've also heard this standing wave referred to as *zero-point* energy.

The *Scalar Wave* is a term in physics for this type of energy. Dr Valerie Hunt (1916-2014), an American scientist, university professor, and author, explains this energy when used within the body as the *Bioscalar Wave*. (For a more in-depth explanation, check out an excellent article called "Healing with Bioscalar Energy," posted June 30, 2016, on Awaken.com).

After I bring this energy in, I get lovingly bossy and tell it specifically what to do, according to the needs of the individual animal, such as: "Increase blood flow and circulation in the right paw."

Finally, while this energy is still at that zero-point place in the animal's body, I create the perfect, healthy cell and replicate it exponentially until it has spread throughout the body.

A typical session takes 30-40 minutes. Animals love it and often fall asleep while I'm doing it, both remotely or in person. While I target physical healing to help facilitate the body to heal itself, the Scalar Wave yields results in many different ways. It can help reduce anxiety while increasing vitality and speed up the healing process. And it even can alter bloodwork, which was the case with Squeaker!

I've learned from experience that illness and disease will first appear at the energetic level before the physical, and so, too, for healing. When the energetic field is healthy, the body will follow suit. Hence, healing takes place at the energetic level first, and physical changes can appear either immediately, within a few days, or usually within a month.

Sometimes, there are amazing results after only one session; other times, it may take more than one to work through more serious health challenges. Often, when combined with other practices such as EFT Tapping, acupressure, better nutrition, veterinary care, or training, amazing results can take place! Scalar Wave energy work is part of a truly holistic approach to healing.

As students, we practice these techniques on our own animals, as well as each other's, and have a considerable number of case studies to complete before we graduate.

I was in the early stages of learning to work with energy, and my instructor, Joan Ranquet, asked us to choose an animal to begin to learn the technique with, so I chose Squeaker, as his health was the most fragile of my remaining four cats. He became my first Scalar Wave Energy Healing case study! His condition wasn't changing – still on thyroid medication, special food for his kidneys, and waiting for the bacteria to be identified with the prospect of another round of antibiotics. I was very worried about him, and figured I had nothing to lose.

I had so much to learn, but was extremely focused on following the guided verbal instructions from my class session on Zoom, completing all the steps I mentioned above. Squeaker was in the room with me, but I was not hovering over him while I moved the energy through him. As this was new territory for me, I didn't know how it would affect him, or whether it would even work! In short, I didn't know *what* to expect!

The next day, Squeaker literally came *running* from the side patio to the front door when I called him! I hadn't seen him run in ages! It warmed my heart that he was obviously feeling so much better. That was my initial hands-on experience with the power of the Scalar Wave.

And then it got even better. I took Squeaker back for more lab work after I'd done the Scalar Wave healing – and the test came back negative. There was no longer any trace of bacteria in his urine. He had no infection!

I sure became a believer on a whole new level that what I was learning to do was powerful, and that I would be able to help so many animals! To say I was excited would be an understatement.

Squeaker definitely had more energy and seemed so much happier. Over the next few months, I gradually backed off from using the thyroid medicine on his ears. Well, okay, so he made it clear in his Squeaker-like fashion that he didn't want it anymore by trying to run away when I grabbed him to apply it. I had also noticed that he seemed to be trying to scratch at his ear, so I believe it was getting uncomfortable and possibly even causing a skin rash.

I also quit the battle of trying to get him to eat the kidney diet cat food, especially when the other cats were eating something different. He was a foodie, and I just let him eat whatever he wanted. Looking at the bigger picture, Squeaker was at least 20 years old, had led a full, happy life for the 10 years he'd lived with me, and the fact that he was feeling better overall was good enough for me to stop these uncomfortable and un-tasty protocols.

But while the immediate crisis was over, there were other health issues happening simultaneously that were never diagnosed, including something he kept pawing at in his mouth. He did have a tooth come out, accompanied by a fair amount of blood, but recovered from that. He would sometimes paw at his face again, but I never knew why, and I couldn't bring myself to take him back to the vet. He had had enough. I'm convinced that's what he wanted as well, so I chose to let the last part of his life unfold naturally and try to make him as comfortable as possible.

I did other Scalar Wave sessions on him to continue practicing the technique, and although we didn't have further blood tests done, there were definitely positive changes in his health. His overall attitude, energy, and demeanor were the most normal for Squeaker that I had seen in a long time. And I've since had clients' animals diagnosed with kidney disease whose blood work returned to normal following Scalar Wave sessions.

Given his improvements, I was taken aback when Squeaker passed away a few months later, in late August 2020, at home in the middle of the night. There were a few signs that perhaps might have indicated his time was drawing near, but they were subtle, and he didn't seem uncomfortable. I'd noticed that he wasn't going outside hardly at all, had been sleeping a little more than usual, and his sleep seemed very deep. The night that he passed, I had been watching TV with him next to me, and so I just let him stay there sleeping while I went to my bedroom, which is the entire basement of my small house. He was in a very deep sleep, and I didn't want to disturb him.

At about 2:00 a.m. I woke up suddenly to a loud, wailing cry in my room. I knew it was Squeaker, and immediately turned on the light and jumped out of bed. He had made his way down the stairs and was lying sprawled out on his side, just a few feet from the foot of my bed. The next few moments became a blur. I crouched down to the floor to start petting him while he lay there, and at the very moment I touched him, he quietly took his last breath. He lay there motionless, and I realized with tears in my eyes that he had put forth a huge effort in coming downstairs to let me know it was time to go; he wanted us to be together when he left. I knelt down next to his still warm body and continued to stroke him, even though his spirit was no longer there. My heart was broken, and I was too distraught to fall back asleep for the remainder of the night.

Later that day, a friend came over to help bury him in my backyard next to Luce and Louie, and when I opened the door to go outside, a butterfly flew right by me. I immediately thought, *That's Squeaker giving me a message that he's free now!* For the next few days, butterflies continued to unexpectedly present themselves in unique ways. They gave me hope and helped reinforce my belief that Squeaker was still there, only in a different way now. It was painful, yet very comforting.

CHAPTER 51

CHRISSY

"Mom, I'm sorry I had to leave so soon after Squeaker, but our souls were traveling together, and I had to go, too. Grieving over two of us within just a few weeks' time was difficult, and we're sorry it happened that way. We sent you butterflies, though, as a reminder of our transformation and rebirth into the afterlife. We hope you liked them!"

— Chrissy

The three-week time period right before and following Squeaker's death at the end of August 2020 became a blur. Multiple events were happening at the same time, too much to process all at once.

Squeaker was spending noticeably more time indoors, and Chrissy, my beautiful, 12-year-old tan-and-white female, was right there with him. I had never seen them together as much as this, albeit sleeping in separate boxes, baskets, and shelves in the living room.

This was out of the ordinary, because both cats were fairly independent, and I had never noticed any particular bond between them. They both usually preferred to sleep outside during the summer months, but hardly ever near each other.

I also made a mental note that Chrissy was starting to look a little thinner. She displayed no signs of illness and had never been sick a day in her life, so I wasn't overly concerned. In fact, when she came back to live with us at age three, she was our largest cat, even surpassing her brother Boots, who had larger front paws that he never fully grew into.

Squeaker's declining health consumed most of my time, and I didn't give Chrissy's seeming weight loss much thought. Looking back, I know I was in a state of denial, not wanting to have to cope with another cat's failing health so soon after months of taking care of Squeaker. Losing one cat after the other, along with my horse Jake, was taking a huge toll on me emotionally.

Chrissy's appetite was decreasing, perhaps due to the summer heat, or maybe she was upset that Squeaker was failing. She showed absolutely no physical symptoms of having anything wrong – only decreased appetite. Very baffling.

After Squeaker passed, Chrissy's smaller size was much more noticeable, and I kept a close eye on her. She was definitely eating, but very small amounts.

While she continued to lose weight, another odd thing happened. I was driving by my old neighborhood on Stocker Street when Boots, Chrissy's brother, came to mind. We sadly never knew exactly when Boots had died. The young couple that was feeding him didn't know either. He just stopped showing up at their house to eat.

But I knew in my heart that some type of predator had no doubt taken his life. I was heartbroken that I hadn't been able to keep him from returning to our old neighborhood after we moved to Crestwood Drive, but I couldn't change his mind about where he wanted to live. I would visit him when I could and think of him with an aching heart when I drove past his old stomping grounds. It was devastating to me that he was no longer part of our daily household.

This time, though, when I drove through those familiar streets, the impression in my heart was *much* stronger than usual. I couldn't get Boots out of my mind. It was odd, too, that when my daughter Kristina and I were eating dinner together, for some reason, she kept calling Chrissy "Boots." She had never done that before. As difficult as it was for her to remember names, she never got the cats' names confused. She even mused, "Why do I keep calling her Boots?"

It was now a week after Squeaker had passed, and Chrissy's decline was increasing exponentially. I was in shock at how fast this was happening and felt totally helpless. Plus, it was now Labor Day weekend, and the vet clinics were all closed.

She didn't appear to be in pain late Saturday night when she was sprawled out on the bathroom floor. And even then, she purred continuously the entire time when I petted her. She was giving me mixed signals, and they only increased my panic and confusion.

As an Animal Communicator, when I'm distraught over one of my animals, I find it difficult to get into a neutral meditative state to communicate with them. And now, I was no longer rational. *What's going on here? How did this happen so quickly? I'm at my wits' end and don't know what to do. I'm not over Squeaker's death yet, and I can't think straight.*

I decided to take Chrissy to the local emergency vet on Sunday. She was very quiet, with just a faint meow, but still purring steadily. I sat in the waiting room at the vet clinic with her for two painfully slow hours, watching various distraught pet parents come and go. Finally, it was my turn to take her to an examination room. I described her symptoms to the vet tech, wondering if there might be a problem with her teeth – still not realizing the gravity of the situation.

The vet tech had a deadpan look on her face and left the room after initially checking Chrissy out. I waited with my beautiful girl, who was now almost fully asleep, still quietly purring as I petted her.

The vet walked into the room about five minutes later, and based on what the vet tech had told her and what she observed, said that Chrissy was in liver failure. Her eyes and face color signaled jaundice. *How could I have not seen this? How could this cat, who'd never been sick a day in her life, suddenly stop eating, and then be in liver failure in less than two weeks?* I had no idea…

There was no hope for recovery, so I told the vet I wanted to have just a few minutes with her alone. I didn't see any alternative other than to have her humanely euthanized while we were there, although she was already starting to drift to the other side, and no doubt would have passed on her own within a matter of minutes.

Those precious moments with Chrissy broke the pattern of the end-of-life emotional torture I had inflicted upon myself over the course of my adult life each time I was about to lose a cat. I generally had no peace, berated myself for not doing more, and stuffed my feelings.

This time, I was more compassionate toward myself. It had been a stressful time for months with Squeaker. I loved all my cats tremendously and have always done my best to take care of them, even when there might have been other choices I couldn't see at the time. I tried to make the best decisions with the information and circumstances at hand.

Ten days earlier, Squeaker had come to my bedroom to find me and be with me when he left. I was hurting but knew that the end of his life happened just the way he wanted. He died at home with those he loved.

And now, it seemed as if Boots had been paying us a visit from the other side all week long. In hindsight, I had no doubt he was present with us, and was waiting to escort Chrissy across the rainbow bridge.

During my Animal Communication and Energy Healing studies, I had discovered a whole new level of understanding of life, the afterlife, and living with a purpose. So in my last moments with Chrissy, I told her it was okay to leave, and that Boots and Squeaker were waiting for her and were there to take her with them. I reassured her that it was going to be okay. Then I asked her a favor. I asked if she could send me butterflies after she passed on behalf of *all* my previous kitties. *But how could she ever do that?* I wondered. *There are so many.*

I sat with her as they inserted the needle, and she transitioned quietly and peacefully. I knew she had escorts to the other side, but my heart still ached. It was way too soon to say goodbye to this beautiful, sweet girl who was only 12 years old and had always been in perfect health. It didn't seem fair. I hadn't even processed Squeaker's death yet, but here I was burying Chrissy less than two weeks later, on Labor Day. She now lay peacefully in my backyard on Crestwood Drive, next to her friends Squeaker, Luce, and Louie.

The next day, when I walked to my mailbox at the end of the driveway, I inadvertently glanced toward the ground near the base of the wooden post that held my box, and there was a plant with pale pink flowers freshly blooming all over it. Hovering over the flowers, flapping their wings, and looking beautiful, were butterflies too numerous to count! *Oh my gosh. They sent them to me!* They were all a similar bluish color, except for one little white one. I figured that one was from Chrissy.

Grieving two cats that died within 10 days of each other was tough, but this time, I allowed myself to grieve rather than stuff my feelings and deny the pain, again changing my previous pattern. I also allowed time for my remaining two cats, Fuji and Pumpkin, to grieve as well. It was a somber time around the house while we all did this together.

I intuitively knew that Chrissy and Squeaker were supposed to leave at the same time. Their souls had been traveling together, and there was nothing I could have done to change the outcome. My mind once again flashed back to the Tiger Kitty in Japan who died from mange the morning I was going to take him to the vet, and the scripture verse I was given that day from the Bible reading at church: "I, the Lord, deal death and give life."

I'm grateful to Squeaker, Chrissy, and Boots for the appointed time we had together, for the joy they brought into my life, and for what they showed me about death – and, of course, for the butterflies!

CHAPTER 52

FUJI'S IMPECCABLE TIMING

"Mom, it's time for you to finally tell the rest of the story of how you put all the pieces together and finally realized that Big Boy had returned as Fuji. (Of course, he made it fairly obvious, as his soul has a flair for the dramatic!) We love this story so much, along with your other discoveries, like the healing power of energy work. We're so glad you became an Animal Communicator and that you opened your heart to new ways of thinking. Fuji was especially gifted, though, and through her soul's amazing connection with you, she showed you that she was with you in your previous lifetimes, and that her beautiful soul will be a part of your future. Her impeccable timing represents ALL of us! Although you were a rather 'slow learner,' when your 'aha' moment came, it was so worth waiting for!"

– The Fur Family

Fuji, the calico we brought home from the apple orchard in 2005, eventually became the feline matriarch. She had gained a fair amount of wisdom over the years, but I believe her most astounding quality was her sensitivity to energy. She was highly in tune with the healing work that I do, often jumping on my lap while I did Scalar Wave sessions remotely on other animals. And, she had the uncanny ability to show up at the most unexpected times.

My greatest "Aha!" moment related to Animal Communication and Energy Healing started out as an EFT Tapping Session with one of my tapping partners through CWALU. Of course, Fuji was present.

Tapping, as I've previously shared, is a way to help remove emotional stress from the physical body. It's administered by literally *tapping* your fingers on a specific set of acupressure points, either directly on the body or from a distance, with intention, in the body's energy field.

I have used this technique with both humans and animals and try to stay within the scope of my training by dealing with emotions related to animals or animal-related trauma. This usually centers around a difficult situation or circumstance involving an animal that my client perceives as traumatic, causing emotional wounds that haven't healed.

I try to target the root cause of the troubling emotions and the subsequent debilitating effect they can have on the person or animal for years. The goal is to release the stored emotions so that my client is no longer triggered by either the memory or a similar event in the present.

Sometimes, the release can happen after one session, or sometimes, it might take two or three. For instance, you no longer cringe every time you see a bee after having been stung multiple times as a child.

Here is an example from my life:

When I was 10, a neighbor's German Shepherd scared me to death every time I walked by their house. He was contained behind a fence, but always ran toward me, barking, when I walked along the fence line on my way to the top of Wellington Street.

Grrr... woof-woof... Grrr... was the sound I heard every time he approached me. I was terrified of that dog before I even left the house, regardless of the fact that he was in a confined space. As a result, I felt uncomfortable and stressed every time I was in proximity to a German Shepherd for the next 45 years!

As an Animal Communicator, it's important to be free of any emotional blocks that would impede my ability to connect with an animal and get correct information. If I did not heal this childhood trauma, it would be difficult for me to have a communication session with a dog I'm afraid of.

I targeted that memory during a Tapping session with one of my homework partners from CWALU and had amazing, immediate results. The next day, I started seeing German Shepherds everywhere, beginning in my Facebook newsfeed. The first post was a heartwarming video of one helping a kitten up the stairs. I had no fearful reaction! I also had no reaction to these beautiful dogs on subsequent walks in the park.

I'm no longer afraid of German Shepherds. In fact, one greets me at my car every time I go out to the barn to visit Nelly!

The story of the German Shepherd seemed like such a small incident, but it had clearly impacted my life. *What about something more traumatic? Could those wounds ever heal?*

Big Boy, the faithful tiger cat that I had an incredible bond with, had died in a way that haunted me for 20 years. The guilt, regret, sadness, and self-hate had never fully left me. Additionally, I lived with the fear of getting too attached to another animal, which manifested in two ways: (1) I was afraid to feel the grief of losing another being that I loved so much, and (2) I was afraid I would be betraying my loyalty to Big Boy if I did.

His death was one of my deepest wounds regarding animal-related trauma, so in April 2020, when I was tasked to practice Tapping with another CWALU student, this was the scenario I chose to try and heal.

My Tapping partner was Dr. Bernadette Spector, VMD, an Integrative Medicine Veterinarian who was also completing the Animal Mastery Program, and we did this remotely, by phone. First, I led her through a session centered on the emotional trauma around the death of her beloved soul-companion dog, who had passed a few years earlier.

Then it was my turn. Prior to this assignment, I had been reluctant to tap over Big Boy's death, because I thought it would be too painful. I'd lived with all those emotions for so long that they had become a part of me. I had a different animal-related trauma in mind that I wanted to address.

But I figured that since we were both dealing with end-of-life issues with an animal we had lost, I felt a tug in my heart to bring up the topic of Big Boy.

What happened next blew my socks off, defying any rational explanation. It totally changed my life and my understanding of the afterlife. It also solidified my belief in the new career field I was embarking on. I couldn't even *begin* to conjure up a story like this.

As I shared the details surrounding Big Boy's death with Bernadette and the emotions I had carried surrounding that trauma for 20 years, Fuji jumped up onto a large plastic storage bin on the floor directly in front of me.

At the *exact moment* my eyes landed on her – and I mean *exact* moment – I heard a sarcastic voice inside my heart that said very confidently, "Can't you see it's me?"

Oh, My God – that's Big Boy's voice! I'd know it anywhere… This is unbelievable…

I had communicated with over 100 animals by this time as an Animal Communicator and knew immediately when I was hearing them speak. Big Boy's presence filled my heart the same way it had done for over 15 years when he was with me! It was the first time I'd felt this familiar presence since he passed.

A new wave of excitement hit me as I realized what had happened. Big Boy *did* come back to me in another incarnation, and it was in the being of Fuji! My eyes peered at her, and every intuitive sense within me knew it was real. My heart welled up with that familiar sense of his soul.

I didn't understand it, yet at the same time, it made sense. It seemed like I was hearing Fuji from the soul level, from the part of her that was Big Boy. I don't know how to explain it any other way.

Big Boy was talkative that day, because he came through to Bernadette, too, right at the end of our Tapping session. He said that he was not in pain or miserable during the last stages of his life when he had cancer. It was only at the very end that it bothered him. He didn't want me to feel guilty or blame myself for his death. He loved me very much and wanted me to focus on the positive aspects of our relationship and the love we shared, because that was the most important thing.

Not only was I blown away by his shocking revelation about Fuji, coupled with the fact that I could *feel* him as Big Boy, but now he imparted this beautiful message to me through Bernadette. It was a combined effort, along with the Tapping, and I knew I was 100% healed from the circumstances surrounding his death 20 years earlier. Massive waves of relief ran through my body... What a day!

This knowledge brought up some questions that I began to ponder. First, what does it *feel* like to know that an animal has returned and to be aware of which animal they were in a previous incarnation?

Fuji was a different being, yet the same soul. My relationship with her was different than mine with Big Boy, because his soul had evolved since his death, and so had mine. Our relationship could never be identical to what it was previously.

Fuji had a different genetic background, yet there was a sense of familiarity. There was the same strong connection between us – yet different – although I didn't perceive it until that moment when I saw her on the storage bin.

Another sign of reincarnation I looked for in both animals and humans was behavior. When I had done the past life regressions, there were *behavioral quirks* in my current life that seemed to be remnants or carryovers from previous ones. Could this be the same for animals? When I notice these quirks, I make a mental note that they are unique to that person or animal, and they become permanently etched in my memory.

I spotted these quirks in Fuji, but were they strong enough to indicate that she might be another incarnation of Big Boy? To me, yes, because they were specific, and to teach me something important. But for my own peace of mind, I wanted more evidence. I didn't want to be conjuring up some wild idea, trying to force it to be true because I *wanted* it to be.

In observing Fuji and her *quirks*, there were definitely two that were foremost in my mind.

I recalled how surprised I felt when she was a young cat, the first time she had wriggled her body up around my neck as I held her, and camped out on my shoulders. This became her favorite place to sit when she wanted to be with me. I remember thinking to myself, *That's the first time I've had a cat up near my head since Big Boy!*

A second intuitive hit with Fuji happened when she slept on the bed with me. She didn't sleep on the pillow wrapped around my head like Big Boy, but she curled up next to my neck and shoulder on the side I was facing. Then, when I turned over to face the opposite direction, she followed suit, climbing over my body to get to the other side. *Big Boy used to do that,* I thought to myself. *Whatever side I was facing, he would turn and do the same.*

These seemed like random observations at the time, but as I continued further along my spiritual journey, their importance became clearer and clearer.

Were there other funny quirks that seemed unique to both Big Boy and Fuji? Absolutely! Big Boy had the loudest purr I'd ever heard from a cat, and Fuji also purred loudly, but hers was funny because it was often spontaneous, seemingly for her own amusement, or just for the fun of it. I didn't have to stroke her body to initiate a purring session. Sometimes, she even purred when she was sleeping or when I walked into a room and just acknowledged her.

One of the amazing aspects of reincarnation to me is that we can have some of the quirks or behaviors that are a carryover from a previous lifetime yet have no memory of that lifetime. I've heard it said that our souls are "much bigger" than our human bodies with their limitations, and practically speaking, we don't have the capacity to remember all of its experiences – sort of like not having enough storage space in our computer's hard drive!

I also think it's a huge gift that we *don't* consciously remember the details of previous lives, because if we did, we might be appalled at how "primitive" our behavior probably was. With each new lifetime, we are given opportunities to respond differently to the life lessons we are given, to grow in love and grace, and eventually be reunited with the loving Creator of the Universe. Jesus gave us the example, and this is further explained in a book by John Van Auken, one of the directors at Edgar Cayce's A.R.E., called *From Karma to Grace: The Power of the Fruits of the Spirit.*

Am I able to prove any of this? Absolutely not! I don't even begin to have all the answers. My conclusions are based on my own experiences, but I believe the insights that have been given to me. If you're curious about reincarnation, there are many other books and resources available on the topic.

The changes in my spiritual life as the result of my experiences and exploration in this area of spirituality have impacted my life in a positive way. I'm finally at peace with who I am, knowing that I'm a work in progress – literally, over eons of time! I feel connected to the universe as an integral part, rather than being an observer, which makes me want to learn even more about its vastness and how it works. My life is so much more joyful and has turned into one exciting adventure after another, full of hope and wonder.

My new knowledge of Fuji and Big Boy's "relationship" explained why, when I paid for the medium's reading at the Edgar Cayce Center to get more information about Big Boy, nothing came through except a couple points about his temperament. I'd felt then that the medium was not given any more information about him, because, at the appropriate time, it would be given directly to me. The "appropriate time" was *now* – and I didn't see it coming!

Fuji's impeccable timing surprised me once again during a Silva Method Course I took via Zoom during the Covid-19 pandemic.

The Silva Method is a system of mind development named after its founder, Jose Silva, who was a pioneer in fields such as alpha brain waves, relaxed concentration, visualization and imagination, positive thinking, reprogramming the mind, activating the subconscious mind, and controlled ESP.

I love the Silva Method and have taken several courses online via Zoom from Lee Pascoe, who learned from and worked directly with Jose Silva. It has been a game-changer in that I use many of the techniques daily in my meditation practice, as well as *all* of my Animal Communication and energy healing work, helping me easily shift from using my "logic" brain and sympathetic nervous system to the parasympathetic, where my intuition and creativity can shine.

I fully trust the accuracy of the information I receive while "working" in these slower brain wave states and have seen amazing, immediate results when I do energy healing. I also employ the Silva techniques for other daily tasks, such as problem solving, manifesting future goals and aspirations, making travel plans, and remembering practical information, like multiple items on a shopping list without having to bring the list with me.

The class in which Fuji made her grand appearances at uncanny times was called "Back to Your Future." Lee led us in a past life regression where I set the intention of wanting to know if I had worked with animals in a previous lifetime. Although the class was not in person, it was easy to experience a regression.

I sat at my computer, facing the screen while she led us into a deep meditation and then through the regression process. It was shorter in duration than my previous PLRs, because the questions were general and geared toward a group, and we couldn't respond individually. It hit several key points, though.

As Lee led us deeper into the meditation, we focused on passing through a tunnel into a light that would lead to another lifetime. All of a sudden, at the EXACT MOMENT I entered the light into that lifetime, Fuji jumped on my lap. *Oh no... why is she doing this now, of all times?* I didn't want to interrupt my deep meditative state, so I just let her sit there.

My mind took me to a lifetime where I was dressed first as a young Pilgrim girl playing with dogs, and then as a grown woman who worked with herbs that I used to help heal animals. There were golden retrievers in the scenes. I knew I was in Massachusetts.

Lee told us to ask our "self" from that lifetime to give us a gift that would help us in this lifetime, and the "previous me" gave me the gift of Compassion. *I certainly need more of that!*

That was the extent of the regression, but it was enough information to know that I had worked with animals before in a healing capacity, and that I'd worked with natural remedies for health.

As we were preparing to leave that lifetime, the next remarkable "Fuji moment" happened. At the EXACT MOMENT I left the light to enter the tunnel and return to this lifetime, Fuji jumped off my lap and onto the floor. *What just happened?*

I marveled at her timing amidst my frustration at her interrupting the regression. But it made more sense the next day in class when Lee led us in another meditation, this time jumping ahead to 10 years in our future – to our Future Self.

Once again, at the EXACT MOMENT we entered the setting to meet our future self, Fuji again jumped on my lap! *Are you kidding me? What's up with this cat?*

My future self was gardening, and the advice she gave to help me "become her" 10 years from now was to be patient and stay grounded. She reached down and picked up a handful of dirt as her gift to me from the future.

Then, sure enough, at the EXACT MOMENT I left my future self, Fuji jumped down off my lap and landed on the floor. *This is absurd!*

All at once, I knew what had happened. This remarkable calico had just given me a message: She was with me before, she is with me currently, and she will be with me again. We are traveling through time together! *I always wanted to be a time traveler, but never envisioned doing it with a cat!*

I had another suspicion that Big Boy and Fuji were also my cat Kimba from childhood – the cat that ran away, found his way home a couple years later, and was hit by a car soon after he returned. I was devastated when that happened, and it would explain why I was so drawn to Big Boy the first time I saw him as a kitten. Could that be true?

What an incredible way Fuji had found to teach me this valuable lesson about life and the continuity of the soul. If I wasn't living these extraordinary events myself, I would say I had entered The Twilight Zone!

CHAPTER 53

LILLI

"This was tough for me, Mom, being uprooted from my family after 12 years and losing my vision along the way. Life is full of challenges, but I have a strong spirit, and I'll do my best to integrate into your family. I really like the golden boy you call 'Pumpkin,' but that calico is a b*tch! (Pardon my French.) And please, please give me time to grieve the loss of my other home. We cats also experience loss and need time to recover."

– Lilli

"Mom, I've had enough. I'm sick and tired of training new cats when they join the family. I don't want this girl to live here. Can't you see I'm ready to retire from this line of work? Like it or not, I'm putting my paw down and will show you (and her) who's boss."

– Fuji

After 23 years of a constant flow of 8-10 cats in my house, my feline population had dwindled down to two: my fluffy, handsome 10-year-old ginger boy Pumpkin, the Walmart Greeter, and my snarky, opinionated 15-year-old calico Fuji, the Queen Bee and feline matriarch.

The house was so quiet. *I'm down to only two cats! That's the fewest I've had in almost 30 years…* I pondered those thoughts while still grieving the deaths of Squeaker and Chrissy, who passed within 10 days of each other in September 2019, not sure if and when I would ever be open to welcoming in another one.

To be honest, taking care of so many cats was not easy, but through various circumstances, dying or destitute cats always found me, and I fell in love with each of them. I could never turn one away.

Four months after the passing of Squeaker and Chrissy, I began to feel that familiar tug on my heart that perhaps there was another cat who needed me – or that *I* needed. It had been over six years since I had welcomed a newcomer.

To recap my history of taking in lost and wayward cats, many had shown up in my yard in a decrepit state, usually starving, filthy, or injured, like Muffin, Gray Kitty, Georgie, and Luce. Others had been dumped off somewhere and were trying to survive, like Fuji, who had been left in an apple orchard with her litter mates. Pumpkin showed up at the barn where I boarded my horse, trapped up in a tree by dogs in the rain in winter – cold, starving and filthy, with respiratory issues. Louie had shown up next to a trash can at a gas station in Suffolk, Virginia.

In Japan, Cyclops was wandering around an abandoned Japanese neighborhood, starving and crying for help when Chuck and I went bicycling. And there were the stray, feral cats, like Bashful and Bobtail. Mr. Peabody was rolling around and purring on the ground next to *my* bicycle at a train station, when we returned from spending the day at a waterpark. That's just how things worked with my cat history.

For my entire life, I was used to cats finding *me*; I wasn't accustomed to actively *looking* for one. *How would it happen this time? Would it be from a shelter? An ad on social media? One wandering into my yard?* I didn't have any clarity, so I just waited.

Meanwhile, I was finishing my case studies to become an Animal Communicator and Energy Healer, getting ready to graduate from Communication with all Life University (CWALU).

A week before Memorial Day weekend of May 2020, I went on a reorganizational binge at my house and determined that I needed more bookshelf space for my ever-growing library of books on animal communication, energy healing, and all sorts of other transformational topics, not to mention the tons of notebooks from all the online classes I was taking. I wanted to learn more. *My coffee table overfloweth with books!*

On a whim, I checked the ads on Craigslist to see if there happened to be any local postings for bookshelves. I wanted something simple and not too bulky, because my house was small, and I didn't want it to look crowded.

My eyes immediately fell on a listing less than 10 minutes away that had just been posted. The pictures looked perfect. I contacted the seller and set up an appointment for the next day, thrilled that I had come up with a solution for my coffee table clutter, which included multiple partially read books.

I drove my van to a beautiful, two-story house in the country and had a nice chat with Stephen and Darci, the owners, who were moving and would be living in temporary places indefinitely. The Covid-19 pandemic had thwarted their plans to move into a self-sustaining community.

A black cat wandered into the room while we were visiting, and that prompted me to mention that I was an Animal Communicator. I was new to this field, and still shy about telling people what I did, but each time I spoke about it, I gained more confidence, and it seemed like a natural transition point in the conversation.

Stephen spoke up immediately, "Do you know anyone who might be interested in adopting a 12-year-old blind cat? We're worried that she won't be able to adapt well to moving around indefinitely, given her blindness" *Oh, no... tug on my heart...*

"We have three cats, and we're taking this black one with us. The new owners have agreed to let the second one, who is primarily an outdoor cat, stay here, but we have a third cat, Lilli, that we're still looking to rehome."

From my years of experience with so many needy cats, I was fully aware that it would take an experienced cat person to take on such a daunting task. It would be devastating for Lilli to go to a shelter. Her chances of being adopted would be slim, and she'd be terrified in a cage after having the freedom to roam in a house for 12 years.

My compassionate side began to run full throttle: *I can't let that happen, when I'm fully capable of taking care of this cat. Besides, I've been having this urge to adopt again for several months now, and this certainly fits the bill for unique circumstances surrounding my cat adoptions. Another synchronicity...*

Without thinking, I blurted out: "I might be able to help you."

Meanwhile, my logical side chimed in: *What am I saying? I came here for bookshelves. Do I know what I'll be getting myself into? This is crazy. It's not my job to take in every needy cat on the planet. I'm getting too old for this...*

After we loaded the bookshelves into my van, Darci carried Lilli over to me, and my eyes melted at the sight of this beautiful, smokey gray, peach and white long-haired Norwegian Forest Cat. Darci had adopted Lilli from a feral colony when she was just a kitten. She wasn't born blind, but had lost her sight gradually over the years.

The couple was scheduled to vacate their house in five days, and although the new owners were willing to let Lilli stay on the property, they would not allow her in the house, and she would be relegated to living in the barn. *I can't let that happen to her. It would be devastating...* Still, my logical side had to give this some thought, so I left with the bookshelves, promising to get back to Steve and Darci with my decision. As usual, when it came to my feline family, the compassionate side prevailed and I let them know the next day that I would give this beautiful girl a new home.

Of course, I knew from the moment they told me about her that Lilli was going to join my family, but it was still a big decision with a lot of responsibility. I had to figure out where to put everything – her food, water, and a litter box that she could find easily. I also needed to keep her in a confined area until she was comfortable learning her way around unfamiliar surroundings, with the added complication that she couldn't see.

I used my skills as an Animal Communicator to connect with all the cats involved with the move to help them prepare for what was going to happen: Lilli, her two cat siblings, and my two, Fuji and Pumpkin. That went well, and to Stephen and Darci's surprise, Lilli actually let herself be put in her carrier without a struggle when I arrived at their house to take her home with me.

Fuji and Pumpkin were both accustomed to my bringing new cats into the household. Neither of them had ever had a problem with previous additions – particularly Fuji, who had welcomed at least eight new cats over the years. And Pumpkin was so personable that I doubted he would have a problem, either.

Little did I know about the ensuing struggles I would encounter from Fuji, leaving me at my wits' end, only to discover the importance of *emotional leadership* in the household.

I carried Lilli through the front door and put her carrier next to Pumpkin and Fuji, who were in the living room, so they could sniff each other. Then I carried her to my large basement bedroom and opened her carrier by the foot of my bed.

If I had planted a microphone inside the head of each of my cats to hear things from their perspectives, I'm pretty sure it would have sounded like this:

> **Lilli: Day 1** - *Where am I? I know this lady talked to me and told me I would be going to a new place, and I listened, but I didn't quite get what it would feel like. I let them put me in my carrier without making a fuss, but what was I thinking? I'm scared to death. Everything that was familiar to me is gone – my two brothers and my humans. Now I'm at this new place and I'm too scared to even climb out of my carrier. I'm shaking...*

The lady is talking gently to me, but that's not making me any less scared. I can't see anything except a little light and some shadows. I'm afraid to go anywhere because I don't know what's safe.

Lilli: Day 2 - *I finally walked away from my carrier just a little bit. I found some food and a litter box. But I wonder about those two other cats that I smelled. Who are they? They're not my brothers. There's a boy that seems friendly enough, but the girl – that's a different story. I'd better not get in her way.*

Pumpkin: *A new friend! Woo-hoo! I'm so excited! I love making new friends. She's really pretty, and seems kind. I notice she's having trouble finding her way around, so I'll show her the ropes and protect her. Welcome, Lilli! I'm so glad you're here! We're going to have a great relationship!*

Fuji: *Mom, why did you do this to me? I'm fed up with welcoming new cats into our house, and this is the last straw. I'm just not going to do it anymore. I don't even know her, but I hate her already. This is MY house, and there isn't room for any more girls. On top of it all, she's camping out in your bedroom. I don't want her here.*

Lilli, who do you think you are, coming into my house? Go back where you came from. If you don't, I'm going to make life miserable for you, starting with the litter box. I'm the boss here.

Fuji's instant hostility was *not* the reaction I'd expected from her when I brought Lilli home, but I was determined to make this adoption work. Pumpkin was fine, and it was just Fuji with her uncooperative attitude that tried to thwart my plans.

I thought my bedroom, which comprised almost the entire basement of the house, would be the safest place to let Lilli get oriented to her new surroundings. Plus, she could be close to me. She was scared to death, shaking in her carrier and afraid to get out. I tried to calm her by petting her and reassuring her, and although she put out a somewhat nervous purr, she was still shaking – understandably, as she couldn't see where she was.

I set up a litter box in my bathroom less than 10 feet away, thinking it would be easy to find, with the plan to eventually remove it once she found the primary box in the utility room adjacent to my bedroom and accessible through a cat door. I put the dry food Stephen and Darci had given me in a bowl in my room. *This will be easy enough.* I put a large pet cushion Darci gave me next to Lilli's carrier by the foot of my bed, and tried to let her get comfortable. This, along with a dangling fish toy that she liked, would give her something familiar to cling to.

"Relax, Lilli, you're going to be fine." I repeatedly spoke reassuring words to her, using a calm and loving voice. I was sure that it wouldn't take long for her to settle into her new home.

The first night, Lilli didn't stir from her carrier, and she remained in it the entire next day. The second night, however, turned into a nightmare when I awoke the following morning to find her missing. *This is impossible. How could she have gotten out? Could she have found one of the cat doors?*

> **Lilli: Day 2 (Later in the day)** *I need to get out of here and chill by myself for a while. This is just too much change. I don't know where to go, but I'm going to find a way to escape*

and hide so they can't find me. My whiskers will guide me. Oh, here's a cat door... Adios, amigos!

Lilli: Day 3 – *I hear them calling me and looking everywhere, but I don't want them to find me. I'm not ready to come out of this hiding place yet. I'll decide if and when I'm ready. I need time to take this all in.*

I reached out to all my Animal Communicator friends and colleagues to ask for help in finding her. I was an emotional wreck, to say the least, and my mind raced nonstop in hysteria. *Did she get out through a cat door? Is she trying to find her other home? What do I tell Stephen and Darci? How could I have done this? I'm a total failure as a pet mom. I'll never forgive myself. What if she gets hit by a car?* On and on…

Fuji, meanwhile, tried to calm me down by following me everywhere inside and outside the house, meowing at me as if pleading. I largely ignored her, and focused on scouring every inch of my property. I called Stephen and Darci to come and help look as well, thinking Lilli might hear their familiar voices and come out from hiding. We walked up and down the street to all the neighbors' houses, to no avail.

That evening, I went to bed completely distraught and defeated. I had failed.

Lilli: Day 4 – *Okay, I'm ready. But I'll do it overnight so no one will see me. I'll find my way back to my cushion on the floor. Maybe she'll never know I was gone. Then I'll take my time getting used to this new place.*

When morning came, I was greeted with the biggest shock of my life: Lilli was sprawled out on her cushion at the foot of my bed, sound asleep. *Oh. My. God. Where did she go, and how did she find her way back?* I never found out, but I didn't care, as one of my bleakest days had turned into one of my brightest.

> **Lilli: One month later** – *Things aren't so bad here. The lady gives me lots of food whenever I ask, and I really like that. I'm trying to make friends with the others. Pumpkin has been so kind to me and has taken me under his wing.*
>
> *Fuji is a totally different story. She's a total bully. No matter how nice I am, she's just nasty to me, and sometimes even swats. I'm afraid to get in the litter box because she attacks me, and I can't sleep on the couch next to my new mom without her hissing and growling at me.*
>
> *I don't know what her problem is. I didn't ask to come here. I know that she's the alpha cat, and I'm certainly not trying to take over her role, but I'm so frustrated. She acts like she owns the place.*

Time marched on, and Lilli gained confidence to start exploring the house. I admit that I bribed her with wet food at the top of the basement stairs to help her eventually integrate her mealtime with Pumpkin and Fuji, who ate in the kitchen. *Success! Lilli is a total foodie!*

Lilli used her nonvisual senses to navigate her way around the house, as well as her whiskers to help judge distance from objects without bumping into them. I eventually noticed that she seemed to see or sense light and shadows to help her, so

I don't think she is 100% blind. She's also a huntress who can still catch mice and flying things!

One thing I'm very happy about is that I've never treated her as a disabled cat. I don't pity her and take her dignity from her. I help her be as independent as she can, making accommodations for her only when needed.

She has taught me many things in the process. She doesn't like it when I approach her too quickly because it scares her and she runs away. I've had to retrain myself when I'm around her, walking slower and talking gently when I'm close by. She has taught *me* how to interact with *her*.

Her wet food has to be fresh and not refrigerated. I always tap the plate on the floor in front of her so she can hear it and find the food with her nose. If she can't smell her food, she won't eat it, no matter how many times I tap her plate.

I've had to learn to gauge how much she'll eat so I can minimize the leftovers. She is very vocal around food, and will tell me when she's hungry. If she wants more or something different because she can't smell what I gave her, she will often sit by her plate for long periods of time and just wait for something to magically appear!

As far as integrating with Pumpkin and Fuji, this is where I failed miserably. Pumpkin was great, truly acting like a Walmart Greeter. He took on the role of big brother, welcoming and protecting his new feline sister. Fuji, on the other hand, let it be known that she wanted nothing to do with a new cat in the household. She was a total bully, despite Lilli's attempts at friendship. She terrorized her when she tried to use the litter box, forcing me to keep the extra one on my bathroom floor. *Will my life ever be normal again? There's no peace in this household.*

Every attempt that Lilli made to befriend Fuji was met with hisses, growls, and swats, like a boxer using an uppercut. It was painful to watch. I was out of skills to help fix this horrible situation.

Fuji refused to come into the basement bedroom for months when Lilli was down there, even though she had previously slept with me on a regular basis. The final straw happened one evening when I was in the basement with Lilli. Fuji marched down the stairs and came toward us. *Could this be a breakthrough? Au Contraire!*

My matriarch calico strutted by both Lilli and myself with her grandiose attitude and demeanor, pretending to go toward the bathroom to get some water. Instead, she stopped and positioned herself next to Lilli, let out a very big hiss, then turned and walked away, purring as loudly as she could as she strutted off with a totally smug look on her face. I watched in horror. *This cat is running my household.*

That's when I learned my most important lesson in household dynamics with animals, an area that I had inadvertently overlooked: Emotional Leadership.

My 15-year-old snarky, opinionated calico had assumed the role of emotional leader in my household. Fuji had helped me so much over the years, particularly when I was having major family problems that culminated in my divorce. Now I saw that I had unknowingly allowed her to take over that leadership role and never regained control.

That was a turning point for me. I began to reclaim leadership of my home, a process that didn't happen overnight. I implemented a few *energy-shifting hacks* to help change the relationship dynamics in the household:

First, in my journal, I drew a picture of each of us, with me as the largest image, and a heart around all of us to represent unity with love.

Second, I meditated on that image *daily*, visualizing that I am the boss, and I have their backs. I did this lovingly, feeling it in my heart and body for each animal individually.

And finally, I consciously made an effort to be *present* with them when I was home, and not always distracted with electronic devices. I gave each one of them individual time and immediately interrupted any arguments or unkind behavior they exhibited toward each other.

I continue to use these simple *energy-shifting hacks* to keep order in my home.

As the months went by, Fuji and Lilli began to co-exist with no arguments. They were both able to eat in close proximity to each other without Fuji hissing.

What I considered to be the *ultimate, final victory* happened after two years, when one evening I plopped myself down on the couch to watch a movie, and Fuji sat on the left side of my lap, while Lilli sat on the right – and both cats were purring! *Yes! It's peaceful again, and was worth the wait…*

Fuji: Two years plus – *I let Mom think she's in charge, but* I'm *still the boss… hee hee…*

CHAPTER 54

JAKE'S COMPUTER SABOTAGE

"Mom, you didn't really think that our relationship ended when I passed away, did you? I'm still Jake the Jokester, and when I 'sabotaged' your computer, you wouldn't believe how hard I was laughing! It was all in fun, though, because I wanted to figure out a way to get your attention and let you know I'm still here helping you. It's just that I'm no longer in physical form. And don't you like the picture I chose that appeared on your screen? It's one of my favorites of the two of us, and I think I look mighty handsome, don't you?"

– Jake

When Jake passed away the morning I attended that first Animal Communication Conference, I believed the timing was divinely orchestrated, but I didn't understand its significance at the time. Since then, I've frequently entertained the thoughts: *What do animals do after they cross over? Can they still be a part of our lives, but in a different way? Maybe Jake's death will help teach me.*

A couple years later, I attended the annual Members Congress at Edgar Cayce's A.R.E. I had become a self-professed "Soul Growth Junkie" and immersed myself in everything I could find about Energy Healing, personal transformation, the metaphysical world, quantum energy and, you might say, "learning how to navigate the world of woo-woo."

The A.R.E. Center has become a magical place for me, as synchronicities abound, and I gain an enormous amount of clarity of thought when I'm there. Being in the collective energy of that environment has enhanced my intuitive skills tremendously.

At this conference, one of the speakers held a book signing in the gift shop. I purchased two of his books, and while standing in line to get them signed, within arm's reach was a sales rack full of pendulums, which were not related to the speaker's topic, but were interesting to look at. I'd recently learned that they can be used to work with energy, so the display drew my attention.

I was confused, though, because what little information I had read about pendulums mentioned "dowsing" in the description – the same word that refers to a type of dowsing or "divining" rod used to find water, gemstones, metals or precious ores buried underground. But that's not the purpose of a pendulum, which I now use for many reasons, but mainly to check an animal's chakras when I do an energy healing session.

I stared at the various pendulums and thought they had pretty stones and designs, but didn't want to purchase one until I received a sign that it was something I should pursue. So, after I got the books signed, I went directly back to my hotel room.

That night I had an unusual dream in which friends at the barn where I boarded Nelly were helping me move her to a different location. When we looked around at the new setting, I noticed that Jake was clinging close by me, not just in physical proximity, but also in my heart and mind. He seemed to be part of my consciousness, reminding me that Nelly needed to have different pasture options for her dietary needs. Jake was so close to me in the dream that when I woke up, it felt like he was right next to me. It was definitely an intuitive hit that his presence was more real than just in the dream.

I went back to the A.R.E. that morning as soon as the gift store opened to look around more thoroughly. I was still intrigued with the idea of having a pendulum, but I wanted to learn more and determine whether it could help me with my work as an Animal Communicator and Energy Healer.

As I strolled up and down the aisles of books, my eyes landed on *Dowsing for Beginners*, with a picture of a pendulum on the front cover. I picked it up and randomly opened to the chapter entitled "Dowsing for Animals' Health." *Really? What are you up to, Jake?*

That was my sign. I wanted to know as much as possible about healing and helping animals. I purchased the book along with a pretty pendulum with a horse.

I found another book about learning to work with a pendulum, and once again, as soon as I opened it, the passage pertained to healing for animals – more confirmation that I was on the right path.

I contemplated the dream about Jake for months, still having a sense that he was more present with me than I could imagine.

Although I don't know the fullness of what he is up to on the "other side," his sense of humor still comes through. He's a trickster, and his "computer sabotage" escapades later caught me totally off guard.

I had graduated from Communication with all Life University (CWALU) and was now one of the teachers for the online Animal Communication classes. Like the other faculty, I was asked to present a Facebook Live, introducing myself to the students I would later teach. Navigating technology isn't one of my superpowers, but I was determined to make a good presentation, hopefully with confidence and without embarrassing myself.

When the time came for my live debut on a Wednesday afternoon, my desk was adorned with easy-to-read, colored sticky notes with catch phrases and prompts related to my journey of becoming an Animal Communicator. Nicely dressed, with hair perfectly styled, I sat at the desktop computer in my home office, preparing to do my first live video. Though calm outwardly, my inner state was in turmoil.

Shannon, the moderator for the Facebook group, guided me over the phone through all the technology steps to ensure that everything was working properly. It seemed easy enough to just click on the "live" button when it was time to start. I was nervous, yet ready for the inevitable: going live on Facebook.

While we waited for the bells to strike five, I casually asked Shannon if the picture I had submitted to both her and the school's administrative assistant was posted on the Facebook page, identifying me as the guest speaker for that day.

Neither of us had checked, so at 4:50 p.m., I scrolled down the Facebook page, expecting to see the image of my crazy calico cat Fuji wrapped around my shoulders, both of us with smiles on our faces.

The picture posted on the page, however, caused my heart to skip a beat, because it was *not* the one I had sent to either party. In plain view, for all to see, was a 10-year-old photo of me wearing a silly blue hat, standing alongside my horse Jake who sported a matching blue halter.

"That's impossible," I said. "I've never sent that picture to *anyone*. First of all, it was taken 10 years ago, and I don't look anything like that now. How did that happen?"

I knew immediately that Jake had sabotaged my computer, *replacing* the picture I'd sent with one of the two of us together!

Now, as the Facebook Live was ready to start, I was in a panic, first because of the swapped picture, and then because at exactly 5:00 p.m., the technology malfunctioned. The "live" button wasn't working on the page I had opened, and I desperately clicked on everything I could find to resolve the problem.

Some mysterious adjustment in cyberspace caused the button to eventually work, and I proceeded to talk about my journey into the world of Animal Communication for the next 15-20 minutes.

When I was finished, Shannon and I looked through the comments in the group, knowing that most people would be watching it later, but the names of the viewers were *not* members of CWALU – they were my friends from various walks of life, such as the Air Force, high school, and the town I lived in!

I realized quickly that the Facebook Live had been broadcast on my *personal* Facebook page, and not the school's. The technology "problem" had definitely been solved!

I was mortified. At that stage of my journey, I would *never* have done this presentation on my personal page! Being a professional Animal Communicator was still fairly new to me, and I was a bit shy in sharing it with my friends for fear of being considered too "woo-woo."

I was faced with a huge personal dilemma. The recording needed to be shared with the school Facebook group, but what about my personal page? There seemed to be only two choices: (1) Share it with the school group and hide it from my own page, or (2) Share it with the school group and leave it on my personal page. If I kept it on my personal page, I would be vulnerable, letting everyone know what I was doing with my life. Terror and anxiety reared their ugly heads and held a grip on me.

Just then, Jake's loving presence permeated my heart, filling it with a huge burst of angelic love and white light! I felt it so clearly. His message conveyed to me that the work I do with animals is important, and he is working alongside me every step of the way.

I moved past my terror and vulnerability and kept the recording on my own page, sharing it with the school. In turn, I gained a huge amount of confidence about sharing my work.

Jake was a jokester when he was in his body, and his jokes were continuing from the other side. I recognize his presence because it feels like a massive amount of energy, full of light and joy – almost angelic. I believe he knew I needed confidence to fully embody my work as an Animal Communicator, and his sense of humor thrust me into an uncomfortable situation to help enable it.

Jake's computer sabotage helped me understand that death is not a barrier to our relationships with animals. What a comfort!

With his inspiration, I framed a large copy of that picture of the two of us and have it proudly displayed above my computer. It's a daily reminder that he is one of my biggest helpers.

Thank you, Jake, for your continued sense of humor and support from across the veil.

CHAPTER 55

WE'RE ALL IN THIS TOGETHER

"Keep asking those spiritual questions, Mom! You're getting answers, and we, your felines (and Jake, the 'stray'), are now in the spiritual realm, still teaching you! Although we aren't with you in our physical bodies anymore, we can still make our presence felt. Jake masterminded the plot to dramatically get your attention with his clever computer sabotage, and we have to give him credit for that, even though he is a horse. Plus, he makes us laugh while we teach you serious lessons about life and death."

— All Your Cats Who Have Crossed Over

I loved what I was learning *so much*, and Jake's computer sabotage just tickled me pink. All that I was learning through becoming an Animal Communicator, embarking on my Spiritual Quest, and the vast number of transformational classes I was taking, inspired me to want to learn even *more!*

Okay, I admit that I was — and still am — obsessed with getting emotionally healthier and more spiritually in tune with a Higher Power. I knew there was more healing ahead, although I didn't always understand what I needed at the time. Actually, I was clueless about how much healing I still needed regarding end-of-life issues for my animals. But I now had many tools at my disposal to facilitate this.

I began to change my morning meditation routine from using guided meditations to ones that would allow more freedom and spontaneity. Daily meditation had been a priority since I started working the 12-Step recovery process. Step 11 refers to prayer and meditation and seeking a closer conscious contact with God or a Higher Power, and how I implement this step and others continues to evolve.

I used to think that meditation meant sitting in the lotus position for hours on end, eyes closed and chanting, "OM." Maybe there are monks and yogis who do that, but for me, that was not what I needed. In my experience, many Westerners do not know how to meditate. I believe prayer and meditation go together – one is talking to God and the other is listening. Growing in meditation has helped me learn to listen.

The Bible references meditation multiple times in the Psalms of the Old Testament, but for some reason, most Christians I know are afraid of it. I used to feel that way, too, and I think it relates back to being cautious and fearful of something you don't understand. But at this point, meditation didn't bother me. I wanted to learn more, work the 12 Steps, and get well, and I just happened to start doing it through the guided meditations.

For me, meditation is the practice of mindfulness and being fully present with myself, including body awareness. Throughout my life, I had learned how to dissociate and run away from difficult emotions and experiences. More on that later in this chapter.

Now for the Silva Method. I've taken many classes from Lee Pascoe, one of the International Directors, and love everything

I've learned and the insights I've gained. My meditation practice has truly reached a new level! One Zoom course in particular, called "Silva Manifesting," was a game-changer.

We were guided into a deep meditation, tuning in to the level of consciousness just prior to our current incarnation. The goal was to find answers that give clarity to our life's mission. We were asked the following questions, and these are the insights I gained during the meditation:

Q. What does Universal Source Energy mean to me?
A. The loving presence that created all things. It works in and through me and radiates out to others.

Q. What do I believe is my mission in life?
A. To help animals, to be a healer (physical, emotional, spiritual).

Q. Give me a sign to reinforce my mission.
A. I saw waves of ocean water approaching the shore. At first, there were no creatures, just the water. *What does this mean?* Then the water was filled with creatures. Then there were creatures in the air, all kinds of flying creatures. Then there were creatures on the land. *I was witnessing the dawn of creation.* The sun was now shining. All were alive and working together in harmony.

Q. What do I need to know to understand my mission?
A. All of creation is meant to be in harmony. It's held together by love. Love is the way for it to return to its beginning form. There has to be love to restore it. Many things block love. Removing the blocks will bring the love in. Healing helps restore love.

Q. What do I need to believe about my mission?

A. I need to believe that I can make a difference, being only one person, one soul. I make a difference. I'm joined with other souls who are here to do the same thing. We bring healing. By loving, I am bringing healing. By healing others, that increases *their* capacity to love and brings even *more* healing. My part is important. Just one person can make a difference. I make a difference.

Q. What value most defines my life?
A. To be authentically loving.

These insights gave me the reassurance of knowing I was on the right path in this current life and the confidence to move forward as an Animal Communicator and Energy Healer!

It all made sense. Did I really see the beginning of creation? That doesn't matter. What *was* important was that the images I received were exactly what I needed to get answers about my current incarnation and why I've been drawn to certain things, like animals, healing, spirituality – and music! *Did I say "music?" Yes!*

Music comes into play in terms of healing. To add to my energy healing toolbox, I've become a Vibrational Sound Therapy Certified Practitioner, using singing bowls and vibrational sound to facilitate healing. I've barely scratched the surface in understanding frequency and vibration, and the capacity to heal with sound. But that's a topic for another book! *Back to Silva...*

My favorite tool in preparation for the day is using some of the Silva Method techniques to create visualizations while meditating in the alpha level of consciousness. This is not the same thing as just letting my imagination wander all over the place!

In a controlled state of relaxation, I've found that these visualizations make it easier for me to receive intuitive information. I don't interpret the meditational images in the same way as I do with something that happens in real time, but I compare the experience to reading a fable – a fictional story that is meant to teach a truth.

For example, in Aesop's *The Boy Who Cried Wolf,* a young shepherd boy repeatedly plays a prank on the people in his town by lying that a wolf is attacking his flock of sheep. Eventually, the people stop believing his fabricated story, so that when a wolf *does* appear, they ignore him. The message, or "moral of the story," is about the importance of having integrity and telling the truth.

One of my favorite morning meditation examples was when a beautiful bald eagle appeared in my mind's eye, followed by my horse Jake. The eagle was soaring above us, while Jake and I were on a glorious trail ride through beautiful, wooded areas, waterways and high cliffs.

Jake's presence was strong, different than when I just think about him and remember what we used to do together. I interpreted this experience to mean that he is an integral part of my work with animals, guiding me with the ones I'll be working with during the remainder of my life. I knew from his computer sabotage that he is present with me and already helping in that capacity. I think he's quite happy about that, too, because, like dogs, horses need a job!

Apparently, all my deceased cats do, too, and they also wanted to tell me. While in meditation the next day, all the cats who had passed away in my adult life appeared to me. A massive amount of love came pouring into my heart, which I was able to return to each of them. As I expressed this, their unique memories came back, and I felt the essence of nearly 20 feline fur babies!

This caught me totally by surprise, and I realized that, like Jake, they too are helping me with my new life's work and are very much still with me. What I experienced through both meditations was enlightening and helped me further grasp the concept of "oneness" and the existence of a collective consciousness.

I've mentioned "oneness" before, but what does that feel like to me? Here's an example: As a musician, when I play in a band, my individual part is interconnected with all the others in the ensemble, and together we perform a song. My entire *self* (body, mind, soul, and spirit) is participating in the performance, and I'm connected to everyone else's *self*. If you add an outpouring of love from an outside source (God, the Holy Spirit, whatever term you want to use for the Divine) uniting all the musicians, the performance is transcended, intangibly morphing into what feels like another dimension.

I have performed music most of my life and used to wonder why I feel so good at the end of a concert or those occasions when I perform as a soloist. I believe it's because of that intangible Divine presence, filling my heart and transcending the experience. When coupled with the reaction of the audience, another layer of love is added. However, performances don't happen on a daily basis and usually only last one to two hours. *How can I get more of this?* I wondered.

I found my answer in nature. I started to experience oneness when I spent more time outdoors, like hiking, walking along the beach, sitting on a bench at the park watching the ducks, or even planting flowers in my yard. I can *feel* and sense the life in everything around me, knowing that I'm an integral part of something bigger and not separate from it. At these times, I experience a profound sense of belonging that I'd felt I'd missed out on my entire life. And I'm able to take that sense of belonging everywhere now! It's part of who I am.

Yet, it's not only experiencing the oneness, but also being aware of and feeling the presence of Divine Love (God, Higher Power, the Creator of the Universe – whatever your term) that's holding it all together. This was one of the turning points in my life that helped me understand that I am not separated from God. At long last, I was finally "home!" And while this might not be the best analogy, it was almost like Dorothy in *The Wizard of Oz*, who discovered that she had the power within her all along to get back home to Kansas!

The flip side of oneness is that because I'm so sensitive, I feel the overwhelming sadness and despair of another sentient being when it is hurting. This is especially tough when I become aware of various practices of animal abuse or neglect, such as scientific experimentation, factory farming, backyard breeders, puppy mills, abuse of circus animals, dog fighting, slaughterhouses, cat and dog meat markets, bears put into small cages their entire lives to be used for their bile – the list goes on and on. These realities exist.

The worldwide situation regarding the inhumane treatment of animals grieves me to no end, but if I dwelt on this negativity all the time, I would be contributing energy to it, effectually causing it to grow. I'm grateful to the individuals and organizations on the front lines who are making a difference on behalf of these beings, and I do what I can to support their efforts in the form of donations, signing petitions, or volunteering. I can't fix all the injustices toward animals, but I can put positivity into the world, which, when combined with others doing the same, can help create change.

The feeling of oneness with my deceased animals in meditation was a precursor to the healing I needed after the death of about 20 cats up to that point – it wasn't surprising that I had become emotionally numb over the years. I had closed off my heart to each feline family member when they died, feeling as if a part of me had died, too. I had no skills to process the gamut of emotions that held me prisoner.

I had lived with huge amounts of guilt and regret after most of my cats' deaths and forgotten who they were at their best. It seemed that no matter how my cats died, I felt that I should have done something better or differently.

I've never "done grief" very well, and I became aware that I had *dissociated* from the pain of their deaths so that I wouldn't feel it, which resulted in a total disconnect between my head and my heart. So much so that by closing off *their* memories, I had also blocked the love I was capable of for each *new* cat that came along.

I became aware that I wasn't fully present with my *current* cats, even when I was physically close to them. It seemed like my heart would vanish, and I became a shell, doing my best to love them, yet devoid of emotion.

This realization was a huge breakthrough for me, because now I could recognize what it felt like when I dissociated and break the pattern. I yearned to *feel* the love for each cat again. I had done a fair amount of EFT Tapping to ease the end-of-life guilt and regret I felt, but there was another aspect I had not considered. This became clear when I volunteered to help during the nine-day Intensives for the Animal Communication school.

As a student, I had attended both Intensives the previous year in person. This time, they were held remotely on Zoom, and I was available during the three days that were centered around Animals in Transition: Death, Dying, and Beyond.

Throughout the day, we spent time in breakout sessions, practicing Communication with each other's animals that had already passed. The three students I was assigned to work with each connected with one of my deceased cats.

All their readings captured the essence of who these animals were when they were alive and were a beautiful reminder that their end-of-life scenarios were not the defining factor of their lives or a summation of our relationship. They were merely a fraction of it.

Because of the pain I had been holding onto surrounding the final stages of their lives, I had unknowingly clouded my vision and forgotten other aspects of our relationships. This was such an eye-opener, and I was happily reminded of the many great years we'd shared together.

That's what I love the most about communicating with animals that have passed – remembering their essence and the love that's shared over their entire lifetime, and not just the final stages.

Another way I've discovered to help move past the death of my animals is to commemorate them and celebrate their lives. There are many ways to do this, but my favorite is to frame their photos and hang them on the wall or put them in scrapbook albums. An album (or a journal) provides space to write something special about the animal or what I loved about our relationship together.

I've even written letters directly to my animals, as if I was still talking to them, sharing whatever is on my heart. It's like what some people do after the loss of a human family member, and they want to speak what was left unspoken while they were still alive. This has been extremely healing for me.

The bottom line is that I was finally making space in my heart for the long-needed healing of the trauma related to the death of my animals. I was utilizing all the tools I had been given, along with my own creativity. Best of all, I was finally learning to trust in myself and my intuition again.

My perception of death and the afterlife has also changed, knowing that the souls of my animals live on, and they are helping me build even stronger relationships with *all* animals – past and present. I LOVE that we are all in this together!

CHAPTER 56

PUMPKIN'S DECLINE

"Mom, leaving you was incredibly difficult. I wish my lungs had held out just a little longer. I will always be your golden fluffball, though. Thank you for taking all those beautiful pictures of us and featuring one of them on the back cover of this book! And I don't mind your referring to me as the 'Walmart Greeter.' You know how much I loved making everyone feel welcome in our home, but what I really want is to be remembered as your golden feline knight in shining armor. And I have a little surprise for you. Is there another cat I remind you of? Hint: I've been with you before, and soon you'll discover who I was in that previous lifetime!"

— Pumpkin

In early spring of 2021, I noticed that my handsome, golden fluffball Pumpkin's lifelong respiratory problems were taking a toll on his health. He was sneezing more than usual and sleeping excessively. A couple years earlier, most of his teeth had been removed to treat stomatitis (a painful inflammatory condition where ulcers develop on the gums), so eating was not only a challenge with just two remaining teeth, but even more so when he wasn't feeling well.

To make matters worse, he was losing the lively, playful spark to his personality that I had grown accustomed to. Our fun games of throw and fetch with stuffed mice and ping pong balls had become few and far between, because he lacked the fervor to chase the "prey."

As I witnessed this decline, my heart sank. This wasn't supposed to happen. At 12 years old, Pumpkin was the youngest of my three cats and should have had several good years left.

The vet gave him the usual round of antibiotics to get rid of any infection, and he bounced back briefly, but then the fatigue and congestion returned. I went into denial, not believing that I could lose this guy anytime soon.

I scheduled a photo shoot with a local pet photographer, Vicky Mitchell, to have some professional quality pictures for my website and digital writing. Pumpkin was such a beautiful cat, and I thought that with both him and Fuji as the subjects, I could get some cute pictures. Lilli was still scared of people she didn't know, so I wasn't hopeful about her cooperating with a photographer.

Pumpkin was a trooper and endured the session, even though I knew he wasn't feeling his best. I did Scalar Wave energy healing sessions on him, as did some of my friends, which helped, giving me hope that he was gaining strength and on the road to recovery.

I had planned to visit my daughters Masha and Dasha in California in July and was concerned about leaving Pumpkin while he was sick, but as often happens (I'm convinced that cats *do* have nine lives), he rebounded within a week before I left. I was optimistic that things would get back to normal, but the resurgence of energy only lasted while I was gone.

After I returned, I realized that he had given me the gift of holding on to life a little bit longer, so that I could travel in a calmer state of mind. For that, I'm so grateful! But as I watched him weaken again, I finally accepted that his death was imminent.

In the final two weeks of his life, he did something unusual. I observed him sleeping multiple times on the front porch stoop of the house across the street, and then he would come back home. *What's this all about?* I hated it when my cats even *walked* onto the neighbor's property, much less slept there, because I never want them to be a nuisance to anyone.

I asked a colleague to communicate with Pumpkin to see if she could find out about this peculiar behavior, along with anything else I should know about his final days. I was too emotionally invested to do it myself and didn't think I could get an accurate reading.

Pumpkin showed her that he wanted to observe his home from a distance and see the love that was there. It was part of his way of detaching. When asked if he wanted assistance in transitioning, he was a little puzzled by that question and never directly answered it.

So once again, like watching a rerun of a bad movie, I was in the midst of enduring another end-of-life scenario with a beloved cat. I would have to look for the clues and wait for Pumpkin to show me what he wanted, like many of his predecessors had done. In my heart, I knew he would.

I'd installed many cat doors when I moved into my house, so all the kitties could go in and out whenever they wanted. I didn't want to interfere with their freedom to explore and hunt. Okay, I admit it was a little selfish, because after so many years of continually opening and closing doors and windows for cats, I was worn out!

It was the same with food bowls. I started leaving food out for them overnight so they wouldn't come howling at me in the middle of the night to feed them. Purely selfish, yet practical – and it worked!

I knew I was taking a risk by letting Pumpkin continue to have access to the cat doors, and that he might prefer to die outside by himself. That was my choice, though, in trying to honor his wishes.

His appetite had waned to almost nothing, and he only drank small amounts of water. This stage is one of the most difficult for me to endure, because when their body weight decreases, they become physical shells of who they were in their prime.

During Pumpkin's decline, Fuji and Lilli were also showing signs of stress with their own odd behavior. While Pumpkin remained outside most of the time, Fuji did the same, sleeping on the patio nearly 24/7, then coming inside and *running* across the outer perimeter of the living room floor and into the kitchen to eat. Lilli isolated herself from the other cats, probably because Pumpkin was her best friend and ally, and she could sense things were changing.

Observing the shift in household dynamics was a reminder that it's not just humans who are affected by the decline and death of their animals, but these beautiful creatures have their special, unique relationships with each other.

When one is sick or injured, the others cope in their individual ways, and when they die, everyone in the household deals with the loss and grief uniquely, at their own pace. Then, the entire household structure and dynamics have to reorganize.

That's what happened after Georgie, the best king cat ever, died while living on Stocker Street. From my experience, usually the next oldest male cat takes over the feline leadership, but if that one is not a strong leader and doesn't rise to the occasion, there can be a sense of confusion. My other males were definitely not strong enough leaders to fulfill that role, and the remaining cats lost confidence and their sense of security, evidenced by increased spraying around the house (which had never been a problem). Over time, Fuji, the strongest female, took over that role and became the feline matriarch.

I desperately wanted Pumpkin to convey what he wanted me to do for him at the end of his life – if anything. Waiting it out and letting him die unassisted was also an option. Each end-of-life scenario is different. I don't ever want my cats to suffer, yet I want to honor their wishes. I've also realized that often, *I'm* the one suffering more than they are, feeling both hopeless and helpless from the inability to control what's happening.

Pumpkin's presence at home became so scarce that when I thought he had left permanently and died on his own, I did one of my *pleading prayers* and begged that he would return to the house one more time so that I could hold him and tell him how much I loved him. *Just one more time…*

Two days later, I jumped from my bed when I heard Pumpkin's familiar meow as I was waking up! My heart was immediately filled with warmth, and I scooped him up, held him tight, and told him all those things! I breathed a huge sigh of relief and loved on him as much as I could.

I also made a vet appointment, knowing it would be his last one, but there were none available until the next day. Since Pumpkin had returned to the house, I thought he would stay inside overnight, or at least within view, but once again, he disappeared. And like Louie, he vanished at the time of the appointment, so I had to cancel at the last minute, giving me the answer I was looking for. I knew in my heart that my golden fluffball wanted to die without any extra help. Still, I felt peace in the midst of the emotional pain and knew that the timing would unfold in the best possible way.

I saw Pumpkin one last time, resting under my car, knowing that in his weakened state, he probably had just a few hours left to live. I let him be peaceful and stroked him gently, telling him how much I loved him and that it was okay to leave.

He went to wherever his quiet spot was and crossed the rainbow bridge on his own, similar to what Georgie, the best king cat ever, had done years earlier. I never found Pumpkin's hiding place but knew that it was outside in the natural surroundings that he loved. His death was on his terms and in Divine timing – not mine.

Over the next two weeks, I *know* that I heard his voice more than once, meowing audibly – so much that it startled me – and I cried out to him in a panic, thinking that maybe he was trapped in the house somewhere and needed to be rescued.

I was still quite emotional, and those experiences seemed weird at the time, but I recognize now that he was just letting me know he was still present with me, just in a different way.

Squeaker and Chrissy had sent me butterflies as a gift after they passed, and Pumpkin let me hear his voice. For those gifts, I'm very grateful. Today, I occasionally see "shadows" of my cats for brief moments, like in the kitchen. I'm sure, without a doubt, that they make their rounds to come and check on me!

After Pumpkin passed, I pondered the possibility of his being a reincarnation of another animal I had known in this lifetime. While he was still alive, that never occurred to me, although when he was younger, I used to joke that he must have been a dog in a previous life, because he wagged his tail back and forth *sideways* – not like a cat! I watched this phenomenon with amusement his whole life, along with his desire to play catch with me when I would throw toys at him. Those were only entertaining thoughts, though, and my belief system back then didn't include reincarnation.

But now I was more accustomed to noticing quirky animal behaviors and better able to tune in to the intuitive hits I was getting. It started with the *familiarity* of Pumpkin the very first time I met him 10 years earlier in the middle of a cold, damp winter at the barn where I boarded my horses. He was a newly rescued stray who was temporarily living in the small office next to the feed room until a permanent home could be found.

There was *something about him* that immediately warmed my heart, along with the same feeling I had known so many times: *This is my cat.* Although I kept denying it, once again declaring that we didn't need another cat, the inevitable happened, and we finally brought him home. Of course, we had a special bond immediately.

What about some of the other cats I had cared for over the course of my life? Were there unusual *quirks* associated with any of them that might have given me a clue that they had returned as Pumpkin? Absolutely – and they were becoming easier to perceive.

Mr. Peabody came to mind immediately. *Mr. Peabody? Really?* He was the filthy, emaciated white cat with black splotches that Chuck and I found kneading bread next to my bicycle at a train station in Japan, one of the Core Eight cats that we brought back to the States with us. He had died in 2005, five years before we adopted Pumpkin.

What was Mr. Peabody's "essence?" Did he have any unique traits, personality quirks, physical conditions, or other characteristics that I would use to describe him? Of course! That was easy: He was a happy soul without a mean bone in his body and was plagued with respiratory issues his entire life, which eventually led to his death.

Oh, my gosh, that sounds exactly like Pumpkin! Could it be? Pumpkin's essence was very much like Mr. Peabody's. But there's more…

The real "aha" moment came when I recalled the last stages of Mr. Peabody's life when he walked across the street to sleep on the neighbor's porch shortly after we moved to Staunton. At the time, I made a mental note, thinking it was unusual, but that he was okay. We later found out that the neighbors had called Animal Control to take him to the SPCA, where he was euthanized.

Wow… Watching Pumpkin sit across the street on the neighbor's porch during his last days reminded me so much of Mr. Peabody. Then it dawned on me: Pumpkin had duplicated Mr. Peabody's end-of-life scenario, *sleeping on the neighbor's porch across the street.* How weird was that? It was so unusual that it couldn't be a coincidence – I knew it was Divinely orchestrated.

When I realized the similarities, I immediately felt *the knowing*, and a deep sense of peace filled my heart. Mr. Peabody's soul had returned as Pumpkin and had been a part of my life again. It now made total sense – happening right under my nose, yet I never saw it coming – and I definitely didn't make the connection while my golden boy was still alive.

This beautiful soul, expressed in the lives of Mr. Peabody and Pumpkin, had given me a gift. The correlation between their lives was another example that confirmed my belief in animal reincarnation. And like Big Boy/Fuji, these guys were traveling with me in my soul's evolution.

My spirituality and my work as an Animal Communicator and Energy Healer are inseparable – both parts of the bigger "whole" of the universal, collective consciousness held together by Divine Love. I had been told that my work is "spiritual," but I didn't understand that before. And never in my wildest dreams would I have imagined that my life would unfold like this, but I'm so grateful that it has!

Although the deaths of my animals are incredibly painful, our relationships continue, whether in the physical body through an incarnation, or in the spiritual dimension.

My realization about Pumpkin and Mr. Peabody's connection had heightened my curiosity about whether some of my *other* cats had also been with me before. Could this be more widespread than I previously thought? The extent of this possibility now piqued my interest, and I was on a mission to find out!

CHAPTER 57

I THINK THIS CAT'S BEEN WITH ME BEFORE

"YOU GOT IT, MOM! You finally have the proof you need to verify your suspicion that not only is animal reincarnation possible, but WE – your beloved Fur Family members – have been with you in various cat bodies your entire life! We realized it would take many, many years for all this to come together, but now we are jumping up and down (or should we say, 'flying around'?) in our spirit bodies! Woo-hoo! This was so much fun, watching you have all these 'aha' moments when you realized who we all were, and that we've been with you before. We know there were times when you thought you were crazy, but when you reached out to some friends, and they reported similar experiences, you knew that animal reincarnation was real. We LOVE hearing all these stories and know that readers will, too!"

— The Fur Family

I no longer had any doubts about animal reincarnation. Fuji and Big Boy had sealed the deal with such a profound experience when my eyes landed on Fuji, and at that precise moment, I heard Big Boy's voice in my heart saying, "Can't you see it's me?"

This new knowledge deepened my awareness of animal reincarnation, and it caused me to wonder how my cats regarded the subject. It's hard to explain this adequately, and it's just my perspective, but I don't believe the members of my fur family understand the bigger picture consciously – that they've been with me in different incarnations. I suspect that, with animals, this knowledge comes from a deeper level of consciousness, in the same way that I, as a human, have no conscious awareness of past lifetimes. It's only when I dig deeper within that I've gained this understanding and can "see" a previous life.

Nonetheless, I was so excited about the correlation between these two important beings in my life and felt like I was now swimming in the midst of a multitude of other cats who were also trying to get my attention!

I came across a lot of material about human experiences with reincarnation, but I couldn't find anything about animals except for what I had found in Edgar Cayce's readings. It made sense to continue my own exploration adventure with the plethora of cats I had to choose from!

After my second past life regression, I was certain that Luce (the large, lanky white cat that wanted to see my friend Wally one last time before he passed) had been with me before, but I didn't associate him with any other animal in my current life.

I was certain there had to be others, so I started calling to mind all the stories I remembered about my other cats to see if there were some common characteristics, attributes, or quirks, wondering if I could make any connections. Not surprisingly, the intuitive hits and the *knowing* came very easily.

I started with Boots, Fuji's son, and my gold-and-white boy, who, after we moved to Crestwood Drive, kept returning to the old neighborhood on Stocker Street, now a mile away. Boots had an incredible internal GPS, navigating his way through the woods to his previous home – five times!

Did I have any other cats with a strong GPS? Of course: Samantha, the golden female stray who showed up when I was attending Michigan State University, and who I transported across Canada to my mother as a gift. This little girl did her best to become a part of our family, but it wasn't meant to be. Mom had chosen not to keep her and brought her to a local farm, but the determined little girl found her way back home. Mom brought her to another farm farther away, and that was the end of Samantha's stay.

And even further back was my parents' cat Oliver, who, early in their marriage, they attempted to rehome to a farm over a mile away, but who navigated his way back a month after they left him with his new family.

Many cats have a strong GPS, however, so I wanted more evidence that pointed to reincarnation. Was there something else I could add to verify the connection between Oliver, Samantha, and Boots?

Yes! My mother had become *extremely* attached to Boots after just one visit, when he was a young cat. From that time forward, she inquired about him in just about every phone call, even commenting that she didn't know *why* she was so drawn to him. Now, looking back, it all made sense in light of her previous association with Samantha and Oliver. Even though there didn't appear to be the *same* bond with all three, I believe she sensed both Oliver and Samantha in Boots, and that's what drew her to him.

This association of the continuity of the cats in my family was definitely part of my learning curve. Mom had passed down the story of Oliver, and I was invested in the story of Samantha, which also involved Mom, and then Boots came along and touched both our hearts. I'm convinced that Mom felt the familiarity, but was not able to connect the dots and draw the conclusion about one cat being reincarnated as another.

I've never forgotten these family stories, and it was easy to make the correlations between all three cats. I got a strong, intuitive hit on the continuity of their souls. As I've learned to tune in to my ability to interpret what I receive intuitively, I've learned to trust what I receive.

I would describe using my intuition as being similar to using a muscle. I've shared in an earlier chapter what I learned from Joan Ranquet about developing the "telepathic muscle." It's just like developing a physical muscle: The more you use it, the stronger it becomes. I believe that everyone is endowed with this skill, but some have developed it more than others.

In the case of intuition, I'll reiterate my point that the "intuitive hits" or "knowing" is specific to the individual. What makes sense to *me* wouldn't necessarily have the same intuitive impact on anyone else. In my discoveries, my goal is to share my experiences in the hope that they will propel you to be fervent and diligent in seeking answers to your own questions, no matter how off the wall they might seem.

Another cat that came to mind immediately when contemplating reincarnation was Squeaker, whom I always referred to as "the cat who wanted to live with us." Did I have any others that I would describe this way? Of course! George, the black-and-white cat in Japan that we fed and nursed back to health – the one who inspired my neighbor to bring me two Japanese dolls as a thank you, even asking me to take George back to the States with us. I immediately had the *knowing* that this was the same soul as Squeaker.

It was so much fun to play "Soul Continuity Detective" with my cats! The more I reflected on each of them, the stronger sense I had that they'd *all* been with me before, either in this lifetime or a previous one.

In some cases, I didn't have a lot to base my conclusions on other than the cat's essence and my intuition – unlike the blatant example of Big Boy and Fuji. Nonetheless, all this was making sense to me. Later, I would make more correlations with new cats that came into my life, but here are some others I'd noticed.

- Georgie, the best King Cat ever, who joined us in Virginia Beach after Big Boy passed away, was Goldy, my childhood cat that I had brought to the school science fair. Each had a steady, confident aura of "being in charge."
- Pretty Girl, my tortoiseshell mama cat with the orange mustache from Japan, was my early childhood gray kitten that we hadn't even named yet, who had died young when he fell out of a tree. To me, the connection was the tree. Pretty Girl loved to climb trees, and that's how

she had entered the abandoned house to have her kittens. She also frequently climbed the tree in our yard in Japan, and although many cats climb trees, Pretty Girl was one of the few I've had who did. There was also the strong, intuitive feeling that "this was my cat," and that a part of me had already bonded with her before she joined the family. The dream I had in Japan, where I knew I had to help her, drew my attention to her even more strongly, and I consider the story of her arrival an early sign of my intuitive development.

- Louie, the cat that waited for us at the gas station when I was on my way to Virginia Beach to play in a wedding, was Reggie, another childhood cat. Too many years had passed for me to remember more specifics, but I felt the commonality through my intuition. When I paused and *felt* the dynamics of the relationship I had with each of them, it was the same feeling for both.

- Lilli, the blind cat I adopted at age 12, and who is still with me, was Bashful, the stray we fed for three years in Japan, who was hit by a car before we moved back to the States. They both had/have an aura of aloofness, afraid to fully trust, yet at the same time wanting to be close to me. Like some of the other examples I've given, Lilli feels the same as Bashful did.

Although I had no verifiable evidence for any of these associations, I didn't need it. I was learning to trust the inner *knowing* that revealed the continuity of the soul through my cats, and the intuitive information I was given was specifically for *me*.

Some of my other correlations don't have as much "evidence" surrounding their similarities, so I reached out to my colleagues from the animal communication school and asked if anyone would be willing to share their story. The response was overwhelming, and there were almost too many to include! I'm learning that I am not unique after all!

The first is Amy. She and her husband, Greg, are dog agility trainers, and they have five beautiful shelties. In October 2022, their senior female dog, Desi, passed away, and they decided to adopt another puppy two years later. The new one (Cori) had amazing similarities to Desi.

Amy, Greg, and all four shelties drove together to pick up their newest family member. There were six puppies in the litter (five girls and one boy). It was important that their current dogs knew what was happening, and that the "right" puppy would choose *them*.

From Amy: Desi

One of the girls was so happy to meet our family! Our four seemed to like her, too. She immediately fell in love with Brodie, one of our males (whom Desi was close to when she was alive.) I knew this puppy belonged with our family. We named her Cori, and we brought her back with us that day.

Cori felt quite confident in her new surroundings. She fit right in the day we brought her home, and she knew to go through the back door if she needed to go outside. I thought she was just doing what the other dogs did.

Desi used to sleep with her head on my shoulder. The first night, Cori did the same. Cori is noticeably taller for her age than other shelties, and so was Desi. Cori also seemed familiar with the layout of our house. She loves to zoom around the yard with the two boys. Desi loved to run.

Cori loves going to agility trials with the family. Desi had 10 agility championships during her lifetime. She loved the game! We have agility equipment in our backyard, and Cori went over to the weave poles and weaved through three of them with no instruction. This is a complicated behavior to teach.

Cori was able to follow my directions for turning and reading my body language without me teaching her anything. It was like she could already read my signals and know what to do. That's why I started to think she might be another incarnation of Desi.

From Jennifer: Miss Kitty

I'd been working on my mental and spiritual health after many years of neglect. I know I was beginning to see progress because I started "hearing" more messages from my 15- year-old cat. Miss Kitty was my soul cat. Honestly, I didn't even like cats before I met her. She'd been with me since she was about 6½ weeks old.

One afternoon, I was scooping the litter box (yep, that's really what I was doing!). I clearly heard her tell me that not only had she been the dog that I had before I adopted her in cat form, but she had been one of my pet rabbits, at least one, if not two, of my childhood hamsters, and our family's first cat. Though I didn't have a lot of experience with animal communication yet, I immediately believed it to be true. I could remember the adventurous spirit in all those animals. There was a similar mischievous flavor to all their personalities that other pets I had didn't share.

While Miss Kitty seems to choose to reincarnate as a new species almost every time, that isn't true for all my animals. Our large, muscular, male tabby cat, Oyster, passed away a few years before a conversation that took place with my friend Eddie. Eddie and I were talking about pets that reincarnated, and I told him about Miss Kitty. I told him that she seemed to like the variety of experiences. She wanted to try as many different things as possible. He contemplated a moment and asked if they all did that and said, "Do they switch sexes each time, too?" I clearly felt Oyster shiver in my head as he said, "Eww! Why would I want to be a girl?! Ick!" Oyster is living with us again. Once again, he is a large, muscular, male tabby cat. This time, he's orange instead of gray.

From Noelene: Misty and Monty

I have loved and owned many horses in my life, and two continue to hold a very special place in my heart: Misty, a 12 ½ hands Welsh Mountain Pony, and Dawn, a 16-hand Clydesdale cross. Misty was my first pony, and we were a team. She would buck my brother and sister off and tried but failed to buck me off. I think she had some kind of respect for me.

We lived in an isolated spot (in Australia), and my childhood wasn't particularly happy, so Misty would come galloping when the bus dropped me off. I would saddle her up and would ride until dark.

In 2019, I began an Animal Communication class. We were told to bring a photo of a deceased pet. I found it very hard to believe that this would work, but I took a photo of Misty with me. We had learned about communicating with deceased pets that morning and were given a list of questions we might like to ask. One of them was, "Will you ever come back?"

Very happily, I connected with Misty, and was expecting an incredibly emotional reunion, because that's how I felt. She was very matter-of-fact and showed me her foal that was with her. I had forgotten that she had a foal.

I asked her if she would ever come back, and she said, "I have been back!" and turned around. There was my 'other' soul horse, Dawn! This really took me by surprise, but when I reflected later, they were very different in many ways, but the love between them and me felt the same.

That day, when I learned that Misty had reincarnated as Dawn remains one of the most memorable, emotional, and special days of my life.

After my studies, when I was an emerging Animal Communicator, I was asked to communicate with a dog who had recently moved in with his adoptive family. They felt sure that their new dog, Kevin, was a reincarnation of their deceased dog, Monty. I told them that I would do it, but felt that communicating with Monty might get me the answer more easily, because Kevin may not know.

This was one of the most beautiful communications I have ever done. Monty ran up to me, showing me his eye and saying, "Look, it's fixed! I can see now!" It turns out that he had a brain tumor, which gave him seizures, and every time he had a seizure, his eye turned, giving it an abnormality and making him blind.

I asked him about Kevin and if there was a connection between the two of them. He told me, "I guided him to them." His human family has no doubt that their lovely Kevin is a reincarnation of Monty.

From Terri: Tigger

We adopted Tigger, a tabby, when he was six months old. He had been dumped at the shelter for biting a toddler. Said toddler was bugging him when he was trying to eat.

Tigger fit easily into our group of four cats. He was a gentle, friendly cat. He slept with me and followed me around the house. He greeted me when I came home from work. He would lie on the bathroom counter while I took a shower. I called it his spa time.

One day, he started sneezing constantly. He was around five years old. After taking him to a specialist, we found out that he had developed a sarcoma in his nasal passage. We did not have the thousands it would cost for treatment, and there was no guarantee it would work. When he started to decline, we took him to the vet to let him go. I was completely devastated. For two months, it felt like someone had pummeled my heart.

After a couple of months, I took off work early to go to the local animal shelter. I met every cat and kitten there. I had just about given up when I noticed a white with black patches kitten named Copper eating at the front of his cage. He was kneading the floor of his cage, purring away. I opened the cage door, and I picked him up, and he melted into my arms, purring his contentment. He was mine. I adopted him and brought him home.

It was clear something was special about him. My cat sitter noticed it, too. I changed his name to Twig. He would greet me at the door when I came home from work. He slept with me, followed me around the house, and enjoyed his time on the bathroom counter, soaking up the warmth from the shower steam. Just like Tigger, he would lie there while I combed his long hair. I could see Tigger in his actions and his eyes. I could feel Tigger's presence.

Both Tigger and Twig were what I call "heart cats." I've loved every cat I've ever lived with, but sometimes, along comes a special little soul that you connect with at a deeper level.

Twig lived 12 years until his heart gave out. Again, my heart felt pummeled to pieces. I sat with grief for a week after losing him. For 17 years of my life, I lived with this incredible kitty soul that kept me going through many challenging days. I am grateful for this experience because it changed how I view life and death with my companion animals.

From Melissa: Jag

Jag came to me in the most special way, which is not surprising because he was the most special boy in so many ways. My beautiful Weimaraner, Rock, sired a litter of puppies, and I had the privilege of being the co-breeder. Rock was a once-in-a-lifetime dog – his athleticism, intelligence, and beauty truly broke the mold. To have a puppy from him felt nothing short of magical, and it made the bond with that puppy all the more precious from day one.

From the moment I met him, I knew Jag was meant to be mine. He was my pick of the litter, and my heart was drawn to him immediately. As a puppy, Jag faced a serious health scare, but he pulled through, although it was ultimately the reason he had to leave us far too soon.

Jag and I shared a connection beyond words – a telepathic bond that I didn't fully understand at the time but now recognize so well. I always felt like he could read my mind, and though I didn't realize the depth of our communication back then, it was always clear to me that we were in sync. In agility competitions, we moved through courses as one. I just had to make sure I didn't think the wrong thing or think the next obstacle too quickly or off he would go! Our connection was so deep, and it was so special.

We had six weeks together after his diagnosis. During that time, we cherished our moments, we discussed his leaving as well as his return. He said he had to leave because he needed a new, healthy body. He always told me it was about quality, not quantity, and he thanked me for the quality of his life. I reflect on that often. He left the world peacefully, surrounded by the love of his family. Even after he was gone, I could always feel his presence, and many times he visited through my other dogs.

Several years later, I was on my way to meet the litter of my soon-to-be new puppy. As I was driving, I could feel and hear a dog in the back of my van. I said, "OK, who is that? Jag!?!" It was Jag, I could feel his energy! He was letting me know he would be coming home with me again. Happy thoughts and happy tears!

When Mojo came home, it was clear he was special. He was incredibly smart, already knowing things that most puppies do not know. He could do all the fun tricks and even knew how to walk backwards on cue. His knowledge and abilities were a direct continuation of Jag's — Jag had been a rock star in all those things.

When we went to our massage therapist that Jag used to go to as well, she could sense Jag's energy when she met Mojo. Kathy, the author of this incredible book, did a communication session with Mojo and felt the same energy and confirmation that Jag was back as Mojo. Not that I needed any more confirmation, however, it is always magical when someone else notices it, too.

Mojo does so many of the things Jag used to do. I'm beyond grateful to have my boy back. As we go through life together, there's no doubt in my heart that Jag is with me once again.

From Paula: Riggins

Here is the story of Riggins, my soul kitty, coming back to me in my current cat, Tucker.

Animals sure are amazing, especially if you pay attention and listen to them.

I found my first cat (while living on my own) in a parking lot of a grocery store when he was roughly two months old. He was all white with the most gorgeous copper eyes that changed color from copper to a shade of green. I named him Riggins, and he became my soul kitty, who lived for almost 18 years. He was quite the rascal; very impish, super-loving, was always by my side, and followed me everywhere.

Years later, I rescued my current cat, Tucker, who was approximately two years old. From the minute I saw him, I felt the presence of Riggins in him. When I picked him up, he put a paw on either side of my neck and gave me a light love bite on my cheek, something Riggins used to do. I noticed that, once I got him home, he had a similar impish energy and tons of love like Riggins.

I looked at Tucker and said, "Riggins, if you are in there, please do something only you did so I know that it's you." That very night, I woke up and Tucker was sleeping over my head, which Riggins often did. I reached up, petted Tucker, and then he left, never to do it again. It blew me away. That was all the confirmation that I needed. The longer I have Tucker, the more he reminds me of my soul kitty, Riggins.

I still marvel at the fact that the loving Creator of the Universe knows each of us uniquely and intimately *so well* that when He wants to get our attention, He gives us signs and circumstances so tailored to each individual that we can't miss them – *if* we are open!

I'll end this chapter with one more example from two of my cats that I thought was extremely unusual, and the verification came in a unique way. It was with 12-year-old Chrissy, Boots' sister and one of Fuji's offspring, who along with her sister

Callie came back to live with us when they were three, after we had given them away.

I always described Chrissy as "one of the sweetest cats I've ever had." Did I have another one that I also referred to in this way? Of course! Cyclops, the golden Japanese male that Chuck and I found while out riding our bikes, who was missing an eye and was the first of our Core Eight to die after we moved back to the States.

I found a picture of Cyclops and mused about the two of them, wondering if there was another way to verify their connection. The next day, while Chrissy was sitting on my lap, she gazed up at me very deliberately. As I looked at her sweet eyes, her *left one* closed – as if in slow motion – then opened back up, like she was winking at me! I'd never seen a cat do this.

It impacted me so much that it prompted me to go back and look at the picture of Cyclops to check which eye was missing: It was his left eye – the same one as Chrissy's wink. *OMG, am I making this up?* Nope. My imagination isn't that vivid. I was *not* making this up…

CHAPTER 58

SIMON AND MAX:
I HAVE NO MALE CATS

> *"Mom, having no male cats is truly a dilemma. You need some of that masculine feline energy in your home, so we've developed a plan: Two of your crew from Japan are coming back to you in different bodies. And this is a cool lesson, because we want you to recognize early on which cats have returned in a new body when you first adopt them, rather than later on in the relationship. Enjoy!"*
>
> – The Fur Family

Now that Pumpkin was gone, I faced a serious dilemma – at least, in my mind: I had no male cats…

Imagine a world with only female felines.

For the first time ever, as a cat mom, that was my situation. I'd always had at least *one* male. I loved Fuji and Lilli, but I missed the male feline energy. My question to myself was: *Should I be content with my two girls, or should I add a boy to the family?*

Not only that, but it was the first time since my 20s that I had only two cats! I'd had a 23-year run of being guardian for a continuous flow of eight to ten. Gradually, over the last few years, I'd lost several, and there were only two remaining. The house was *so quiet!* It actually felt "cat-less!"

I remembered what it felt like years earlier, when we lived in Japan and *four* seemed like a houseful: Big Boy, Little Boy, Pretty Girl, and Spunky. Then, little by little, as our feline family grew, it didn't seem to matter anymore. We just adjusted, and *more* became our normal!

But now, in this later stage of my life, how much responsibility did I want to have? And if I decided to increase the size of the family, where should I look, and how many should I adopt? Except for when we adopted Little Boy to be a companion to Big Boy many years ago, all my other purr babies found me through unexpected circumstances.

Even when I found Lilli, although I'd had a sense that there would be another cat joining me in the near future, I wasn't actively looking, and taking in a 12-year-old blind cat was definitely not what I'd envisioned (pun intended!).

Now, here I was again, feeling the nudge inside my heart that alerted me to impending change. Over the years, so many needy cats came to me that I never needed to look in a shelter, but I was certainly open to that possibility. The downside would be that I would want to take them *all* home, and I couldn't do that!

The thought *'I have no male cats'* went through my mind every now and then after Pumpkin passed, but it didn't consume me, and I went about my daily life as usual. Plus, I was still grieving his loss.

Two months after my golden boy passed, I was scheduled to play a gig at a local church, and as I walked out of the house that morning with instruments and music in hand, I casually noted again: "*I have no male cats.*"

When I arrived at the church, Sylvia, a fellow cat lover that I had become friends with over the course of my many years of performing there, started a conversation with me out of the blue that went something like this:

Sylvia: "Hey Kathy, do you remember that feral cat I told you about over the summer that had back-to-back litters of kittens? Well, she had a third, but we were finally able to catch her and get her spayed. We found a home for two of her babies, and I don't know why I'm telling you this, but we still need a home for the other two. They're males, and we've already had them neutered."

Me (in my mind): S*eriously? You've got to be kidding.*

Sylvia: "Are you interested?"

Me: "Let me think about it. I just lost Pumpkin only two months ago, and I'm not sure if I'm ready yet." *Of course, I'm ready. Why else would I have been having these recent thoughts about getting a male cat?*

Over the summer, Sylvia had told me about this mother cat and her kittens, but I was not interested. Pumpkin was sick, and looking for another cat wasn't anywhere on my radar. We had talked about some strategies to help catch the mother cat and get her spayed, but that was all.

Me: "I'll pray about it during the service." *Why did I say that? This is catching me off guard. It's definitely not the conversation I thought I'd be having today. I didn't think it could happen so quickly. And kittens? I haven't raised one in several years. Do I have the stamina to do it again?*

Sylvia: "They're 12 weeks old, born in July. We'd like to find a home soon, but we've been holding off for a while because one of them is still pretty attached to his mother."

Me (intuitive hit in my gut and heart): Oh, my God... Spunky! He was the gold-and-white male really attached to his mother, Pretty Girl, the first cat we rescued in Japan. Is it possible that Spunky was ready to come back in another incarnation? What if I missed this opportunity? And what about the other one? I couldn't separate the two boys.

Were there any signs to confirm that it was really Spunky, and what about the other male? Had I dreamed about any of my cats recently? A big YES to both questions: Spunky, along with Muffin, the skinny, female black-and-white cat with bad breath who had wandered into our yard when Spunky was less than a year old, had *both* appeared in recent dreams. *What if???*

I regularly had cat dreams, and occasionally, they would leave an impression on me, like two of my most recent ones. In the first one, Spunky was walking alongside me through a neighborhood, up a hill. The dream seemed to last for months, and he felt quite present to me. Then, in the dream about Muffin, she was going in and out of a window, from one side to the other, back and forth, like entering and exiting a house.

Both dreams made perfect sense in light of the idea that those two souls might be returning to me in the bodies of these two kittens. Excitement welled up inside me!

Me (after the service): Sylvia, please send me some pictures of them.

I figured that if I saw their pictures and felt a familiarity or tugging on my heart, I would know immediately that these were my cats.

I didn't want to be hasty, though, and bring two kittens into my household unless I was certain it was the right thing to do. It would be a lot of work. *What if I'm just making this all up?*

When I arrived home, waiting on my cell phone were pictures of two of the cutest kittens I'd ever seen! They were both white with gold markings and splotches on their bodies, one a long-haired and one a short-haired.

Of course, these were my cats! I told Sylvia I would come by later that afternoon to see them and make a plan to pick them up.

When I arrived, both boys ran and hid in a corner under the furniture of the sunroom they were living in temporarily. Their mother, a small calico, was also in the room. This was going to be another challenge: the offspring of a feral cat.

I had experienced that scenario before with Bobtail, the female tiger cat from Japan with the curly tail that slept next to me for 19 years and never bonded with anyone else. But I knew it would be manageable, and these boys would at least bond with me. I would take them both and never separate them from each other.

I decided to wait until the end of the week to come back and pick them up, partially so I could get the house ready, but also because I had some unfinished business to do in the realm of emotional healing.

I had a big skeleton in the closet that I had to face: separating a mother cat from her kittens. *How could I do this again, even though she's not my cat?*

Sylvia's neighbor planned to keep the mother, but the kittens would be given away or brought to a shelter with the hope of being adopted. Regardless of what I chose to do, they would be separated from their mother, and there was no guarantee that *they* would even stay together.

I couldn't let that happen. I knew in my heart that these were my cats, and I was ready to face my skeleton. I now had skills as an Animal Communicator, so I took their pictures, and during the week, I connected individually with each boy, and then the mother, letting them know what was going to happen, trying to reassure everyone that they would all be safe and loved.

What I received from the mother cat totally surprised me. She told me that she was worn out! This was her third consecutive litter, and she was exhausted. She didn't know who *she* was and needed time to just grow up. She was barely more than a kitten herself. I assured her that her babies would be safe, loved, and never go hungry.

I breathed a huge sigh of relief and *almost* felt total peace about my decision, but there was still one more huge fear that I had to face: I still bore the guilt of giving away Pretty Girl's kittens, and I knew that I'd have to confront that pain. And then, one night, that mustache-faced, tortoiseshell cat appeared in a dream – and she let me know that she wanted to help me heal.

I don't remember the details, but it was clear to me that I was still full of trauma from having given away her kittens in 1993.

But the message was clear: It was time to let go of the guilt and regret I had held onto for nearly 30 years!

I knew that EFT Tapping would help release those stored emotions. I don't have a clue why I hadn't done this sooner, but I think that sometimes when we have painful, deeply engrained emotions that we've lived with for so long, in a sick way, they become "comfortable" when they're hidden – until something triggers them again. It's easier to store them in the subconscious rather than bring them to the surface, only to feel the pain once more. When you use the EFT healing technique, you have to allow these emotions to *come through and be felt*, so they can finally be released.

Prior to picking up the boys, I did two extensive self-Tapping sessions, targeting the guilt and regret I'd stored from giving Pretty Girl's kittens away, the merciless, highly emotional way I'd treated myself, and the deep shame I felt whenever I thought about the situation. And even though I had practically duplicated my actions with Fuji and her kittens, the root cause lay with Pretty Girl. When you target the earliest memory of an issue with Tapping, any later ones that are similar are usually also resolved.

It was a beautiful experience to finally release the emotions from that trauma. I felt lighter and free, like a new person! And I was now ready to bring these sweet little boys to their permanent home! *Thank you, Pretty Girl, for helping me face this.*

Sometimes after Tapping, it can take a few days or longer to reinforce the effects of the emotional changes, and I admit I was still nervous about picking up these kittens and separating them from their mother. I had communicated with all three cats and knew without a doubt that I was doing the right thing, but I was still a little fearful about being physically present when the boys were placed in the carrier. The best I could do was to let Sylvia and her neighbor do that, so I waited in the car.

When they returned just a few minutes later, two very cute and scared little boys were huddled together against the corner of the carrier. Sylvia commented, "I can't believe how easy that was. We just picked them up and put them inside without any problem!" That was the confirmation I needed that both the Tapping and Communication had been effective.

Yes, these were my boys! I didn't know what to call them, though, so I came up with an innovative idea to find the perfect names: I held a contest for my Facebook friends and offered a free Animal Communication session to the winners! The results? "Simon" and "Max"! (And of course, I communicated with each of them to see if they liked their names before I chose the winners!) *Welcome to the family, boys!*

In keeping with the pattern of what I'd discovered about animal reincarnation up to that point, I was curious to see if either of these kittens had any behavioral patterns and/or personality quirks that I could associate with Spunky and Muffin. I was having fun!

With Simon and Max, it was my first time gaining insights into "which cat they were previously" at the *start* of our relationship. Up till now, it was when a cat was older, or even after one had passed. It was a different feeling, and I didn't want to just "make it up to fit a pattern." I took my time with this personal investigative process, and this is what I observed:

(1) Spunky had been the one attached to his mother, but he also had a behavioral quirk of slamming his body down on the floor next to the cat he wanted to be friends with (namely Little Boy), or whomever he wanted to like him.

Max, the short hair, totally fit that bill. He tried the body-slam with Fuji, but she wasn't interested. Instead, he does it to *me*, especially in the kitchen when it's time to eat, but his affectionate move now occurs throughout the house. (I have to be careful where I step!)

This little guy has totally warmed up to Lilli and treats her like his mother. It's actually quite precious to see him grooming her and sleeping next to her. Like Spunky, he needs to bond with a mother figure.

(2) Muffin had been my "bathroom kitty" and loved to lick my chin, sometimes accidentally biting it! *Ouch!* Simon is the king of the bathroom, perching himself on the closed lid of the toilet seat daily, waiting to be groomed. And he loves to lick around my nose, my chin, and everywhere else on my face, with the occasional bite as well. *Ouch again...*

These are subtle behaviors, but important similarities to me. I recognized them as *intuitive hits* immediately. I'm grateful to Simon/Muffin, Max/Spunky, and Pretty Girl for being wonderful teachers in this recent adventure!

To me, Simon and Max are like angelic beings that fell out of the sky and landed in my living room. They are the purest and most innocent of all the beings that have joined my crew thus far, and I feel so blessed. And these little guys brought an immeasurable amount of welcomed fresh energy into the house after so much loss. I didn't realize how much I needed that.

Do I dwell on the fact that I've made associations between Simon and Max and two previous cats? Nope! They are different beings with different genetics. Their souls have evolved, and so has mine. My relationship with them is different than it was with Spunky and Muffin.

What's different now is my perception of life and the calmness and assurance I experience with the changes in my spirituality. Death is not the end, and our love remains, whether in another incarnation or across the veil. That has been the biggest blessing.

Watching these boys grow up together and learn about the world has been pure joy for me, beginning with their youthful energy as kittens. They hardly ever stopped moving!

I loved this early phase, observing them together as they figured out how to climb stairs to explore everything in the house, practiced their hunting skills, and tried to mimic and learn from Lilli and Fuji.

One of my favorite moments was watching them learn how to use the cat door when they were eight months old. Max intently studied Lilli as she magically disappeared from the living room through what seemed like a wall. He just *sat and sat and sat* on the floor about a foot away from her, watching her tap the in-and-out flap, push herself through it, and vanish.

I could see his wheels turning as he desperately tried to figure out how it worked, no doubt wondering where she went. Then *he'd* tap on the flap, but nothing happened. Eventually, he started pushing it harder – and voila! The outdoor world now opened up to him. Simon quickly followed suit.

Lesson learned.

My little boys were growing up...

CHAPTER 59

A FAIRY TALE OF TWO KITTIES

"Mom, we really like the story, A Tale of Two Cities, but it was too long for us to insert here, so we wrote something different: A Tale of Two KITTIES! And we turned it into a fairy tale! (Of course, we are the stars!)"

— Simon and Max

Once upon a time, in a cat kingdom far away, there lived a brave and noble Queen named Kathy, who dwelled in a modest palace along with her two handsome, young knights, Simon and Max.

The knights were domesticated little feline brothers adorned in gold-and-white fur, with gentle dispositions and playful spirits, who spent most of their time guarding the castle by night and sleeping by day.

During the daylight hours, they looked quite innocent, with their relaxed, outstretched bodies basking in the rays of warm sunspots scattered throughout the palace. Yes, they looked harmless enough, but underneath those sleeping kitty bodies lay fierce warriors!

In the middle of the night, they would stalk their prey, decimate it, and with great enthusiasm carry it back to the Queen's bedroom, howling a war cry to wake Her Majesty and let her know that all was well.

The brave young kitties were always quite eager to share their bounty. One chilly night, however, they deposited their gift in *live* form on *top* of the sleeping Queen's bed, awakening her with their haunting bellows. Startled, and disoriented, she quickly bounced up, leaving her warm satin sheets behind, and put on her glasses, only to see a frightened mouse desperately pleading for its life.

Adorned in only her nightshirt and slippers, the noble Queen quickly grabbed a royal napkin in the form of a paper towel, captured the hysterical rodent before it could escape, and flung open the door to face the below-freezing temperatures and gusting wind, *all by herself!*

Bracing against the cold, she gently released the mouse on the other side of the moat that surrounded the castle, relocating it to a safer place. Closing the door with the wind and cold now behind her, she removed her glasses, crawled back underneath the cozy royal blankets and satin sheets, and praised her two handsome, young knights for doing such a splendid job protecting the kingdom.

The Queen and the ferocious hunters, who had completed their duty for the evening, then quieted down and fell back asleep. And they all lived happily ever after.

The End

CHAPTER 60

MOM, I BROUGHT YOU A PRESENT

> *"Mom, we've brought you present after present, yet your reactions are puzzling. After all the work we go through to catch them and carry them inside, they often disappear. Do they escape? Do you hide them when we're not looking? We hope you're grateful. We only share with you the VERY BEST things we catch, because we love you so much!"*
>
> – The Fur Family

Cats are hunters. Simple fact. I watched an episode of *Animal Planet* that named the "Top 10 Deadliest Killers" in the animal kingdom, and cats were at the top of the list. I don't know if that claim is backed by statistics, but this killer instinct permeates through the lions and other wild cats, down to the tame, domestic versions that rule my household.

Wild cats kill for food and survival, but my household rulers seem to kill just for the fun of it, with the exception of Fuji, my calico, who eats not only what *she* catches, but what *everyone else* catches as well.

I've witnessed repeated scenes of excitement over the kill, yet disinterest in consumption many times over the years. They insist on bringing *everything* they catch into the house, often depositing the poor victim next to my feet, an action that I interpret to be a "gift to Mom." If there is a dead critter on the kitchen floor, they nonchalantly walk around it en route to their food bowls, devour their store-bought wet or dry food, and leave their prize kill to do nothing but decay.

That always bothers me – killing only for sport. For my part, I try to rescue *everything* that's in harm's way, inside or outside the house. Once, while attending an open house on a Sunday afternoon in Georgia when we were house hunting, I rescued a honey bee trapped between two panes of glass in one of the windows. I successfully maneuvered the windows and freed the bee, allowing it to fly away.

I do my best to be kind to everything and everyone, especially the wayward creatures who have unknowingly made their way onto the premises, courtesy of my killer cats. In my numerous attempts to rescue these unfortunate victims, sometimes I'm successful, but other times I'm too late, and the ending doesn't turn out so well for the captured.

I often observe changes in the demeanor or body movements of my cats when they have been hunting and quietly try to sneak something into the house. Muffin, the sweet, dainty, black-and-white female cat from Japan, is a prime example.

One day, while living in Virginia Beach, I glanced at Muffin with her head held low, walking quietly into the house through the sliding glass patio doors. I noticed her slumped-over posture as she cautiously walked past the table where I was sitting and into the living room, but didn't pay close attention and continued going about my business.

About five minutes later, I heard a noise coming from that direction, which I recognized as a bird trying to escape. The feather-flapping became louder, along with the squealing. I darted into the room, saw a frantic sparrow that Muffin had carried inside, and quickly tried to rescue it.

I find that birds are often the most difficult captured creatures to rescue, because when they're scared, they hop and flap their wings at the same time. When they attempt to fly to safety, they bump into windows, curtains, doors, or items hanging on the wall – not to mention the hundreds of feathers scattered about in the process. (I've never figured out whether those come from trying to escape the jaws of their captor or the stress of the situation.)

Much to Muffin's dismay, I opened the front door and was able to guide this flustered bird outside to freedom. *Poor Muffin!* I had curtailed her playtime with this prize catch, but I was very happy to have given the bird a new lease on life.

Fuji wins the prize for her skillful ingenuity in capturing the most unexpected "gift." Shortly after we moved to Stocker Street in Staunton, I was sitting on a couch in the den reading and facing the backyard, which you could see through sliding glass doors. I heard a rattling sound that caught my attention, but couldn't pinpoint where it was coming from. *click/clack/click/clack... Maybe it's from the backyard... Maybe it's my imagination...* I continued reading my book and heard it again: *click/clack/click/clack...* This happened a few more times. I slowly and nervously scanned the room with my eyes, afraid that I might see a rattlesnake, but didn't notice anything. I was puzzled.

I continued to read, but the sound got louder. *CLICK/CLACK/CLICK/CLACK... What is that?* I finally gave it my full attention. My quirky calico was lying on top of something on the white tile floor, several feet in front of me. *What did she catch?* I wondered.

There on the floor, no doubt suffocating underneath her in broad daylight, was a bat! I have no idea how she caught it or brought it into the house unnoticed. The most likely possibility was through a window entrance in our upstairs master bedroom we had rigged for the cats. We had opened the window just wide enough for a cat's body to fit through, used a small piece of cardboard to make a flap, and attached a curtain to minimize heat loss or insects coming inside the house. We thought it was an ingenious way for the cats to enter the house without waking us up at night! (Years later, on Crestwood Drive, I would discover premade "cat doors" that you simply installed in your windows or doors.)

First, they would jump onto the carport railing, then the carport roof, and then the lower roof of the house, giving them access to the makeshift cat door to have their own entrance to the house. It was the only entrance they could use without us assisting them. *I'll bet she brought it in through the window…*

However it got in, I froze when I saw it and had no idea how to get it back out. Thankfully, Chuck was home and came to the rescue. He grabbed an empty box, and with a broom, navigated the bat into the box and carried it through the sliding glass doors to freedom. The thought of rabies occurred to me. It was daylight, and after all, how could a cat possibly catch a *bat?* But there were no signs of rabies in Fuji or anyone else after that episode. I marveled at her hunting prowess.

After I moved to Crestwood Drive with Kristina, a slithery critter made its way onto the living room floor while I was out of town for the day. Kristina called me to report the news of the crawling visitor. I had seen a harmless garden snake outside on the front porch before I left, but the key word is *outside*. It was no doubt the same unsuspecting reptile that would soon become another hunting victim, although this time not a fatality.

Thankfully, Kristina followed my example when it came to putting wildlife back outside and skillfully put it in a box, safely escorting it over the chain-link fence in the backyard. I praised her for her bravery!

I've always loved snakes, and the only time they scare me is when I come upon them unexpectedly. When we were still unpacking boxes on Stocker Street in 2005, I was carrying some freshly laundered clothes upstairs to the master bedroom in the dark and stepped on something soft and mushy near the bed. *Cat poo,* I thought immediately. But there was no smell.

When I looked down, it was *not* cat poo, but instead, a rather stunned brown snake coiled up in a ball. I seemed to have awakened him from a nap! Thankfully, he was too shocked to move, and Chuck came to the rescue once again with a box and broom and escorted him outside.

After Chuck and I parted ways and Kristina moved out of the house and into a supported-living apartment in February 2021, I lived by myself for the first time in over 30 years. The burden was now upon me to rescue any critters that came into the house.

One afternoon, when I casually opened my basement utility room door to check on the laundry (like I'd done hundreds of times), my eyes bugged out as I saw a *large* brown snake at least 5 feet long on the floor right in front of me! I stopped dead in my tracks, and immediately, my nervous system shifted into fight/flight/freeze mode all at once, complete with a fast heart rate and lack of rational thought.

When I realized I was alone in the house, I tried to regain my composure and come up with a plan. *There's no way I can catch that snake and put it in a box. Maybe one of my cats can help me? Not a chance…*

I startled the snake as much as it startled me, and it slithered away quickly, hiding under the washing machine. The only plan I could come up with to facilitate its escape was to prop open the cat door in the utility room that opened to the outside and try to convey to it that through that door was the path to safety. I left it propped open for two days.

Although the cats didn't carry this one in, the result was the same — me trying to rescue a critter that belonged outdoors. The unexpectedness of its visit scared me to death, and for months, I had to take a deep breath every time I opened the utility room door. The element of surprise from that snake's appearance had paralyzed me.

I had to follow-up with this large snake, though, and after the two days, finally managed to muster up the courage to go into the room again. I slowly and cautiously opened the door, thankful to find that it was nowhere in sight. I was afraid to look under the washing machine, because that would mean crawling on the floor and getting "up close and personal," taking the chance that the snake was still there, I would have screamed again, causing it to come charging toward me! I still wasn't rational.

I don't know if it went out the propped door or climbed into the ceiling rafters and died in the attic, but I never saw that visitor again. I have to believe it made its way to safety. To this day, I still open my utility room door cautiously.

* * *

Springtime is the most prolific time for hunting, and during Easter week of 2023, the cats brought in a multitude of visitors.

It started while we were sitting at the dining room table for Easter Sunday brunch. My brother Dave was in town and seated where he had a clear view of the living room.

Lilli, my 15-year-old blind cat, was sleeping in one of the empty baskets under the coffee table when we heard a rustling noise near the furniture. She woke up and quickly scooted out of her basket to get a better read on a mouse that Dave saw scurry underneath the TV cabinet.

In spite of her compromised vision, Lilli is very attuned to energy, can smell anything except her food that's been sitting in the refrigerator, and has a heightened sense of hearing. I suspect that she can still see lights and shadows, but is definitely visually impaired. And she is still a successful huntress.

The mouse made its way to the closet and squeezed through the small space below the folding door that didn't quite extend all the way to the floor. Lilli parked her body outside the closet, ready to pounce.

We continued to eat our brunch, figuring the little rodent wasn't going anywhere immediately. Ten minutes later, Dave saw the mouse poke its body out from the bottom of the door to see if the coast was clear.

Meanwhile, Max, then almost two years old and a skilled hunter himself, walked into the living room just as the mouse poked its body out. He made a beeline for the closet door next to Lilli, who also reacted, and as the mouse tried his best to escape from certain death, Max grabbed him with his mouth. Then, with a confident demeanor that said, "I'm Max the Hunter! Look what I caught!" he carried the stunned rodent into the dining room. Lilli was no doubt disappointed that she came up empty-handed – or rather, empty-pawed!

We had left our seats by this time to watch the drama unfold. I followed Max into the dining room, pleaded with him to "Drop it," (which he did not, of course) and then tried to pick him up and carry him outside with the mouse in his jaws. But as I lifted his 10-pound body, the terrified mouse fell out of his mouth and ran the perimeter of the room. *Oh no...*

As fate would have it, I had left my leaf blower against the far wall of the dining room, and the little mouse ran straight into its long, black nozzle that looked like a tunnel! The timing was unbelievable. (Thank you to all my helpers across the Rainbow Bridge who now help me with these household animal crises!)

I picked up the leaf blower, my brother opened the door to the patio, and I brought the terrified little fellow outside to a much calmer environment, free to leave the safety of his temporary hideout whenever he was brave enough to show his face again. We kept the cats inside for the remainder of the day!

Less than two weeks after the brunch mousecapade, another rescue – this time with a bird as the helpless victim – took place. I had completed all my morning "wake up" rituals of prayer and meditation, stretching, and journaling, along with the bathroom schedule of brushing my teeth, putting in contact lenses, etc. I was finally ready to go to the gym.

I hustled up the stairs into the kitchen to grab some fruit for breakfast and feed whichever cats showed up, but was shocked to find the kitchen in disarray. Cat food cans were knocked over into a disorganized mess, and a plethora of bird feathers were scattered all over the floor with no sign of a body. *Oh no… This doesn't look good. I'd better be on the lookout for the victim.*

There was nothing in the immediate vicinity or underneath any furniture, so I turned my attention to finishing the tasks at hand and getting my belongings together to take to the gym.

I went into the living room to open the curtains and greet my plants, when all of a sudden, there was rustling and vigorous movement behind the window curtain closest to the couch. I opened it and stepped back: *The bird!*

It was a robin, a larger bird than I could envision a cat carrying in, but one of my cats was obviously in rare form that morning. The bird flapped its wings furiously, trying unsuccessfully to return to its outside home – through the window glass.

There are three floor-length windows in my living room, and the frantic bird painfully tried to fly through each of them. This is always a disturbing sight, because they don't see the glass and keep bumping into it.

Determined to help the bird escape, I did what I usually do when they are trapped in my house: I hurried to the front door and propped it open, while three of my four cats were now in the room watching me, salivating at the prospect of another kill.

I grabbed a broom from the nearby closet and tried to direct the robin toward the door, but it kept climbing up the curtains, flapping its wings and perching on the curtain rods. It took a few minutes, but my strategy worked, and the confused bird made its way back outside through the open door, flew away, and gained its freedom.

Thankfully, this was a happy ending to the robin's escapades. Everyone in the house calmed back down, and I went back into the kitchen to clean up the feathers…

My trip to the gym was not going to happen yet, though. There was a bee trapped inside, trying to get out the same windows as the bird, also unsuccessfully. I spent another five minutes helping the bee and eventually trapped it with a plastic cup and piece of cardboard that I put flat against the window; then I took it outside.

Too much excitement for one morning. And yes, I did finally make it to the gym…

CHAPTER 61

THE BABY RABBIT

"I'm so grateful to you, Miss Kind Lady. My life was short, but you cared – and loved me – even for a short while. Many years ago, a Tiger Cat named TC taught you that 'even the smallest act of love will be remembered.' This small act of love from you gave my life purpose."

– The Baby Rabbit

Not all of my cats' hunting expeditions have a happy ending, and some of the more emotionally devastating ones are permanently etched in my heart, like the story of the baby rabbit.

A week after the Easter Sunday escapade, when the mouse ran inside the leaf blower, I had a terrible night, woke up more times than usual to use the bathroom, and then had a very disturbing dream, after which I couldn't fall back to sleep.

At exactly 5:50 a.m., I heard the utility room cat door being opened on the opposite side of my bedroom, followed by the screeching sound of a "critter." I couldn't pinpoint what it was, so I listened for more information as I jumped out of bed, donned my bathrobe, grabbed my glasses, and turned on the lights.

I didn't hear the unique growling noise that Simon makes when he catches something, so I knew it must be Max. Sure enough, as I looked around the corner of the L-shaped room to see what creature was pleading for its life, I saw a very young baby rabbit dangling from Max's mouth, thrashing its hind legs, trying to escape.

First, I opened the door and tried unsuccessfully to get Max to carry it outside. Then, like I had done a week before when he was holding a mouse in his mouth, I tried my useless command of "Drop it," but of course, it didn't work this time, either. *For real, Kathy, do you think a cat with prey in its mouth is going to listen to you? Max is not a dog...*

Instead, my two-year-old male hunter got nervous as I raised my voice and ran upstairs with the baby rabbit still in his mouth. I followed him into the dining room where he finally *did* drop it.

It was still alive but appeared to be injured. Over the years, I've witnessed countless animals go into shock as if dead, then later escape and wander off to safety, having "played possum." *Perhaps this baby rabbit might be doing the same.*

I grabbed the nearest kitchen towel and draped it over the rabbit, then gently carried him outside to the far end of the property, laying him down on a bed of soft leaves behind the chain-link fence. I never touch wildlife directly when I first pick them up, because I don't want to get bitten or scratched when they're in a frantic state, or squeeze them too hard as I try to keep them from escaping. The towel is the safest way to protect both of us from getting injured.

When I set him down, he was motionless but still alive. At that point, he was calm enough for me to pet, so I did so as he gently rested, speaking encouraging words and telling him he was safe and loved. (I also apologized for what my cat had done.)

I had previous obligations to attend to that would take a couple hours, so I left him by himself in hopes that the injury wasn't fatal and that he'd have the courage and strength to get away. I felt that if he was one of those animals playing possum, my presence might scare him, so I would check again when I returned.

I couldn't stop thinking about this little guy, and when I arrived back home, I immediately ran to see if anything had happened. He was still there in the same position as when I'd left. I petted him, and his body was still warm, but at that very instant, I felt his spirit leave. *Did I just imagine this? Was his body really still warm?*

His body temperature started to drop almost immediately, and I knew he was gone.

I was sad and puzzled at the same time, so I reached out to one of my Animal Communicator friends to ask if she would try and connect with the rabbit to find out more information.

Communicating with an animal that has passed is one of the most rewarding aspects of being an Animal Communicator. I've found that it brings closure and peace to the humans, and often the animals have a lot they want to say.

At the same time, when I am very emotionally involved in a situation regarding an animal – especially my own – I'm not afraid to reach out for help, because I don't want my prejudices or filters to get in the way of the information I receive.

Although I have learned how to practice detached compassion and can handle most of the situations that come my way, there are still occasions when I need help.

My friend was more than willing, and this is what she received from communicating with the baby rabbit:

> "He told me his home was destroyed, and he had nowhere to go. His mother and a sibling had been killed. There was mud and tree branches. He had no shelter, and he was all alone. He was grateful for your kindness and compassion. In an odd way, he was also grateful for the cat bringing him to you. He got to spend the end of his life in a place where he felt safe and cared for. He did wait for you to come back before he left his body."

That message brought incredible joy to my heart amidst the tears and sadness of the rabbit's death. To know that I had made a difference in the life of this small creature was an incredible gift to me.

Although the baby rabbit's story took place over the course of just a few hours, it was a life-changer for me and increased my awareness of the connectedness of all life, reinforcing my belief that even a small act of kindness can make a positive impact in the life of another creature. It didn't matter that this little rabbit was not a domesticated pet. We had formed a bond in that brief time.

* * *

A week after the baby rabbit passed, I awoke at 5:00 a.m. to the once again familiar sound of the cat door being opened, this time accompanied by Simon's growling noise, meaning: "I caught something, and it's mine!"

I heard movement across the floor of my bedroom, but no squealing or painful moans. I didn't get up right away, because the sounds stopped almost immediately. I presumed the situation was under control, and that everyone had left the room. I admit that sometimes I don't want to deal with these stressful situations because I'm afraid of how they will turn out.

But after about five minutes of quiet, I was still suspicious, so I forced myself to get up. As I slowly walked around the room, I saw Simon and Max staring at my laundry basket, which is situated next to a wall. *What are they looking at? Oh no...*

I cautiously walked toward my little hunters, a bit nervous about what I might find, and looked in the basket but didn't see anything – dead *or* alive. Then I moved it away from the wall, and right before my eyes, crouched in the corner like a statue, was another baby rabbit about the same size as the one that had died just a week earlier. This one was fully alive. *I've been given another chance!*

Once again, I quickly grabbed a towel, covered the scared rabbit to confuse him and remove him from the cats' sight, then scooped him up into my hands with the towel, holding him firmly enough so he couldn't escape. I quickly carried him outside and released him over the side fence into the neighbor's backyard, where he darted away faster than any rabbit I'd ever seen!

Could that first baby rabbit somehow have helped me save this one? I probably will never know the answer to that question, but I was grateful that this little one had lived to hop another day! (I think my cats are still downstairs looking for him…)

I can't save every animal, but I can love the ones I meet, if only for a short while, like these baby rabbits, knowing it will make a difference in their lives.

Maybe it's the only love they will ever know. Isn't that really what it's all about?

CHAPTER 62

LOSING FUJI

"Mom, my journey with you as Fuji is now coming to an end. My soul's presence as Kimba, Big Boy, and now me, has been part of your life longer than anyone else – human or feline! Leaving you is really difficult, but my body is frail and can't hold on any longer. We've shared amazing adventures, and I assure you that we will be together again. Can't tell you when that will be, but my timing is always perfect! Soon, though, I will be with you from the other side whenever you need help from an opinionated calico. Please remember your best girl when you eat those apples you named me after – and we'll smile together!"

– Fuji

I had always hoped that Fuji would live to be at least 20, but when I noticed her health starting to decline as she was approaching her 18th year of life, I went into my usual state of denial, not wanting to face another death.

Somehow, I lived under the delusion that if I had enough wishful thinking, I could make my cats live longer. I knew the timing was not for me to determine, yet, in my love for them, I stubbornly tried to keep them around forever. During Fuji's decline, as with many others, I seemed to find a logical explanation for any health issue that arose, in order to avoid reality – ever the optimist.

My feisty calico, whom we had found as a kitten at an apple orchard 18 years earlier, began to lose her mobility as she lost muscle tone in her hind quarters. It became more of a challenge to climb up and down the stairs, so I helped by occasionally carrying her. She was no longer able to "go hunting" in the hallway to capture her favorite green, stuffed mouse that I would throw.

From the communication I had done with her, I knew that Fuji loved being independent and having her space, doing as much as she could by herself, and eating "people food." And as much as she was able, she still wanted to wrap herself around my shoulders and walk through the house together. I wanted to honor those things and did my best to incorporate them as she continued to decline.

About a month before she passed, she started having some chest congestion. Her breathing was fine, and she had a good appetite, so I thought it would improve. But when one day her appetite seemed to be gone, I lost all objectivity about what to do next. Then I felt a small growth in her throat. *What if she starved to death because she couldn't eat?*

I had an immediate flashback to Spunky, the gold-and-white cat from Japan, who was throwing up his food and making wheezing noises when he tried to breathe. When I took him to the vet, they found a cancerous tumor in his throat. They put him under anesthesia to see if it had spread, and finding that it had, they euthanized him on the operating table. I couldn't bear to go through that type of scenario again.

I panicked and reached out to a local vet who made house calls to consider having her euthanized at home. But first, I wanted to know Fuji's wishes. I knew I was too emotional to trust my ability to connect with her telepathically, so I contacted one of my colleagues, who did it on my behalf.

Fuji told my friend that she wasn't ready to go yet, that her work here wasn't complete. She said she didn't want to have the end of her life "planned." She wanted it to be in the course of her daily life, and to be at home. Thankfully, though I'd left several messages and emails for that vet, I never got a response.

I was relieved to know what my girl wanted, and that gave me the courage to connect with her myself. I told her that I didn't want her to hurt or to suffer, and that I would be okay if she felt it was time to go. I thanked her for her life and everything we had shared together. She wanted to just wait, with no advance preparation as to when she would die, so again I dismissed the idea of having her put to sleep at home.

While connecting with her, I felt the same familiar bond that I had with Big Boy. That was the most incredible part of our communication, and I will carry that feeling of closeness forever.

With Fuji, I reached out to other colleagues for more scalar wave sessions, in addition to what I was doing, along with prayers and any well wishes they could supply. All of my losses have been difficult, but I've found it even more brutal to lose an older animal companion because of the length of time they've been with you.

Shortly after the healing sessions, this determined girl began to eat again, and the lump in her throat seemed to have shrunk, so I made an appointment with a holistic vet she had been to before, in hopes of trying acupuncture to help clear her lungs. But the vet recommended we go a different route and check for other things that might be affecting her health.

Fuji was the most *ideal patient* at that appointment that I had ever seen. She purred and did the famous cat kneading movements of "making bread" while they were drawing blood and pumping fluids into her with an IV.

The blood tests showed that her kidneys, thyroid, and magnesium levels were normal, much to the vet's surprise. I knew, however, that the scalar wave sessions and changes I had made in her diet had played a significant role in those positive health reports.

Her heart was also strong, but she was anemic with a small amount of pneumonia in her lungs. There was also some gas or blockage in her abdomen. We treated her with several medications to try and help her regain some strength and were scheduled for a return visit in two weeks. From her positive attitude at the appointment, I thought she would recover.

The next day, though, I was outside doing yard work, and she was doing her best to follow me around, like she loved to do. I noticed she was somewhat hunched over, trying to walk down the sloped backyard, and then she stopped to rest. I walked over to her, and it was then that I realized just how tired she was.

My self-talk went like this: *How could I have missed the incredible fatigue she must have been feeling? I was trying so hard to let her be independent and self-sufficient that I missed the obvious. Wait… be easy on yourself, Kathy. You love this girl, and you're doing the best you can.* At least, I wasn't so hard on myself this time. Progress!

Fuji continued to eat that day and seemed to be in good spirits. I still hoped for her recovery, while also recognizing that I wanted to dissociate myself from the pain of this phase of her life, as I did my best to stay emotionally present with her.

The next day, Friday, September 15, 2023, I checked on her in the early afternoon and found her asleep under the corner of my bed. It was an unusual place for her to sleep, and I made a mental note that her body was a little cool, but the laminate wood floor beneath her also had a chill to it. She was resting comfortably, so I didn't disturb her. She hadn't eaten that morning, but because of the medication, I thought she was probably extra-tired.

I did another scalar wave session on her, and when I finished, I checked on her again. I approached the corner of the bed, got down on my knees, and as I moved the comforter out of the way to see her, I heard a groaning, exhaling sigh. Then nothing. She was gone…

Fuji had positioned herself in a place where I could find her and waited for me to be with her when she passed. I was taken aback, as it caught me off guard when I heard her groan. It happened so quickly, like it had with previous animals who'd waited to die in my presence. When they breathe their last, as I come close to them, it usually takes me a minute to catch on that their spirits are departing, and this time with Fuji was no exception. I knelt beside my girl in disbelief, stroking her now lifeless body.

Then I gently moved her out from the corner of the bed, finding that her body was now mostly cold all over and had started to stiffen – except for the area around her stomach and heart that were still warm and had kept her alive while she waited.

My beautiful calico, the matriarch of my cats, who stood by me faithfully for 18 years, helping me through every major emotional upheaval of my life, was now gone. She had passed on her terms, when she was ready, and she'd waited for me to be with her. The last gift I gave her was the scalar wave session, which I now realize was my way to help send her across the Rainbow Bridge for her next great adventure.

Starting as my childhood cat Kimba, then returning in another incarnation as Big Boy, and finally again as Fuji, this amazing soul had accompanied me throughout my life. What a tremendous gift I had been given!

Once again, I was reminded that it's not for me to determine the days or seasons when an animal will pass. I remembered that special Tiger Cat in Japan that I was unable to save, who had died from the scabies, and the scripture verse that showed up that day in the daily mass reading from I Samuel 26: v.2-6: "I, the Lord, deal death and give life."

It was now time to clear my head and begin the grief process. I went for a hike the rest of the afternoon, and my brother Dave, who now lived in North Carolina, arrived later that evening for a planned visit. Fuji's timing was always perfect, and having my brother with me for the weekend was a huge blessing. He helped me bury her in the backyard next to Squeaker, Chrissy, Luce, and Louie.

Fuji had one more surprise for me. The next morning, Dave and I went out for breakfast, followed by a quick trip to the Farmer's Market in downtown Staunton. We arrived just as the vendors were starting to pack up and happened to pass by a booth that was selling locally grown apples.

The owner called over to us and offered both of us a sample. I never turn down fresh apples, so I said, "Sure!" There were about seven different varieties, and the one he gave us was very tasty. "What kind is this?" I asked.

"Fuji," he replied. Of course, it was!

Thank you, my beautiful girl, for this special gift, your impeccable timing, and for letting me know you're OK. I treasure the strong love we've shared throughout your different incarnations during my life, and although my heart is grieving because you're gone, I know that the separation is only temporary. I'm looking forward to when we will share more adventures together.

Eighteen years earlier, my family and I had found this feisty, opinionated calico cat at an apple orchard and named her "Fuji" after the apple…

I couldn't make this up if I tried.

CHAPTER 63

LESSONS I LEARNED FROM MY CATS

"Mom, we've had so much fun writing this book with you and have done our best to teach you some of life's greatest spiritual lessons from our perspective. As we start to wrap things up, we're going to leave you with some of our greatest pearls of wisdom. Don't be sad, though, because there will be more stories to tell and more felines to love. And remember: Whenever a dying, destitute, or homeless cat crosses your path, there's ALWAYS room for just one more!"

– The Fur Family

1. Appreciate the sunshine by day and the moonlight by night – all night!
2. Persevere in chasing your goals, and don't be afraid to roll on the ground and get dirty in the process.
3. After you get dirty, take a bath.
4. If you sit at the table long enough, eventually you will get served.
5. If you don't like your food choices, keep waiting long enough, and they will change.
6. Make sure you do your business when nobody is watching.

7. When someone you love is hurting, curl up next to them and just be present.
8. When you wear someone down long enough, you'll be able to catch them and bring them into your house.
9. Appreciate everything that moves – it might have a lesson to teach you.
10. If you knock on someone's door long enough, eventually they'll let you in.
11. When you find someone to take you in and love you, go back and get all your friends.
12. Be persistent: When one door closes, another one opens.
13. If something is stressing you out, take time to go outside and play.

And the best lesson of all:

When you get tired, go take a nap!

EPILOGUE

A LIFE REFLECTION

"Well, Mom, we did it! We wrote our book! Bravo! And as we come to the conclusion, we want to remind you that we are always here, whether in physical form or across the veil in the spiritual realm. Please call on us whenever you need our help or a reminder that we're watching you. We will give you signs of our presence. And as much fun as it was to teach you about animal reincarnation, ultimately, there were greater lessons you were meant to learn, such as the 'oneness' of creation and the unity of all life within the collective consciousness.

It thrills us that you no longer live with the mindset of 'separation consciousness.' More important is the realization that the Divine Creator loves YOU so very much! These lessons are paramount in the ultimate understanding of your soul's purpose and mission. Well done! Yes, there are challenges throughout life, but you always act with good intentions and do your best in every situation you face. Your unwavering perseverance pays off.

Now it's time to relax and give yourself a break. Go have some chocolate (hee... hee... we know where you keep your stash!). Finally, even though you sometimes want to give up in the midst of your trials, we've seen you realize that everything really does work together for good. In fact, it always turns out PURRRRFECTLY!"

– The Fur Family
(Showering you with purrs, chin licks, body slams, head butts, snuggle hugs, and a happy whinny from Jake!)

I often wonder what my life would be like today if I'd made different choices along the way, resulting in different outcomes. For example:

- What if my family didn't have cats when I was a child?
- What if I had stayed in Catholic schools all through my educational years and never played a musical instrument?
- What if I had chosen not to join the Air Force Band, but instead became a band director after I finished college?
- What if I had turned down the assignment to Japan and not reenlisted, but became a civilian instead?
- What if I had not heeded the dream in Japan about Pretty Girl, the tortoiseshell cat with a mustache, and left her to fend for herself and her four kittens?
- What if Chuck and I never took care of more than two cats at a time?
- What if we had never adopted our daughters or never divorced?
- What if I had given up my Spiritual Quest before I received any answers and continued to live in a manner that felt disconnected from the universe?

I'm glad I will never know the answers to those questions, but more than ever, I'm a firm believer in the Bible verse from Romans 8:28 quoted earlier in this book: "All things work together for good to them that love God, to them that are called according to His purpose."

I know that I can't change any of these major turning points, but in hindsight, I wouldn't want to! There were painful and challenging moments, but I'm so grateful for the life lessons that resulted.

One aspect of my soul's journey in this lifetime has been maintaining a sense of humor as much as possible and *trying* to learn not to take myself so seriously. That is definitely still a work in progress.

I would never have imagined that all my cats would be part of this incredible spiritual journey, and as the result of unknowingly becoming a Crazy Cat Lady, I have gained insight into the collective consciousness and oneness of all life. I have such peace that I never thought was possible, and being able to "connect" at the soul level with animals and other sentient beings has brought an immeasurable amount of joy!

My cats' arrivals and departures – not only when they first appeared in my life, but when they came back via reincarnation – have been the best teachers of Divine Timing, miraculously showing me that death is not the end. And the awareness of reincarnation of both humans and animals was the icing on the cake! What a tremendous gift that has helped ease the sting of death, knowing that my furry companions are accompanying my soul throughout its evolutionary growth.

Reflecting back on my heartfelt, desperate prayer, "God, who are You, and do You love me?" the Divine Love has more than answered that plea. What I've learned didn't come from a book or a church. Instead, they've been lessons of the heart, from the heart of the Divine to mine.

These answers were not instantaneous, but rather unfolded gently, as I persevered through the healing and recovery process, which included removing barriers to God's love that I had created, such as shame, guilt, unforgiveness, and resentments.

I came across a prayer from another faith tradition that I love, and I incorporate it in my daily morning meditation. It goes like this:

A Buddhist Prayer of Forgiveness

If I have harmed anyone in any way,
either knowingly or unknowingly.
through my own confusions,
I ask their forgiveness.
If anyone has harmed me in
any way, either knowingly
or unknowingly,
through their own confusions,
I forgive them.
And if there is a situation I am
not yet ready to forgive,
I forgive myself for that.
For all the ways that I harm
myself, negate, doubt, belittle
myself,
judge or be unkind to myself,
through my own confusions,
I forgive myself.

I've been blessed with many fellow travelers along this journey. I no longer live with a separation consciousness, because I have learned that we are not separate after all —from each other or from the Divine. I understand that we are all part of a collective consciousness held together by Divine Love.

Previously, that was only a concept to me. Now, I can touch it, taste it, feel it, and experience it. I know without a doubt that God loves me immeasurably!

Since I lost the feeling of aloneness and separation, I have a serenity that I've never experienced before, despite all my years as a churchgoer. For now, I no longer attend a church on a regular basis, but I've never been more connected to God/Divine Love/the Creator of the Universe in my entire life! I am so grateful!

To me, what I consider to be "churchy language" is a stumbling block. It caused my concept of God to be skewed and ingrained within me that I've had to separate myself from its effects. But this has been *my* experience, and I would not begin to speak for anyone else. We each have our own unique path to travel.

During this spiritual journey, I found myself pondering some passages from the Bible whose meaning used to puzzle me, but now I've *experienced* a better understanding of them:

In the Gospel of Luke, 17:21, Jesus says:

"For, behold, the kingdom of God is within you" in response to the Pharisees asking when the Kingdom of God will come.

I love this verse, because it's exactly where I've found many of my answers, going to deeper levels of consciousness through meditation, intuition, and the promptings of Divine Love.

In the Gospel of John, 17: 21-24, Jesus says:

"I pray that they will all be one, just as you and I are one – as you are in me, Father, and I am in you. And may they be in us, so that the world will believe you sent me. I have given them the glory you gave me, so they may be one as we are one. I am in them, and you are in me. May they experience such perfect unity that the world will know that you sent me and that you love them as much as you love me." (NLT- New Living Translation)

I don't believe that the "oneness" Jesus was referring to has anything to do with everyone on the planet being part of the same church denomination – or even 'church' in general! It goes much deeper and transcends human faith traditions.

In 1 John 4:16, there is another verse I carry in my heart:

> "God is love,
> and whoever abides in love abides in God,
> and God abides in him."

To me, this is truly what life is about, and I'm all in! I don't always measure up to this ideal, but I've learned to give myself a break if I don't. It's with this understanding of love, unity, and oneness that I now live my life, and it propels me forward to help make a difference for humanity.

In one of my daily meditation books, I came across a beautiful quote from Mechthild of Magdeburg, a German Christian mystic (c.1207- c.1282), whose writing describes the love affair between God and her soul:

"I was created in love. For that reason, nothing can express my beauty, nor liberate me, except love alone."

Thank you for sharing what has been an extraordinary journey of my soul through this lifetime, as experienced with my animal companions. May you follow your own path and find the answers you are looking for, knowing that you are not alone!

EPILOGUE TO THE EPILOGUE

REALLY?

Why, might you ask, would I write an Epilogue to the Epilogue?

Well, let me tell you a story… It's been a year and a half since Fuji passed, leaving me with just three cats – Lilli, Simon, and Max. A couple months ago, as I was finishing this book to turn in to the publisher, I started feeling that familiar tug on my heart that meant: "Open your heart to another cat."

I felt like I was ready and had a sense that one of my previous cats wanted to return and show up this time as a young female. I just didn't know which of my fur babies it would be.

While the publisher began the proofreading process, I went to California to visit my oldest daughter Masha, and as we were talking, I shared my willingness to adopt another cat.

Literally the next day, my close friend and hiking partner Scott called from Virginia and said he had another cat for me to replace the one I had lost over a year ago. He was speaking casually, but little did he know how prophetic his words would be. Without hesitating, I said, "I'll take her!"

The young female kitten had either been dumped off or wandered onto his brother-in-law's yard next door, and he and Scott's son brought her to Scott's house. Although he has a cat and wasn't interested in adopting another one, he agreed to take care of her until I returned home and could pick her up.

"Send me her picture!" I said – and he did. The moment my eyes gazed at this pretty little girl that would soon join my family, my heart skipped a beat. OH.MY.GOD. I felt the familiar presence immediately and knew without a doubt that this was Fuji (AKA Big Boy and Kimba). I was overwhelmed with so much love and gratitude.

This time, my beautiful, soulmate cat was a tortoiseshell/calico mix known as a "tortico." The name that popped into my head was "Sally," so that's what I figured she wanted to be called. Or, as my veterinarian friend Dr. Jill Todd calls her, "Mustang Sally Einstein" (tortoiseshell + calico = intelligence). And of course, the spunky, confident personality and determined spirit of the soul I had shared so many years with was evident right away.

Although I totally trusted my intuition on this one, I *still* wanted verification, so I showed my daughter the picture and asked, "Who does this cat *feel* like?" Masha, who is also highly intuitive, responded "Fuji" – with no prompting or hesitation. That was all I needed to hear, especially since I had literally just told her of my desire to add another feline family member.

Once again, Fuji showed up with her impeccable timing, and I am *so happy!* My quirky, opinionated calico had decided that our book needed a surprise happy ending for the readers, so I will gladly let her have the last word:

"Hey, Mom! I'm back! Just like I promised. I know you weren't expecting to see me again this soon, but I felt this was the perfect time because, well, your biological clock is ticking… hee hee… and I want to have enough time for more adventures with you. So, hold on tight, because Mustang Sally wants to go for a ride!" - Fuji

"Thanks for adopting me, Mom! And by the way, did I mention that I'm pregnant?" -Sally

You feisty little tortico…

Golden Years

Pumpkin - March 2021

Lilli - Feb 2021

Boxing Day - Pumpkin, Squeaker, Chrissy

Dave & Steve - Malone 2022

Fall in Malone 2022

Family Pic - Malone Oct 2022

Family 2023

Simon & Max on arrival - Oct 2021

Simon & Max - May 2024

Fuji in the Fall

Fuji's favorite place: riding on my shoulders

With Mom - 2022

Malone - Oct 2022

In Malone - March 2025 after the snowfalls!

In Duck, NC - Dec 2024

Piping for a Burns Night - Jan 2024

Max & Simon - Fierce Hunters in a staredown - 2023

Lilli - Feb 2025

Simon - Feb 2025

Max - Feb 2025

Simon & Max Twinning - 2022

Lilli, Max, and Simon

Simon - Feb 2025

Sally

Me with Max & Lilli Dec - 2024

Continuity of this cat's spirit throughout my life

ABOUT THE AUTHOR

Kathy Boyer is a professional musician of nearly 40 years and is retired from the U.S. Air Force, which she entered while attending graduate school at Michigan State University as a music major.

She's originally from a small town in upstate New York but has lived in numerous places and traveled all over the world as an Air Force band clarinetist, saxophonist, and bagpiper. Although music has been the driving force in her life, her heart has always been with animals. Wherever she traveled to or lived, she sought them out – from having breakfast with the birds in Singapore or riding elephants in Chiang Mai, Thailand, to feeding kangaroos and cradling koalas in Australia!

It was during her five-year assignment in Japan with the Air Force Band of the Pacific that she "accidentally" accumulated eight cats – and returned to the United States with all of them! That's when she began to label herself an *official* Crazy Cat Lady.

Those years in Japan marked the beginning of a 23-year span of being a cat mom to a continuous flow of 8-10 cats in her daily household. This was a steppingstone to finding her soul's purpose of helping animals.

Through a series of synchronicities, she attended a four-day Animal Communication Conference in Virginia Beach, Virginia, in September 2018, taught by Joan Ranquet, a world-renowned animal communicator, energy healer, author, and TEDx speaker. During those life-changing four days, Kathy discovered that she, too, could learn how to communicate with animals telepathically through the transference of words, pictures, and feelings – the same way animals communicate with each other.

Immediately following the conference, she enrolled in Joan's school, Communication with all Life University (CWALU), and upon graduation from the "Animal Mastery Program" began her career as an animal communicator and energy healer.

Kathy considers herself a "Soul Growth Junkie" and continues to add to her understanding of the collective consciousness and "how things work." That exploration led to training with the Vibrational Sound Association to become a Vibrational Sound Therapy Certified Practitioner (VSTCP). She loves conducting Sound Baths with her singing bowls!

Music is still a huge part of her life, and she is a member of several bands, along with being a freelance musician. She performs extensively as a solo bagpiper throughout Virginia's beautiful Shenandoah Valley, where she currently lives. It's also the perfect location to hike and play pickleball – two of her favorite hobbies!

Kathy loves her life and shares it with her feline family of Lilli, Simon, Max, Sally, Daphne, and Kasper.

Feel free to read more about her and contact her by email or on her website: kathyh@drnetwork.com and https://www.thepetconnector.com

Connect with the Author

To Schedule a Reading or Energy Healing Session
https://www.thepetconnector.com
email: kathyh@drnetwork.com

To be added to my Email Newsletter list:
Email me your name, email address and a picture of your pet

To connect with me on Facebook:
Look For: Kathy Boyer
(Animal Communicator and Energy Healer for Animals)
Post a pic with you and your pet and tag me in it, or send it through Messenger, and
I will send you a friend request

For Information about Sound Healing Sessions:
Monthly Sound Baths and Individual Sessions Available
Sound Healing sessions are also available for your animals
(local clients)
https://www.goodvibrationskathyboyer.com
email: kathyh@drnetwork.com

For Additional Copies of Memoir of a Crazy Cat Lady:
Contact me directly to receive a signed copy and a free bookmark
Books may also be purchased through Amazon.

Additional Resources

Joan Ranquet
Founder of Communication with all Life University
https://www.joanranquet.com

Communication with All Life University
https://www.cwalu.com

Dr. Bernadette Spector, VMD
Veterinary Medical Doctor
Integrative, Traditional & Holistic modalities
https://www.grayfoxanimalhospital.com

Dr. Jill Todd, DVM,
Holistic Veterinary Medicine
Certified Veterinary Acupuncturist and Chiropractor,
advanced training in Veterinary Cold Laser Therapy, Energy Medicine and Healing
email: jilltodd@jsquaredhealing.com

Val Smith
Artist/Graphic Designer
(Photo Pages layout designer for this book)
http://ValSmithSacredArts.com
email: val@lavendercommunications.com

Vicky Mitchell
Pet Photographer
(front and back cover photos photographer)
https://www.victoriafinley.photography
victoria@victoriafinley.photography

In Memoir of a Crazy Cat Lady, Kathy Boyer takes the reader on a fantastic journey. As the title indicates, this is a journey that plays out amongst a plethora of feline entities. Yet, although the author certainly qualifies as a "Crazy Cat Lady," a moniker she bears with pride and dignity, this is the story of a spiritual expedition. Among these pages, we join in the evolution of Kathy's understanding of our human spiritual nature as well as that of the animals in our lives. Her special connection with cats, and other creatures, facilitates her soul development. As we travel along, we eventually realize that she is not just accompanied by her beloved animals, but that her four-legged friends are actually guiding her on this mystical path to the realization of the Oneness of all life and the presence of the Creator in all.

Kathy takes one step after another that leads her to training in animal communication and various forms of energy healing. Her animal communication skill allows her to offer a fun and fascinating look into the purr-sonal thoughts and interpurr-sonal relationships between and with the animals that share in our lives. Kathy's struggles with end-of-life issues is a matter that every pet caregiver can relate to. Interestingly, again, her animal communication talent provides a rich source of purr-spectives to consider when faced with the impending death of a beloved pet. Her insights into reincarnation and the continued spiritual presence, and sometimes physical return, of a four-legged loved one into our lives is a comforting perception. Our almost instantaneous connection with certain animals is surely a sign that we have been with them in previous incarnations.

This book is full of valuable life lessons and fun animal anecdotes. In the end, the reader walks away deeply moved and thoroughly entertained. You do not have to be an animal lover to enjoy this genuinely revealing memoire, but if you are, you will totally relate to the stories within it.

Bon Voyage.
— Dr. Doug Knueven, holistic veterinarian

This is a wonderful book about a great lady and her journey with a group of cats that have been sent to her over multiple lifetimes. The cats and one beautiful horse gently guided her to the woman she is meant to be in this lifetime. You don't need to believe in multiple lives to enjoy this lady's story; you just need to believe in yourself. Kathy might be "slow to catch on," as she says, but her cats make sure she stays on track.

— Tracy Smith, holistic pet health coach

A strong, compelling case for animal reincarnation from both a human and animal point of view. Kathy Boyer takes you on her surprising journey from Air Force musician to Animal Communicator (spiked with irreverent comments from her feline friends) and shows how you can learn to hear what your animals are trying to tell you.

— Jean-Noel Bassior, author,
Space Patrol: Missions of Daring in the Name
of Early Television

Memoir of a Crazy Cat Lady is an invitation into the author's interesting life experiences and connection with animals which led to transformation and spiritual growth. Having no personal experience with cats, I found the cat stories and the messages given from the cats themselves opened me to a different perspective. An enticing journey whether the reader is a 'cat' person or not.

— Deny Clark,
retired NP, energy healer & instructor

As you read Kathy's book you will learn about the many reincarnated lives of her cats and the adventures she had experienced with them. This is a fun and want to see what's next book. I had the honor of communicating with her cat "Big Boy" after he had transitioned and what he had me tell Kathy was life-changing for her. I will never forget that time …precious. This book will open your eyes and heart to the lessons the animals that come into our lives teach us. A very interesting read. ♥🐾🐾

— Bernadette Spector V.M.D.

Kathy takes you on her musical journey in the U.S. Air Force as she finds a passion for communicating with cats. No matter where her travels take her, her compassion only grows as she finds time and energy in taking care of her cat family.

After leaving the great musicians in the Air Force, her love for music and passion for cats never changed. Her life of adopted cats, takes us on a journey of how time and love work together.

Kathy is one of those souls who tells cat tales through her special ways of communication - a communication that still finds the next kitty searching for her, and finds her always when the time is right.

— Larry Lohnes, USAF musician, retired

Love this book! Animal lovers of all kinds will enjoy it, too. So much content, including past life regression, animal communication, and the author's own experiences. This book is a wonderful example of the human/animal bond that lasts throughout the years. All you need is love.

— Amy Tabor, dog agility trainer

More than a memoir, this is a weaving of military service with the mystical discovery of the soul's journey through beloved cats. From bagpipes to fur family, Kathy Boyer moves from her distinguished role as a musician in the Air Force into the hilarious, touching, and spiritual lessons revealed through her animals. Along the way, we encounter remarkable reincarnations, the practice of animal communication, and a profound spiritual transformation into the oneness of the collective consciousness of Divine Love. A delightful tale of the timeless quest for soulful connection and life purpose, this is the extraordinary story of one woman and the timeless wisdom of over 30 cats.

— Dr. Heather Shea,
author, speaker, animal communicator,
and everyday mystic

From Big Boy the guard kitty, to Max's mischief, to sweet Samantha with the great GPS, followed by mama cat happily known as Pretty Girl, to the love sponge Cyclops (who handsomely has one eye like me!), to Pumpkin the golden fluffball, joined by Lilli's gentle grace, and Louie's reminder of the flow of life—they form an ensemble of whiskers and feline wisdom. Alongside them, Jake's happy nicker will make you laugh! Read carefully, dear humans: within these pages, the fur family leads you back to the music of your own heart and soul.

— Captain Nemo (the cat)
author and communicating animal,
as translated by Heather Shea

www.ingramcontent.com/pod-product-compliance
Lightning Source LLC
Chambersburg PA
CBHW050416170426
43201CB00008B/432